Harvard Business Review

Behind the Productivity Headlines

Printed in U.S.A.

ISBN 0-86735-232-9 (soft cover)
0-86735-233-7 (hard cover)

Many of the articles we include in this series were written before impressive numbers of women started to play an important role in management. For this reason, the authors of certain pieces treated all readers as men and assumed that the typical manager was a "he" instead of a "he" or "she." We hope that the archaic use of the masculine gender does not undermine the effectiveness of such articles. The expense of resetting them would increase the price of this series sharply and thus limit its distribution.

The editors ask that whenever you read the words "he," "him," or "his" in an article, you take it to mean "she," "her," or "hers" as well. Whenever you see "man," either alone or as part of a word, think of the more appropriate "person." And throughout the series, let the substance of each article, carefully selected for its continued relevance and insight into the problem of productivity, be more important than any problem with language.—*The Editors*

Table of contents

Preface

No managerial problem has generated the amount of material and analysis as has productivity. In fact, company executives are probably tired of the overwhelming emphasis on our "fundamental productivity problem" in five minute spots by media economists on the Six O'Clock news, from politicians anxious to lay blame for America's economic difficulties anywhere but on their own policy shoulders—and even from their children learning about the "decline of American industrial power."

The attack comes at industry from every conceivable front. But is it warranted? Is our productivity really sagging? Most important, is there really anything companies can do about it?

This HBR series takes a very pragmatic look at the problem, and many of the solutions experts have offered for it. It begins with three different viewpoints of the economics. Campbell R. McConnell goes over the most prominent economic explanations for the productivity slowdown and asks that we view it as good, a chance for Americans to live "better" and not just with "more."

Burton G. Malkiel, on the other hand, provides a more traditional look at productivity as well as several solutions for companies and government. Stanley B. Henrici is more pragmatic; he points out that we may all be barking up the wrong tree, that the "productivity disease" may not be as terminal as we think because the U.S. index that measures it is based on faulty statistical assumptions. Instead, Henrici believes companies should monitor their individual productivity and offers tips on how they can find the specific source of their own difficulties, if there are any.

Traditional remedies

No matter whether we suffer from a national productivity problem, however, companies can always benefit from an enrichment of their individual productive capacities. Once an organization decides it should change, how to go about it?

Several articles investigate tried and true solutions for motivating employees whose sagging on-the-job spirits are often cited as the major source of productivity difficulties in industrialized countries. One popular answer is "openness and communication" between management and employees to improve the work environment. Fred K. Foulkes' impressive research into the management of 26 nonunion companies shows how progressive and equitable policies achieve long-term results through nine techniques that range from fostering a sense of employee security to giving workers a management that listens. Stanley D. Nollen's short piece investigates the reality of flexitime and how it can work, depending on the method of implementation.

Various pictures and prescriptions provide the reader glimpses of the specific forms "openness and communication" can take. They range from in-depth analyses of famous innovative cases like Robert H. Guest's look at GM in Tarrytown to interviews like that with Robert N. Noyce of Intel, who proves that an open workplace need not necessarily be a relaxed one and that motivational success still lies in providing employees with the opportunity of learning the joy of daily discovery under competitive pressure, of "working on the edge of disaster." The discussion with Renn Zaphiropoulos centers on the unique, circular organization of Versatec. He envisages a company as a series of concentric circles, which emphasize accessibility and communication between management and employees rather than the hierarchy of the classic pyramid organization.

In a turnabout, the series also shows the problems with various solutions that are based solely on productivity numbers and do not take into account the feelings or expectations of employees. For example, John F. Runcie investigates what has happened to Henry Ford's first dream of productivity enrichment, the assembly line, while Robert Schrank offers an imaginative look at the future impact of the current fad, robotics. Thomas H. Fitzgerald's classic HBR piece from the early 1970s deflates for all time the myth of motivational theory.

The Japanese edge

The fascination with the Japanese way of doing things is reaching the level of a cult in this country, and this HBR series cannot ignore it. But the series does show companies that the answers do not lie abroad, but rather in everything we have always known about ourselves but were afraid to admit.

The series' "international" component takes off with Peter F. Drucker's classic, "What We Can Learn from Japanese Management." The venerable management guru goes behind the myth of the invincible power of Japan Inc. to show just what companies in that country offer their employees. He sees it as an ability to offer a worker "a human relationship that is job-focused and work-focused, a contact they have access to, a mentor who is concerned with them." In short, better human relations.

Ten years later, Robert H. Hayes' visit to Japan results in a realistic appraisal of the workings of Japanese manufacturing operations. As the foreword to that piece says, the answer is not elusive. "No exotic gimmickry, only deliberate attention to the humdrum details of operations management. No secret formulas, only painstaking sensitivity to the strategic implications of those operational details."

Finally, a life's work of investigation into the automotive and other mature industries yields surprising answers for productivity problems in "The New Industrial Competition." William J. Abernathy, Kim B. Clark, and Alan M. Kantrow show how some companies will survive the economic crisis and some won't, and offer advice for managers that is hard-hitting but not impossible to achieve. In fact, they end with a description of Henry Ford by Alfred P. Sloan, as a successful entrepreneur who, nevertheless, "'failed to master change.'" For these authors, that is the message to be learned from productive foreign competitors, "... still the crucial challenge—and opportunity."

A concluding financial note

While most analyses deal with current industry problems, the most nagging difficulty may lie in the future. How can a company foster tomorrow's productive growth with capital investments today? Bradley T. Gale points out that some of the shop-level approaches to productivity improvement may even exacerbate the problem. Rather, he offers companies specific techniques to improve productivity through selective investments. Finally, Lawrence Revsine advocates a revolutionary accounting approach, which will tell companies realistically whether they have the capital needed to make the most productive investments.

Despite the ballyhoo given the subject of productivity, the answer to its improvement lies, as it alway has, in fostering intelligent management techniques. It is a simple, but effective response. The problem, in this age of business science, is to convince managers that they cannot necessarily come up with the answer by "systematization." That good relations with their employees, productive use of investments, and a sound analysis of the problem *from their own point of view* will yield the best results. This is what those successful foreign competitors know. And what the best and most effective U.S. corporate executives still do.

Douglas N. Dickson
Associate Editor
Harvard Business Review

Biographical update

Some of the articles in this series were written several years ago. Although many of the authors' professional activities have remained the same, here are a few additions to the biographical sketches that precede each article (information current as of November 1981):

Peter F. Drucker
("What We Can Learn From Japanese Management") is the author of two new books to be published in 1982, *The Changing World of the Executive* and *The Best of All Possible Worlds.*

Thomas H. Fitzgerald
("Why Motivation Theory Doesn't Work") is director of organizational planning and development for the Chevrolet division of General Motors. He coordinates quality of work life activities there and continues to be interested in alternative systems (and values) for organizing various kinds of work.

Fred K. Foulkes
("How Top Nonunion Companies Manage, Employees) is the coauthor (with E. Robert Livernash) of *Human Resources Management: Text and Cases* (Englewood Cliffs, N.J.: Prentice-Hall, 1982).

Bradley T. Gale
("Can More Capital Buy Higher Productivity?") has written an additional article on productivity, entitled "A Strategic Approach to Productivity Management," *Planning Review,* March 1981.

Robert H. Guest
("Quality of Work Life—Learning from Tarrytown") is currently consulting for one of Ford's large transmission plants. He reports that in one year the company has set up 25 problem-solving groups made up of workers, supervisors, and support personnel, along with a management coordinator. The Tarrytown effort continues to be successful, and a new Buick plant at Flint, Michigan has eliminated time clocks and now calls first-line supervisors "advisers," not "foremen."

Stanley B. Henrici
("How Deadly Is the Productivity Disease?") formerly general manager, organizational sytems, Heinz U.S.A., is also a registered professional engineer.

Burton G. Malkiel
("Productivity—The Problem Behind the Headlines") is currently dean of the Yale School of Organization and Management; director of Prudential Insurance Co., Amdahl Corporation, and the Vanguard Group of Investment Companies; and a Governor of the American Stock Exchange.

Campbell R. McConnell
("Why Is U.S. Productivity Slowing Down?") is the author of *Economics,* which was published in its eighth edition in 1981 by McGraw-Hill.

John F. Runcie
(" 'By Days I Make the Cars' ") is senior researcher at Public Systems Evaluation, Inc., Cambridge, Mass. His most recent research has been on the technological impacts on work, interface between people and machines, and productivity. He is currently managing a project on police patrol practices and their impact on police work, productivity, and attitudes. His article, "Dynamic Systems and the Quality of Work Life," was published in *Personnel,* November-December 1980.

The Editors

1 Is there a productivity problem?

Keeping Informed

Five economic explanations for what many see as an unsatisfactory gap between output and hours worked

Why is U.S. productivity slowing down?

Campbell R. McConnell

Whether it comes from changes in the capital supply and in the labor force, a preoccupation with war readiness, workers' discontent, limitations in natural resources, or overweening government interference, the gap may be indicating a new prerogative for our economy. "More" may not be "better," or even possible. We have something to learn from each of these explanations, the author of this article says, and, after due consideration, we may not find the slowdown in U.S. productivity so bad after all.

Mr. McConnell is professor of economics at the College of Business Administration, The University of Nebraska-Lincoln. He is the author of Economics, *seventh edition (New York: McGraw-Hill, 1978), and he has edited two other books—*Economic Issues, *fifth edition (McGraw-Hill, 1975) and* Perspectives on Wage Determination *(McGraw-Hill, 1970). His major research interests are in labor economics and economic education. Mr. McConnell is past president of the Midwest Economics Association.*

Reprint number 79205

If we can believe the evidence, the rate of productivity growth in the United States has declined markedly since the mid-1960s. The Council of Economic Advisers (CEA), for example, has found that the growth of output per labor hour, which averaged 3.3% per year over the 1948-1966 period, declined to 2.1% during the 1966-1973 period.[1] Official data for 1973-1977 indicate a further deterioration to 1.2%. And the U.S. Department of Labor has noted that all of the major noncommunist economies have had faster rates of labor productivity growth in recent years than has the United States (see the *Exhibit* on page 5 for details).

One implication of this slowdown is that, since the growth rate of the average level of real wages and the growth rate of productivity correlate highly, our living standards will not rise as rapidly as they have in the past. Primarily because of our productivity slowdown the United States no longer enjoys the highest per capita gross national product in the world.

Another implication is that inflation may increase. A rapid rate of productivity growth would offset increases in labor wage rates and would thereby have an ameliorating effect on cost-push inflationary pressures.

Finally, the implication is that our international trade may be thrown out of equilibrium even more than it is now. By slowing down the rise in unit labor costs, a rapid rise in labor productivity would make U.S. output more competitive than it has been in international markets and would thereby have a favorable effect on our balance of payments.

Although there is widespread agreement about the occurrence of a slowdown in U.S. productivity growth, there is considerable controversy about its ultimate causes. It is my objective in this article to summarize several divergent views of what is causing this slowdown. I shall consider:

1. The "mainstream" position of the neoclassical economists.
2. The "war economy" argument associated primarily with Columbia University's Seymour Melman.

Author's note: I am indebted to Professors John R. Felton, Harish Gupta, and Jerry Petr, all of The University of Nebraska-Lincoln, for helpful comments on an earlier draft of this article.

Editor's note: All references are listed at the end of this feature on page 10.

3. The "neo-Marxist" interpretation espoused by radical economists.

4. The "doomsday" stance derived from the writings of those who predict, and often advocate, an end to economic growth.

5. The "noninterventionist," or free market, perspective of the libertarian economists, who adhere to the doctrines associated with Milton Friedman and the University of Chicago school of thought.

Several caveats are in order. Each view is necessarily presented in attenuated form; no pretense of comprehensiveness is intended. Each author associated with a given view may acknowledge the importance of factors stressed in other interpretations of the productivity slowdown. My objective is only the modest one of summarizing; space does not permit a thorough evaluation of each viewpoint.

Mainstream position

The conventional wisdom of the neoclassical economists explains the rate of productivity growth largely in terms of changes in the stock of real capital relative to labor, changes in the composition and allocation of the labor force, improvements in human resources, and technological progress.

The Council of Economic Advisers, for example, attributes the productivity slowdown primarily to four factors.

Decline in the capital-labor ratio: The growth in the amount of capital employed per manhour of labor has gone down. Capital per labor hour grew by 3.1% per year in the private sector during 1948-1966, declined to 2.8% per year during 1966-1973, and diminished further to 1.7% after 1973.[2] A prime cause of this diminishing growth, according to the CEA, is the increased participation of women in the labor force and the entrance of postwar baby boom members to the labor market. They have caused the work force to expand more rapidly than our capital stock.

Change in the demographic composition of the labor force: The proportion of young workers (those having less experience and training and thus lower-than-average productivity) has been increasing. Simultaneously, early retirements, undoubtedly prompted by liberalized social security benefits and the option to obtain those benefits at age 62, have removed substantial numbers of experienced workers from the labor force. The fact that the level of educational attainment in the labor force has been going up at a slower rate than in years past, says the CEA, no doubt reinforces the lowering of productivity.

Shift in labor from agriculture to industry: This long-term change has contributed to the rise of labor productivity. Despite an increasing rate of productivity in agriculture, its average level is below that of the economy as a whole. Given that agricultural labor is only 3.5% of the total labor force, the exodus of labor from agriculture has necessarily slowed down. The consequence is a slowing of the rate of productivity growth overall.

Progress in technology: The fourth factor the CEA considers important is the improvement we have had in the quality of capital goods and in the efficiency of ways to combine inputs. Although the relationship between research and development expenditures and productivity growth is not firmly established, the CEA assumes such a relationship exists and notes that, despite rapid growth over the 1955-1969 period, R&D spending has declined in real terms since 1970. Furthermore, R&D as a percentage of the gross national product fell from a peak of 3% in 1964 to 2.3% in 1975 and 2.1% in 1977.[3]

Bureau of Labor Statistics economists have offered a similar analysis. According to their calculations, annual productivity growth declined from 3.2% in the 1947-1966 period to 2.1% in the 1967-1973 period. Intersectoral labor shifts—primarily the slowdown of the farm-to-nonfarm shift—account for approximately one-fourth to one-third of the overall 1.1% drop in productivity growth. Changes in the age/sex composition of the labor force account for about one-fifth to one-fourth of the total decline. Only a very modest fraction of the decline—about one-tenth at the most—is attributable to voluntary changes in capital formation.

However, capital expenditures mandated for environmental and worker protection are more significant, accounting for approximately one-tenth to one-fifth of the productivity decline. The Bureau of Labor Statistics leaves the remainder of the decline either unexplained or attributed to the interaction among these factors.[4]

War economy argument

In a series of books and articles, Seymour Melman attributes declining productivity growth and a host of related problems to the presence of an overly large military sector in the economy.[5] He marshals statistics showing a decidedly negative correlation between the percentage of GNP a nation spends on its military sector and the growth rate of its labor productivity. Japan's very high productivity growth, for example, is largely attributable to the fact that only a miniscule percentage of its national output is for defense. In the United States, productivity has fallen for two interrelated reasons, according to Melman.

Unproductive military sector: Melman argues that military production is inherently unproductive and wasteful in that it does not have any true economic use. War goods do not satisfy current wants, as do consumer goods; nor do they contribute to future production, as do capital goods.

According to Melman, "Whatever worth may be attributed to military products on other than economic-functional grounds, it is apparent that you cannot live in, wear, or ride an intercontinental missile or an antipersonnel bomb. Neither can such products be used for further production."[6]

The massive shifts of resources to the development and production of military goods have stripped the private sector of resources that are vital to prosperity and growth. To Melman, military production is parasitic, "weakening the host [civilian] econ-

Exhibit
International indexes of labor productivity, 1960-1977 (output per hour of manufacturing workers, 1967 = 100)

Year	United States	Canada	Japan	United Kingdom	France	West Germany	Italy
1960	78.8	75.5	52.6	76.8	68.7	66.4	65.1
1961	80.6	79.6	59.3	77.4	71.9	70.0	67.4
1962	84.3	83.9	61.9	79.3	75.2	74.4	74.1
1963	90.1	87.1	67.1	83.6	79.7	78.4	76.5
1964	94.8	90.9	75.9	89.7	83.7	84.5	81.5
1965	98.1	94.4	79.1	92.4	88.5	90.4	91.6
1966	99.6	97.2	87.1	95.7	94.7	94.0	96.0
1967	100.0	100.0	100.0	100.0	100.0	100.0	100.0
1968	103.6	107.3	112.6	106.7	111.4	107.6	108.4
1969	105.0	113.3	130.0	108.1	115.4	113.8	112.2
1970	104.5	114.7	146.5	108.6	121.2	116.1	117.8
1971	110.3	122.8	150.5	112.9	128.5	121.4	123.5
1972	116.0	128.1	161.0	121.2	136.8	128.7	132.9
1973	119.4	133.4	179.0	126.3	143.7	136.6	147.8
1974	112.8	135.6	180.3	127.6	147.8	145.0	155.9
1975	116.3	133.4	172.4	124.4	151.1	150.4	150.2
1976	124.2	137.8	194.8	128.7	165.3	162.8	161.5
1977	126.9	143.3	206.6	126.6	171.6	169.6	162.3

Source: U.S. Department of Labor.

omy that feeds it." [7] The relative decline of our steel, shipbuilding, and electronics industries and the deterioration of our public utilities and medical services can all be traced, he feels, to this resource shift.

Melman contends that in the early 1960s the relationship between the Department of Defense (DOD) and the producers of military goods changed. The buyer-seller relationship was transformed into one "fundamentally similar to the type of unit that has operated in central-office-controlled, multidivision, major manufacturing firms." That is, "the relation of the military-industrial firms to the single customer shifted from one of, primarily, seller to buyer towards that of submanagement to top management." [8]

The significance of this change lies in the fact that the DOD's economic interaction with military contractors has shifted the latter's decision-making processes from cost minimization to cost maximization. Defense procurement is largely based on what amounts to cost-plus contracts; hence, the higher the cost of a weapons system, the greater the profit to a company.

Another author, James M. Saurez, lends support to Melman's opinion: "If a private sector firm devises a lower cost method of production, it is rewarded with bigger profits. Defense contractors are not rewarded for cutting costs and may in fact be penalized. The defense firm's negotiated profits are a direct function of the estimated cost of the contract. Lower costs mean smaller profits. . . . A labor-saving capital investment can have particularly harmful effects on profitability. The cost-reducing plant and equipment will lower the expense base for determining profits." [9]

In short, the traditional market pressures that compel the private sector to use resources frugally do not, according to Saurez and Melman, exist in the military sector.

'Countermechanization effect': Historically, a rising capital-labor ratio (i.e., the use of more real capital per manhour of labor) has been an important source of productivity growth. Rising labor and materials prices have induced cost-minimizing organizations to substitute capital for labor, thereby increasing labor productivity.

It is Melman's contention that the military sector has been responsible for reversing the historical relationship between the prices of capital and labor, so that the price of capital has increased relative to wage costs. The consequence has been a "countermechanization effect"—a tendency for labor mechanization to decrease and in turn for productivity growth to slow down.

The depletion of the civilian economy by the military sector has had an especially adverse effect on the critical machine-tool industry, Melman points out. Military production has been highly competitive with this industry, and the shift of R&D effort and technological manpower to the military sector has caused a sharp drop in productivity growth in the machine-tool industry. This drop has been reinforced to the extent that machinery-producing industries have become associated with military production and its cost-maximizing objectives.

In sum, diminished productivity and cost maximization, coupled with the ability to pass higher costs along to buyers via price increases, have caused machinery prices to rise more rapidly than industrial workers' wage rates.

This syndrome has in turn eroded the incentive to substitute capital for labor. Melman argues that the export of U.S. capital reinforces this whole process. As diminished productivity growth causes labor costs per unit of output to rise relatively in the United States, U.S. capital tends to flow abroad. Hence our domestic capital stock becomes increasingly antiquated, and productivity growth declines further.

Neo-Marxist interpretation

Radical economists are inclined to associate diminishing productivity growth with worker alienation and discontent. Worker dissatisfaction in turn, they say, is rooted in the systematic stratification of labor processes and markets that has accompanied the maturation of capitalism.

Such segmentation simply means that labor markets and processes are divided into submarkets and subprocesses, each of which entails its own working conditions, behavioral rules, wage rates, degrees of employment stability, and promotion opportunities. It is the contention of the radical economists that labor market segmentation has evolved in large measure from the conscious strategies of capitalists.

The transformation of capitalistic society from one of handicraft production to one of factory production created the basis for a Marxian proletariat, as the radical economists see it. The evolution of factory production tended to create an unskilled, homogeneous, largely urban labor force, which Marx envisioned as the basis for a unified, class-conscious proletariat and ultimately as the means for the overthrow of the capitalistic system.

But the response of the capitalist class has been to stratify labor markets and labor processes. That is, monopoly capitalists have followed a divide-and-conquer strategy designed to undermine the unity of the labor class.

The development of large unskilled and semiskilled work forces has prompted large corporations to search for new forms of worker control. The ultimate result has been the "bureaucratic" form of the modern corporation, and for workers the effect of bureaucratization has been "to establish a rigidly graded hierarchy of jobs and power by which 'top-down' authority could be exercised." [10]

In the neo-Marxist view, the importance of the segmentation process is that it is accompanied by a proliferation of hierarchy, work rules, and worker supervision. Beyond some point, workers react adversely to this proliferation. Their reaction may take the form of absenteeism, work of poor quality, production slowdown, or, in the extreme, spontaneous walkouts and sabotage. In any event, one consequence of an alienated, disgruntled work force is a declining rate of productivity growth.

This sequence of events and the workers' resulting discontent have been exacerbated in several ways.

First, workers' priorities have been shifting away from bread-and-butter issues to the question of improving and controlling the character and content of their jobs. What accounts for the shift?

Through the efforts of labor unions, workers have been capturing a rising share of "surplus value" (profits). Furthermore, appropriate fiscal and monetary measures have mitigated the severity of the business cycle. As a result, what some call the "disciplining effect of material insecurity" has been reduced. Workers' desire to control their jobs and work environments can conflict with their employers' capitalistic interest in fostering rapid productivity growth.

The neo-Marxists' point is that labor's increasing desire to achieve worker control has been frustrated by the bureaucratization and segmentation of work processes and that this frustration has intensified the deterioration of worker morale and productivity.

Second, although workers have in the past 30 years realized higher levels of education than their counterparts in earlier decades, the character of most jobs today has not been adjusted for accompanying changes in workers' attitudes, values, and aspirations. A special task force of the Ninety-third Congress found that:

"Simplified tasks for those who are not simple-minded, close supervision by those whose legitimacy rests only on hierarchical structure, and jobs that have nothing but money to offer in an affluent age are simply rejected. For many of the new workers, the monotony of work and scale of organization and their inability to control the pace and style of work are cause for a resentment which they, unlike older workers, do not repress." [11]

Third, the capitalist response to the problem of declining productivity growth is to speed up production and/or to further fragmentize the work process. This response, it is argued, merely intensifies the workers' discontent and antagonism and thereby precipitates further declines in productivity.

As economist Howard M. Wachtel interprets these considerations, a fundamental contradiction emerges:

"Initially, capital responds with a larger dose of the same medicine, namely increased work supervision, hierarchy, and work speed-ups. But part of the problem is caused by the very character of the labor process under monopoly capitalism, which is characterized by work speed-up, hierarchy, and supervision. So the medicine of monopoly capitalism merely feeds the disease." [12]

This radical view has received some support from an unexpected source. Arthur F. Burns, former chairman of the Board of Governors of the Federal Reserve System, has suggested that growing worker absenteeism reflects "decided changes . . . in the basic work attitudes of employees." He has also noted:

"It is not at all clear that people actually perceive that lessened work effort inevitably must be reflected in the material benefits we as a people can enjoy. That linkage was inescapably evident earlier in our history—when, to a much greater degree than is now the case, men and women could literally see what their individual effort yielded in consumable products; but the linkage has been blurred as our productive and distributive mechanisms have grown in complexity." [13]

Doomsday stance

In the past decade, an extended debate over the desirability and feasibility of further economic growth has occurred. The cornerstone of this controversy is the notion that resources are ultimately finite on "spaceship earth."

On the one hand, there is concern that we will run out of natural resources like oil, coal, copper, and arable land, which are critical to the productive process. On the other hand, there is fear that the increased waste that inevitably accompanies economic growth will overwhelm the absorptive capacity of the ecological system.

These problems are rendered even more complex by rapid population growth, which calls for expanded output and therefore puts increasing demands on both inputs and the environment.

Using elaborate computer models, the Club of Rome triggered a worldwide controversy with its conclusion that continued economic growth is impossible. According to its prognosis, the current growth paths of population, output, and pollution are on a catastrophic collison course:

"If the present growth trends in world population, industrialization, pollution, food production, and resource depletion continue unchanged, the limits to growth on this planet will be reached sometime within the next 100 years. The most probable result will be a rather sudden and uncontrollable decline in both population and industrial capacity." [14]

Elements of such doomsday views can be readily reinterpreted as an explanation of the slowdown of American productivity growth. Bluntly put, labor productivity must decline because (1) the law of diminishing returns is, in some sense, applicable to all sources of productivity growth, and (2) society must redress certain imbalances generated by past efforts to sustain productivity growth.

Diminishing returns: Growth advocates put great faith in the ability of technological progress to offset the law of diminishing returns, but doomsdayers cite mounting evidence that the sources of productivity growth will be increasingly subject to this law.

Given the rapid expansion of world output, they say, it is inevitable that diminishing returns will become increasingly pronounced in the extractive industries, where only finite amounts of land and natural resources exist. In the past, the highest grade and the most accessible natural resources have been brought into production first.

However, further expansion of output will necessarily bring the lower grade, less accessible resources into use. In the case of the United States, domestic policies designed to reduce our dependence on foreign resources for energy will obligate us to use qualitatively inferior resources and will thereby hasten the productivity slowdown.

Until now, a substantial portion of our productivity growth has been derived from the increasing speed of our transportation and productive processes, but such gain is also subject to diminishing returns. In transportation, stepping up speeds requires disproportionately large increases in fuel input, on the one hand, and collision with constraints imposed by societal objectives like safety on the other.

Similarly, there may be biological limits to the speed at which workers can perform. Edward F. Renshaw, for instance, contends that "the age of spectacular advances in practical working speeds is rapidly drawing to a close. . . ." Even the offsetting effects of making machines larger and giving each worker more machines to control through automation have, according to Renshaw, inherent limits.[15]

The most significant—and perhaps the most controversial—component of the doomsday position is the pessimistic contention that the discovery of new knowledge may itself be subject to the law of diminishing returns. Renshaw argues that:

". . . there has been a significant diminution in the power of science and technology to counteract natural resource scarcity and propel our economy forward at a steady, exponential rate of growth.

". . . persons engaged in research and development may be finding it more difficult to discover and invent new products and productive processes which are unambiguously superior to older commodities and ways of producing goods and services." [16]

Renshaw feels there is substantial evidence for his view: despite abundant financial support, there has been an apparent slowdown in the rate of progress in medical science; space research has resulted in meager payoffs, and there has occurred a "profound technological depression" in the development of important new consumer goods. The critical point, of course, is that, if it is in fact subject to diminishing returns, technological progress will no longer offset declining labor productivity.

Living beyond our means: Doomsdayers also argue that in the past we have been living beyond our means in productivity growth and that we must now accept a lower rate of growth to redress our past prodigality. They say that, for example, in a variety of industries—in particular, petroleum and natural gas—we have kept productivity at high levels by drawing down reserves discovered in earlier years. If consumption (output) had been restricted to newly discovered reserves or if exploration and drilling (and hence inputs) had been increased to bring reserves up to consumption levels, past productivity in these industries would have been significantly lower. Society cannot live beyond its means in this fashion indefinitely. Now, as we seek to expand exploration to replace diminished reserves, productivity growth must necessarily decline, the limits-to-growth advocates assert.

They apply the same line of reasoning to the environment. Until recently, society has tended to ignore the adverse effects of production and consumption on the environment. As they see it, society has accepted the debasement of the environment as a "free input" in the production process, and this acceptance has kept productivity (the output-input ratio) high.

But the advent of environmental protection regulations is now forcing companies to include the inputs required for environmental protection in their production processes. Hence the output-input ratio, or productivity as currently measured, has diminished; the additional inputs needed to preserve the environment are included, while the resulting cleaner environment is not measured as a part of output.

Forced expenditures on pollution-abatement equipment divert investable resources from productive capital equipment per se. The result is a smaller and/or older stock of capital goods than would otherwise be the case and a subsequent decline in labor productivity growth.

The primary impact of antipollution laws, not to mention OSHA and oil price increases, has been concentrated on a small number of generally high-growth, high-productivity industries (e.g., petroleum refining, aluminum, industrial chemicals, and pulp-paper paperboard). The resultant higher costs imposed on these industries have necessitated price increases and redirected demand away from these high-productivity industries toward the products of other lower-productivity industries. The obvious result, doomsdayers say, is a decline in the aggregate rate of productivity growth.[17]

Noninterventionist perspective

Free-market, or libertarian, economists contend that the private sector has been subjected to increasing intervention and control by the public sector. Although they believe there are legitimate economic reasons for some government interference in the market economy, such noninterventionists contend that in practice government activities and policies are frequently misguided, overextended, and inappropriate to the problems they are intended to resolve.

Relevant to the current discussion is the allegation that the unfettered free enterprise system comprises a powerful mechanism for productivity growth. According to the libertarians, the productivity slowdown is rooted in deviations from the traditional institutional and ideological characteristics of that system.

Perhaps the basic component of the free-market interpretation of the productivity slowdown focuses on the trade-off between equity and efficiency. In particular, it is held that government efforts to redistribute income have weakened the incentive to work. Edgar K. Browning, for example, estimates that for most American families effective marginal tax rates are approaching 50%, causing substantial deterioration of work incentives:

"High marginal tax rates are inimical to productivity in general, and not just to the amount of time people work. . . . The incentive to undertake job training or get a good education is weakened, since the student will get to keep only part of the higher income that a better education makes possible. Insofar as the return to savings is also subject to tax, the flow of savings, so important to economic growth, can be adversely affected by high marginal tax rates.

"Occupational choices can also be influenced: people will be led to take lower paying jobs that do not involve as much risk or responsibility. . . . Although it is convenient to conceptualize the problem by thinking in terms of work incentives, it should not be forgotten that the incentives issue really relates to productive activity in general." [18]

Many other facets of government intervention also have detrimental implications for productivity, the noninterventionists say. For example, government activity in the areas of pollution control and occupational health and safety have allegedly been pursued beyond their optimum points. These forms of government intervention require larger amounts of input to produce any given output and therefore diminish measured productivity growth.

Furthermore, according to Lewis A. Engman, government regulation of the so-called natural monopolies is counterproductive in that:

"Much of today's regulatory machinery does little more than shelter producers from the normal competitive consequences of lassitude and inefficiency. . . . most regulated industries have become federal protectorates, living in the cozy world of cost-plus, safely protected from the ugly specters of competition, efficiency, and innovation." [19]

Similarly, labor unions are seen as government-sponsored monopolies that resist technological advances and other productivity-increasing efforts of management. Labor views such efforts as threats to job security rather than as sources of benefits to workers. In fact, regression analyses indicate that, for manufacturing industries, rates of productivity advancement and the degree of unionization are negatively correlated.[20]

The absolute and the relative growth of the public sector per se also contributes to the productivity slowdown. Specifically, the competitive pressures and incentives for personal gain that foster efficiency in private companies are largely absent in public bureaucracies. There is no tangible personal gain—no counterpart to profits—for the bureau chief who achieves efficiency within his own domain; there is no compelling incentive to be "productive" in the public sector.

Cynics argue that, in fact, a public agency that uses its resources inefficiently may be in line for a budget increase. In the private sector, inefficiency and monetary losses lead to the abandonment of certain outputs. But government, Peter F. Drucker contends, is loath to relinquish activities in which it has failed: "Indeed, the typical response of government to the failure of an activity is to double its budget and staff." [21]

This bureaucratic mentality means that public sector inefficiency may be sustained on a large scale. A related argument is that public programs tend to spawn new constituencies of bureaucrats and beneficiaries whose political clout causes programs to be sustained or expanded after they have fulfilled their goals or, alternatively, even if they have failed miserably in their mission.

At the level of macroeconomics, Milton Friedman contends that government policies have given rise to an inflation-prone economy.[22] The consequences have been manifold and adverse insofar as productivity growth is concerned.

First, inflation is conducive to business uncertainty and therefore to restrained investment spending. Similarly, inflation tends to divert resources from productive to speculative uses.

Second, the periodic application of restrictive monetary and fiscal measures to control inflation also has had a particularly adverse effect on capital formation and, hence, on productivity growth. Business profits bear a disproportionate burden of demand-restriction policies to the end that investment spending is retarded.

Third, the occasional use of incomes policies—wage-price guideposts and controls—to ameliorate inflation has the side effect of diminishing the efficiency with which resources are allocated among various industries and companies. Effective guideposts and controls breed input misallocations and shortages, which adversely affect productivity.

To the libertarian, the solution to the productivity slowdown is as obvious as the cause. If the productivity problem is rooted in too much government, clearly the remedy is less government intervention and the promotion of competition.

Some reflections

This summarization of contrasting explanations of the productivity slowdown gives rise to several observations.

Measurement difficulty: Perhaps mainstream economists tend to concentrate on too narrow a range of factors in explaining productivity growth. The methodology of the neoclassicists' wisdom tends to shun less tangible, less measurable factors such as workers' discontent (the neo-Marxist view) or institutional changes (the war economy and noninterventionist theses) in explaining the decline in productivity growth.

It is significant to observe that, after assessing the quantitative impact of a number of "conventional" factors in the productivity slowdown—the decline in the growth of capital per manhour, the real decline in R&D outlays, sectoral and demographic shifts in the labor force, and so forth—the Council of Economic Advisers admits that "the reasons for the slowdown are not fully understood at this time because the decline in productivity growth appears to be larger than the sum of the estimated effects of these factors." [23]

In short, it is precipitate of mainstream economists and policymakers to discount too severely the arguments contained within the less conventional views.

Policy complications: If each perspective on the productivity slowdown does embody some degree of validity and if the determinants of productivity growth are diverse, no simple, straightforward measures can be relied on to stimulate the rate of productivity growth. To the extent that the unorthodox explanations of the productivity slowdown are relevant, the task of policymakers is greatly complicated.

The orthodox, mainstream economists have a variety of apparently manageable and practical policies to recommend—for example, tax subsidies to accelerate capital formation and R&D spending by private organizations, increases in public spending for R&D, and subsidies for education and manpower development. But if the roots of the productivity problem lie significantly in fundamental changes in societal values with respect to work or in strongly entrenched institutional changes, then appropriate remedial measures are both less evident and decidedly more complex.

The future: Given the great divergence of views with respect to the causes of the productivity slowdown, it will come as no surprise that there is fundamental disagreement concerning its persistence. Generally speaking, mainstream economists are inclined to be somewhat optimistic, predicting a substantial improvement in productivity growth if not a return to the historical rate.

The Bureau of Labor Statistics in its aforementioned analysis anticipates that productivity growth will rise in the near future. It projects that productivity will grow by 2.4% per year over the 1973-1980 period and by 2.7% annually during 1980-1985. Although less than the overall postwar (1947-1973) figure of about 3%, these projections are obviously substantial improvements over the 2.1% figure of the 1966-1973 period.[24]

John W. Kendrick, in a 1976 report on productivity trends and prospects, is also optimistic:

"Briefly, it appears that productivity advance during the decade 1976-1986 will be stronger than it was during the past decade, reflecting the cyclical factors and the mitigation of the negative effect of most of the factors depressing productivity growth after 1966." [25]

Supporters of the unconventional views appear to be less sanguine about the future. Doomsdayer Renshaw, for example, flatly asserts that "the prospects for further improvements in labor productivity . . . appear to be quite limited." He predicts that "real GNP per worker in the United States will never again increase by more than about 30% and that most of the remaining increase will occur in the next two decades." [26] The war economy and the libertarian views are tacitly pessimistic because they imply that rather profound institutional changes are requisite to a reversal of the productivity slowdown.

Productivity & the 'good life': Finally, I would be remiss not to recognize the view that the relationship between productivity growth and life at its best is quite loose. A permanent decline in the rate of productivity growth is not necessarily incompatible with a bettering of social welfare. Let us briefly consider two variants of this theme.

On the one hand, David P. Eastburn has dramatized the distinction between "economic man" and "social man." [27] Economic man is preoccupied with production, quantity, monetary values, work and discipline, and competition. Social man is concerned with distribution, quality, human values, self-realization, and cooperation.

Perhaps society, in some subtle fashion, is rendering a more or less conscious decision that "more" is not "better." A tacit consensus that social man should prevail over economic man may be emerging. A decline in productivity growth is an expected consequence of such a decision.

On the other hand, Staffan B. Linder has suggested that the growth of labor productivity may have harmed the overall quality of our lives.[28] As labor productivity has increased, time has become more valuable in the labor market or, stated differently, time devoted to pure leisure, cultural pursuits, and consumption per se has become more expensive.

As a consequence, Linder argues, we make an effort to increase the productivity of nonwork time in order to maintain an equilibrium with the growing productivity of work time. In leisure and cultural pursuits, this effort does not work, however, and these activities are simply allotted less and less time. We attempt to increase the productivity of time devoted to consumption by making consumption more goods-intensive or by consuming two or more items simultaneously. The result is a harried life-style and the unattractive deployment of nonwork time.

In short, Linder's point is that total affluence—an abundance of *both* goods and time—is a logical fallacy. One cannot reject out of hand the suggestion that more time and less output might improve the human condition.

References

1. *Economic Report of the President* (Washington, D.C., 1977), p. 45.

2. Ibid., pp. 45-48.

3. Ibid.

4. Ronald E. Kutscher, Jerome A. Mark, and John R. Norsworthy, "The Productivity Slowdown and the Outlook to 1985," *Monthly Labor Review*, May 1977, pp. 3-8.

5. Seymour Melman, "Decision Making and Productivity as Economic Variables: The Present Depression as a Failure of Productivity," *Journal of Economic Issues*, June 1976, p. 230; *Our Depleted Society* (New York: Holt, Dell Books, 1965); *Pentagon Capitalism* (New York: McGraw-Hill, 1970); *The Permanent War Economy* (New York: Simon and Schuster, 1974), and *The War Economy of the United States* (New York: St. Martin's Press, 1971).

6. Melman, *War Economy of the United States*, p. 4.

7. Melman, *Permanent War Economy*, p. 2.

8. Melman, *War Economy of the United States*, p. 2.

9. James M. Saurez, "Profits and Performance of Aerospace Defense Contractors," *Journal of Economic Issues*, June 1976, pp. 399-400.

10. This section draws heavily on Howard M. Wachtel, "Class Consciousness and Stratification in the Labor Process," in Richard C. Edwards, Michael Reich, and David M. Gordon, editors, *Labor Market Segmentation* (Lexington, Mass.: D.C. Heath, 1975), p. 95; and on Michael Reich, David M. Gordon, and Richard C. Edwards, "A Theory of Labor Market Segmentation," *American Economic Review*, May 1973, p. 359.

11. *Work in America, Report of a Special Task Force to the Secretary of Health, Education, and Welfare*, Ninety-third Congress, First Session (Washington, D.C., 1973), p. 16.

12. Wachtel, "Class Consciousness," p. 119.

13. Arthur F. Burns in a speech entitled "The Significance of Our Productivity Lag," May 14, 1977.

14. Donella H. Meadows and D.H. Meadows, *The Limits to Growth* (New York: New American Library, 1972), p. 29.

15. Edward F. Renshaw, *The End of Progress* (North Scituate, Mass.: Duxbury Press, 1976), pp. 35-40.

16. Ibid., pp. 14 and 58.

17. This point is the main theme of John G. Myers, Leonard I. Makamura, and Norman R. Madrid in "The Impact of OPEC, FEA, EPA, and OSHA on Productivity and Growth," *Conference Board Record*, April 1976, p. 61.

18. Edgar K. Browning, "How Much More Equality Can We Afford?" *The Public Interest*, Spring 1976, p. 95.

19. Lewis A. Engman, speech before the 1974 fall conference of the Financial Analysts Federation, Detroit, Michigan, October 7, 1974.

20. See John W. Kendrick, "Productivity and Business," in Jules Backman and Harold S. Geneen, *Labor, Technology, and Productivity* (New York: New York University Press, 1974), p. 131.

21. Peter F. Drucker, "The Sickness of Government," *The Public Interest*, Winter 1969, p. 13.

22. Milton Friedman, "Using Escalators to Help Fight Inflation," *Fortune*, July 1974, p. 94.

23. *Economic Report of the President*, 1977, p. 45.

24. Kutscher et al., "Productivity Slowdown and the Outlook to 1985."

25. John W. Kendrick, "Productivity Trends and Prospects," in *U.S. Economic Growth from 1976 to 1986: Prospects, Problems, and Patterns*, vol. 1 (Washington, D.C.: Joint Economic Committee, 1976), p. 15.

26. Edward F. Renshaw, "Productivity," in *U.S. Economic Growth from 1976 to 1986: Prospects, Problems, and Patterns*, vol. 1 (Washington, D.C.: Joint Economic Committee, 1976), p. 21.

27. David P. Eastburn, "Economic Man in Conflict with His Economic Self," *New York Times Magazine*, July 26, 1970, p. 10.

28. Staffan B. Linder, *The Harried Leisure Class* (New York: Columbia University Press, 1970).

Productivity–the problem behind the headlines

Burton G. Malkiel

Declining productivity growth affects both inflation and unemployment; what causes it and what can we do about it?

Although most people fear inflation, at least they understand how it affects them: prices rise and the value of the dollar sinks. But what is behind inflation, why is the economic pie not sufficient anymore to solve our national problems? The author of this article asserts that low productivity growth may be the single most important factor in determining the national economic well-being. Without growth in productivity, struggles over income shares lead directly to inflation. Economists disagree about the causes of the slowdown in productivity; and in any event some of them, such as shifting patterns in the labor force and in occupations, cannot be altered. Some of them, however, we can affect: the level of business investment, the state of research and development efforts in the United States, and the degree to which government regulations help or hinder our economy. The author discusses how these affect productivity growth and then reviews some policy proposals in the light of the productivity problem.

Mr. Malkiel, chairman of Princeton University's Department of Economics, served on President Ford's Council of Economic Advisers from 1975 to early 1977. He is director of the Vanguard Group of Investment Companies and the Prudential Insurance Company, and is a governor of the American Stock Exchange. This is his second article in HBR, the first one being "Moral Issues in Investment Policy" with Richard E. Quandt (March-April 1971).

Reprint number 79311

Despite a recovery that has celebrated its fourth birthday, the U.S. economy is not well. Symptoms of the disease are publicized in newspaper headlines. In 1978 inflation fever intensified, with the consumer price index advancing 9%, and, throughout much of that year, the floating dollar sank in international currency markets, further heightening the fever. Inflation has continued at extremely high rates in early 1979, and many people now express fears that the economy will also soon suffer from anemic growth and recession.

Yet the news media may be focusing on surface symptoms only and ignoring a more fundamental economic problem behind the headlines. The recent decline in U.S. basic productivity may ultimately have the greatest impact on the nation's well-being. Indeed, the present inflation problem may be intimately related to the clash between declining productivity growth and escalating claims on our national product for environmental, safety, and social needs. And our lagging productivity has, in turn, been affected adversely by low levels of long-term business investment and by the apparent decline in Yankee ingenuity, otherwise known as innovation.

What is this measure called productivity, and how can we be sure it is declining? It is an estimate of output per labor hour worked. Let us grant that it is a notoriously poor measure and that short-term swings in productivity estimates may signify little more than the random numbers generated by a lottery. Over the longer pull, however, the produc-

Author's note: This work was supported by the John Weinberg Foundation and the Charles E. Merrill Trust.

tivity estimates do indicate real trends. As *Exhibit I* shows, there can be little doubt that the creative pulse of the country is slowing down. In the exhibit, productivity is measured by dividing the total output of the economy (real gross national product) by total civilian employment. The productivity locomotive of economic growth, which had been pushing ahead at a rate between 2.5% and 3.00% per year, has clearly stalled.

The parallel performance of the U.S. economy with that of Great Britain in the early 1970s is chilling. While productivity has slowed in other developed countries as well, our rate of growth is far below that of our major trading partners. The United States, which always prided itself on being the undisputed leader in technological innovation, has seen its lead erode alarmingly. From the boardroom to the research laboratory, the consensus seems to be that U.S. enterprise may have lost its innovative touch.

Why do we care about productivity growth? Because the major problems we want to solve as a nation depend on it. Without increases in output per hour, real standards of living cannot increase, poverty cannot be reduced, and environmental quality cannot be improved. Without improved productivity performance in certain key industries, we may continue to see the value of the dollar erode with attendant inflationary pressures.

Indeed, the slowdown of productivity growth may well have contributed to our current stagflation condition. If labor groups have become accustomed to, and thus insist on, increases in real wages larger than the *present* growth in productivity, their living standards will increase only at the expense of others. Only productivity growth can provide the increases in real output per person that make possible overall gains in real living standards. Without such growth, the resulting struggle over income shares leads directly to inflation.

Any wage settlements larger than productivity gains tend to increase unit labor costs. (Think of a log splitter who gets paid $4.00 per hour and splits 10 logs an hour. The unit labor cost of splitting a log is 40 cents. Now if the log splitter's wage increases 10% to $4.40 but her output per hour—productivity—is unchanged, then the unit labor cost of splitting a log increases by 10%.) As a general rule, unit labor costs go up by the amount by which compensation per hour exceeds productivity growth. Since labor costs are an important component of total costs, business tends to increase its prices so that profit shares do not shrink.

This struggle over larger income shares in a pie that can only serve so many can also lead to unemployment. The real wage (wages expressed in real purchasing power) may be pushed up to a level inconsistent with full employment.

What is causing the slowdown?

Although the fact of stagnating productivity growth is clear, the relative importance of various responsible factors remains something of a mystery. A full quantitative explanation of our productivity slowdown is not yet available, but one can make a partial list of causes—some that we can affect and some that we cannot.

Little can be done about those causes of slower productivity growth arising from broad social trends. For example, the composition of the labor force has changed significantly; it now includes many more young and untried workers with less experience and training. Moreover, changes in the composition of output have probably lowered productivity somewhat. We no longer benefit from an exodus from the farms, and we find ourselves being transformed from a nation of industrial workers to one of lawyers and travel agents, occupations where productivity growth is harder to come by. The quintupling of energy prices since 1973 must also have lowered output per worker as companies have tended to shift from a more energy-intensive to a more labor-intensive method of production.

But we do have a say over some important causes of the productivity slowdown. Three of them deserve special mention: (1) the recent low level of business fixed investment; (2) the apparent malnutrition of our research and development effort; and (3) the effects of escalating government regulation. While they are not unrelated, it will be useful to treat each of them in turn.

According to the 1979 report of the Council of Economic Advisers, one important reason for our poor productivity performance is the weakness of business fixed investment over the past several years. From 1948 to 1973, the amount of capital stock per unit of labor grew at an annual rate of almost 3%. Since 1973, however, lower rates of private investment have led to a decline in that growth rate to 1.75%. Moreover, the recent composition of investment, at least until 1978, has been skewed toward

Exhibit I
The recent behavior of productivity in the United States

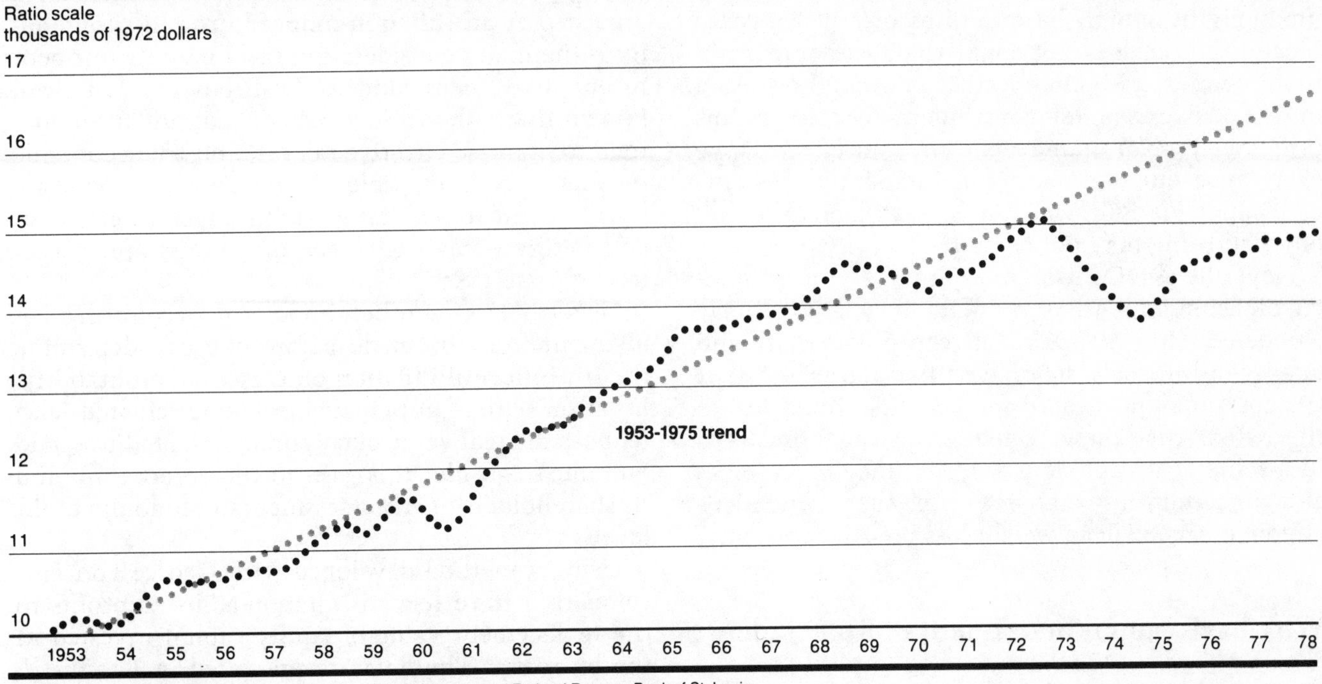

Source: U.S. Department of Commerce, U.S. Department of Labor, and Federal Reserve Bank of St. Louis.
Output per worker (real GNP/civilian employment) seasonally adjusted.

equipment and relatively short-term projects and away from structures and relatively long-lived investments. Thus our industrial plant has tended to age, and labor has had to work with increases in capital goods that are well below those of past years. The result has been a decline in measured productivity growth.

The slowdown in research and development expenditures also appears to have affected productivity growth. Although it is hard to put a precise quantitative estimate on the relationship between a dollar of R&D expenditures and innovation, all available evidence indicates that R&D makes a positive and significant contribution to technological progress. Total spending for R&D by industry, government, and universities dropped from 3% of GNP in the post-Sputnik days of 1964 to an estimated 2.2% of GNP in 1978.

This decline is largely explained by a reduction in space-related government research. Research by private industry has remained stable as a percent of GNP. Nevertheless, evidence from individual companies suggests that the R&D that is done by industry has tended to turn from longer-term research studies to short-term development projects, especially ones devoted to regulatory compliance. Indeed, many scientists have suggested that a similar compositional change characterizes much of government R&D as well.

In our search for instant remedies to satisfy regulatory problems in the areas of pollution control and occupational safety, our basic long-term research effort appears to have atrophied. As in the case of investment, one can also see a shortening of horizon periods. The investment and R&D problems are thus two ends of the same mustache. Our willingness to take risks, to commit resources to the future, is declining. We seem now to be motivated by the promise of a quick return rather than long-term growth.

While new investment and R&D expenditures can be called the engines of productivity growth, government regulatory policy serves as the reins. While regulatory activities can stimulate certain categories of technological innovation, the net effect of the Environmental Protection Agency (EPA), the Food and Drug Administration (FDA), and the Occupational Safety and Health Administration (OSHA) appears to throttle the productive energy of the country.

While such a decline is almost impossible to measure precisely, Edward Denison of the Brookings

Institute, a man who has spent his life sorting out the various influences on productivity, has suggested that such regulation may have recently lowered productivity growth by one third of 1% per year.[1] Since Denison does not count the abandonment of investment and R&D projects that would have been undertaken except for government regulations, his estimates probably understate the full effect. However, since our GNP does not include the benefits of cleaner air and water, the aggregate effect on our well-being may not be quite so devastating.

Nevertheless, Denison and, implicitly, the Council of Economic Advisers in its 1979 report, have wondered if the trade-off between productivity and quality-of-life goals may have tilted too far—so that the costs may far exceed the benefits. Moreover, to the extent that these regulations are administered in a somewhat capricious manner, they create risks and uncertainties that may, in the economist's jargon, create a "dead weight loss" for the economy.

Why have capital investment & R&D fallen?

Now that I have reviewed the important role of new investment and R&D, let us go on to discuss why such investments are so low. Again, the lack of clear consensus among economists reminds us of George Bernard Shaw's crack that if you laid all the economists in the world end to end, they still would not reach a conclusion.

Some analysts have suggested that the poor behavior of business fixed investment during the present expansion in the business cycle to the next peak can be explained fully by the existing unused capacity in manufacturing industries. To be sure, capacity utilization is an important factor in explaining the sluggishness of investment in recent years. The 1974–1975 recession carried utilization rates far lower than in other previous cycles, and the upturn in investment has clearly been associated with increases in capacity utilization.

Nevertheless, my own analysis suggests that, over the whole rise in the business cycle, business investment has been somewhat lower than would be expected on the basis of utilization rates alone.[2] In its 1978 report, the Council of Economic Advisers reached a similar conclusion: "It appears, however, that total investment outlays during the expansion have fallen somewhat short of those implied by historical relationships of investment to its determinants." And in 1978, capacity utilization rates have climbed to within 1% of what is considered (reasonably) full utilization.

Other analysts have suggested that lagging investment can more satisfactorily be explained by falling profit rates. Arthur F. Burns and others have argued that an inflation-induced drop in profitability is the major consideration in explaining our poor recent investment (and R&D) behavior.[3] It is well known that, other things being equal, inflation does tend to increase effective tax rates on true economic income: tax deductible depreciation charges are based on historical rather than replacement cost, and fictitious realized inventory profits are subject to corporate taxes.

Nevertheless, another important accounting adjustment must be made before one can determine the true effect of inflation on corporate profitability. Inflation—either anticipated or unanticipated—also reduces the real value of corporate indebtedness, and one must consider this gain to the corporation and its shareholders in any assessment of economic profit levels.

Using a method developed with George von Furstenberg, I have related inflation-adjusted profits to the replacement value of equity capital invested in the business.[4] The data are presented in *Exhibit II*. While profits are undoubtedly lower than they were in the Vietnam War, super-boom years of the mid-1960s, the data for 1977 and the estimates for 1978 stand up quite well compared with historical figures. There is no evidence of a persistent deterioration in the profit picture.

Of course, as an economist I must hedge and say that one must interpret these data with some care. They measure average profit rates on past investments, not the anticipated future rates of profit that are relevant for optimal decision making. Nevertheless, it is comforting to know that properly adjusted profit rates reveal a picture that is far more favorable than has been commonly supposed. Although investment and R&D expenditures may well be hindered by poor expectations of future profitability, evidence that profits have been damaged thus far in the United States does not exist.

Uncertain climate for risk taking

If the sluggishness of investment cannot fully be explained by either low capacity utilization or inadequate current profitability and cash flow, are other promising explanations available? I believe one can make a strong case for a number of economic developments of the early 1970s having raised the risk premium attached to investment decisions. Such increased risk premiums have increased the

Exhibit II
Inflation-adjusted profits related to replacement value of equity capital

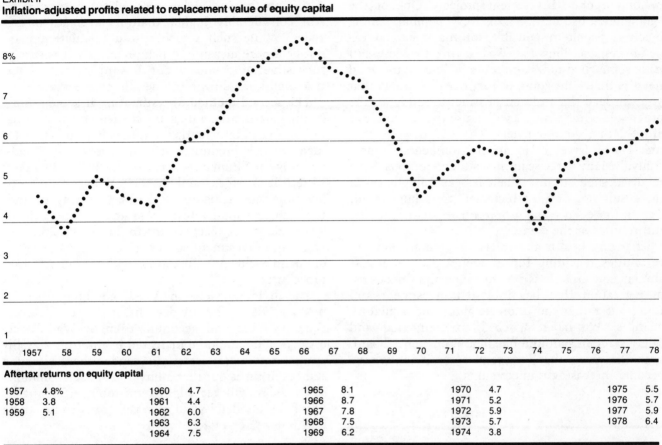

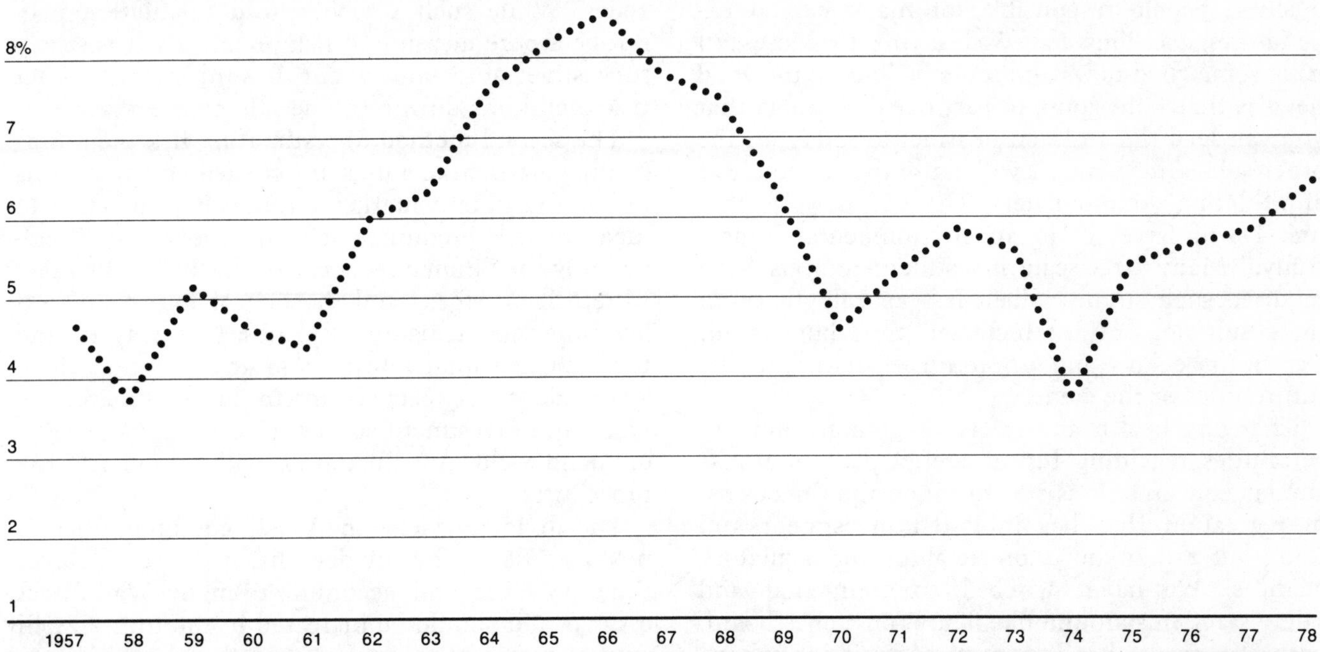

Aftertax returns on equity capital

1957	4.8%	1960	4.7	1965	8.1	1970	4.7	1975	5.5
1958	3.8	1961	4.4	1966	8.7	1971	5.2	1976	5.7
1959	5.1	1962	6.0	1967	7.8	1972	5.9	1977	5.9
		1963	6.3	1968	7.5	1973	5.7	1978	6.4
		1964	7.5	1969	6.2	1974	3.8		

Note: The aftertax profits of nonfinancial corporations are also adjusted to exclude inventory profits and to put depreciation on a replacement-cost basis. As inflation reduces the real value of corporate debt, this reduction is added back to profits. These adjusted profits are then divided by the nonfinancial corporate capital owned by equity holders (and valued at replacement cost). The latter figure is determined by subtracting from the replacement value of nonfinancial corporate assets the total amount of all debt.

hurdle rates of return that must be surpassed by new corporate investment projects (or, alternatively, they have increased the discount rates used to evaluate net present values). As a result, many investment and R&D projects that otherwise would have been undertaken have been cut off by the increased risk premiums.

In the economic area, we Americans are no longer as confident as we once were. A decade ago, we believed that deep recessions were curious anachronisms and that even mild recessions could be fine-tuned away. Few would have believed that the United States could experience double-digit inflation or that the unemployment rate could climb to 9%—let alone that these events could happen simultaneously. While the economy was recovering from the sharp 1974–1975 recession, inflation remained at a high rate despite considerable slack, and later, as we approached fuller capacity utilization in 1978, inflation accelerated.

Inflation, like love, is a fickle thing. High levels of inflation are associated with considerable variability in its rate and with large relative price changes, which make long-run corporate prospects and future planning especially hazardous. Thus, even if total profits increase along with inflation, the dispersion of profits among businesses increases with its rate. And once inflation becomes rampant, mandatory price controls always threaten, creating further instability, especially with respect to corporate profits.

Uncertainty has also increased because of escalating business regulation. Changing environmental regulations have considerably added to the cost, in-

1. Edward F. Denison, *Effects of Selected Changes in the Institutional and Human Environment Upon Output Per Unit of Input* (Washington, D.C.: Brookings Institute, 1978).

2. See my article, "The Capital Formation Problem in the United States," *Journal of Finance*, to be published.

3. Arthur F. Burns, "The Need for Better Profits," speech delivered at Gonzaga University, Spokane, Wash., October 26, 1977.

4. See my article, "Reports of the Death of Common Stocks are Greatly Exaggerated," *Fortune*, November 1977, for an explanation of the procedure.

creased the delays, and added to the risks of many major corporate investment projects. One of the "good-news bad-news" jokes very popular among business people responsible for major capital expenditure decisions has God saying to Moses, "I have some good news and some bad news: the good news is that I am going to part the Red Sea so that you can lead the children of Israel to safety on the other side, after which I will cause the sea to close, annihilating your pursuers. The bad news is that first I will have to do an environmental impact study." Many large-scale investment projects have required such studies, albeit less apocalyptic, with the result not only of increased costs but also of significant delays and uncertainties regarding the future rules of the game.

Changing health and safety regulations and uncertainties regarding future energy policies arouse similar concerns. It is not so much the direct cost of regulation that has inhibited investment and R&D but rather the unpredictability of regulatory changes. We have switched environmental and safety standards around like figures on a chessboard, with the result that long-term commitments have become increasingly uncertain.[5]

Evidence of higher risk premiums

I have suggested that an important explanation of the sluggishness of business fixed investment and R&D in the United States is that risk premiums have increased in financial markets during recent years. This has raised the cost of capital for companies and increased the hurdle rate that investment projects must surpass if they are to be undertaken. While the argument may seem reasonable enough, what evidence can be adduced to support this hypothesis and how do we know that these effects have had a substantial impact?

Although it is difficult to measure the precise extent to which risk premiums have increased in financial markets in recent years, one may employ two indirect methods. Both methods use the yields of long-term government bonds as a measure of the rate of interest on the highest quality securities.

The first method calculates the spread between these bonds and the yields of medium quality (BAA) corporate bonds. As the bottom line in *Exhibit III* shows, this spread narrowed through the mid-1960s and then expanded sharply, reaching a peak in 1974. Although the spread has receded since 1974, it is still considerably higher than its average in the 1960s. While such a yield-spread calculation may not be a pure measure of risk premiums, it is surely suggestive of a movement toward much higher risk premiums during the decade of the 1970s.

The second method for estimating risk premiums in financial markets uses anticipated equity returns rather than bond market returns. It is possible to measure risk premiums in equity markets by calculating the differences between the anticipated rate of return on stocks and the rate of return on riskless long-term treasury securities. One way to find the expected total return from any common stock is to add the expected growth rate—estimated by value and investment survey—of the company to its dividend yield. An illustration will help clarify the procedure:

The dividend yield on AT&T common stock is now about 8%. This dividend has been growing over time, however, and, according to many Wall Street estimates, it should be increased in the future at an annual rate of (at least) 5%. Under these circumstances, it turns out that a buyer of AT&T common stock today will get a long-term total return made up of the dividend yield plus the growth rate; that is, 8% + 5% or 13%.

The reason for the addition of the dividend growth rate to the dividend yield to obtain the total return may not be immediately clear. Perhaps two examples will provide some clarification:

☐ Suppose that an investor buys AT&T this year on an 8% yield basis. Since, by assumption, the dividend grows at 5% each year, the price of AT&T must be 5% higher next year if the stock's yield is to remain at 8%. Thus the investor receives a total return of 13% (8% from the dividend and 5% from capital appreciation).

☐ Now assume the investor buys the stock with the expectation of holding it "for keeps." The investor then buys a stream of dividends that keep growing at 5%. The long-term total return that the investor earns will be the discount rate that makes the current value of the stream of dividends equal to the purchase price.[6]

5. A recent study concluded that the impact of environmental controls on five pollution-intensive industries was to reduce investment in these industries by 5% to 17%; see M. Cary Leahey, "The Impact of Enviromental Controls on Capital Formation," in George M. von Furstenberg, *The Government and Capital Formation*, a study for the American Council of Life Insurance, to be published.

6. The effects of growth rates on security returns and prices are more fully explained in chapter 4 of my book *A Random Walk Down Wall Street*, rev. ed. (New York: W.W. Norton, 1975).

Exhibit III
Estimated risk premiums in financial markets

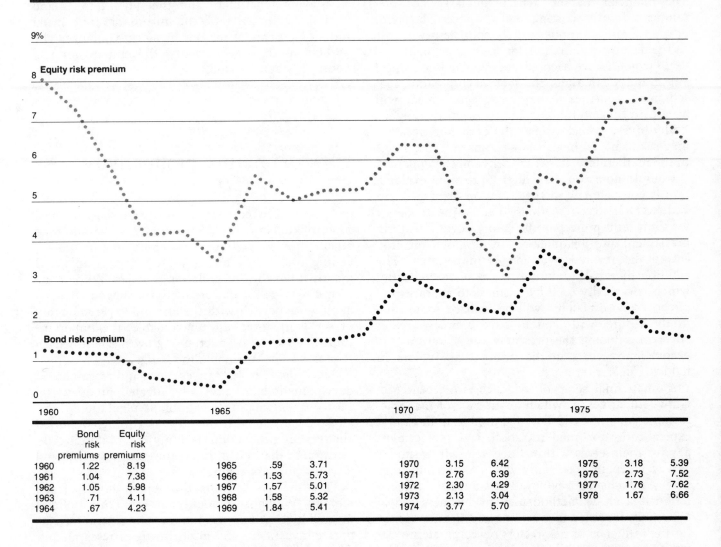

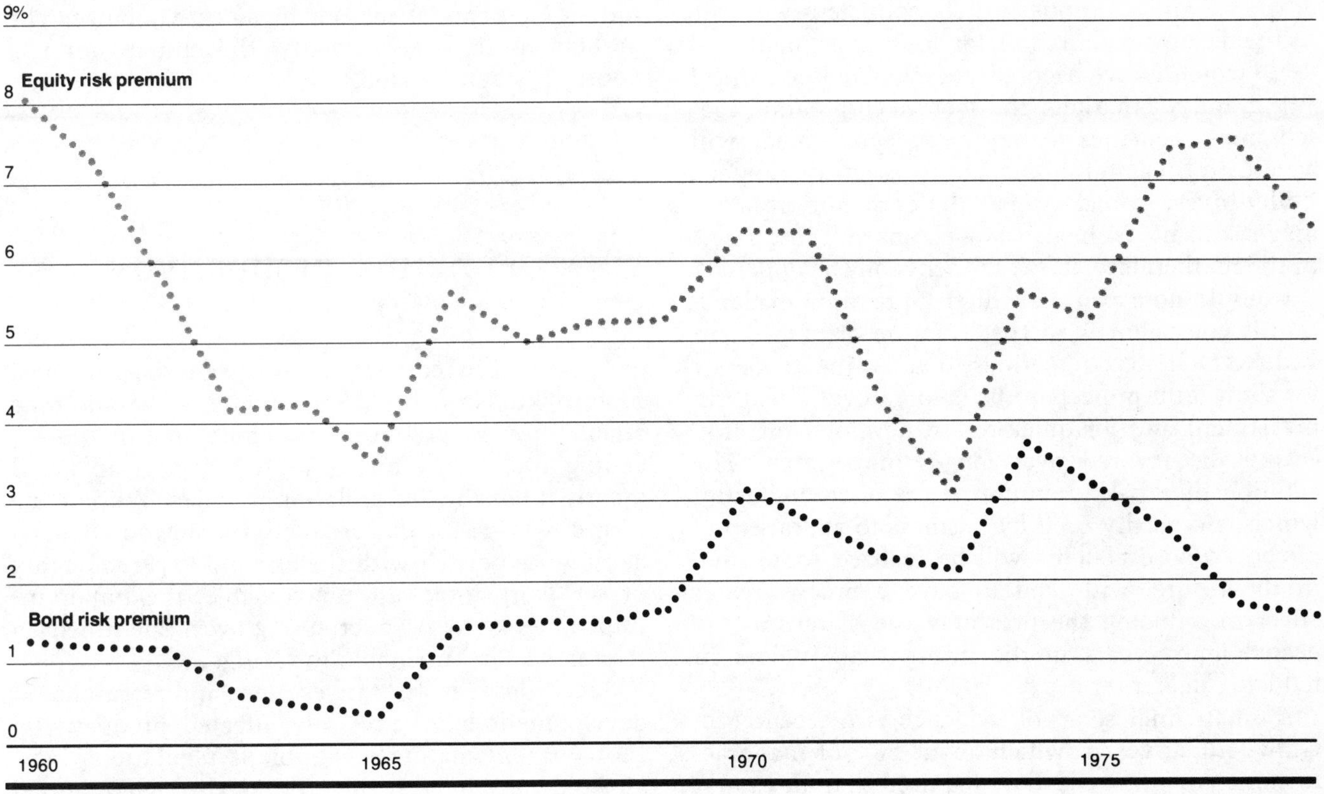

	Bond risk premiums	Equity risk premiums									
1960	1.22	8.19	1965	.59	3.71	1970	3.15	6.42	1975	3.18	5.39
1961	1.04	7.38	1966	1.53	5.73	1971	2.76	6.39	1976	2.73	7.52
1962	1.05	5.98	1967	1.57	5.01	1972	2.30	4.29	1977	1.76	7.62
1963	.71	4.11	1968	1.58	5.32	1973	2.13	3.04	1978	1.67	6.66
1964	.67	4.23	1969	1.84	5.41	1974	3.77	5.70			

A similar calculation was done each year for the Dow Jones Industrial Average in order to obtain the implied long-term rates of return for stocks in general. The yields on government bonds were then subtracted to obtain the equity risk premiums in the market, which are plotted along the top line of *Exhibit III*. Other ways of estimating the risk premium yield similar results.

It will be noted that movements in the estimated equity-market risk premiums follow the bond-market risk premiums remarkably closely. Estimated risk premiums fell until the middle of the 1960s and then rose into the early years of the 1970s. Unlike the risk premiums measured in the bond market, however, the risk premium derived from the equity market did not peak in 1974 but rose again in recent years.

Another way to review risk premiums is to look at the "valuation ratio," the relationship between the market value of a company's stocks and bonds and the replacement cost of its assets including plant, equipment, land, and inventories. In the mid-1960s, the (average) valuation ratio in the economy was approximately one and one-quarter—that is, corporate plant and equipment was being valued in the market at one and one-quarter times its replacement cost. As might be expected, the inducement to invest was great since investment in new plant and equipment would tend to create capital gains for a company's security owners. Thus the share of business fixed investment in GNP was high.

By 1978, however, the ratio of corporate market values to asset replacement values had fallen to about three-quarters—that is, corporate investments were on average being valued in the marketplace at less than three-quarters of the cost of replacement. The financial markets reflect the large risk premiums currently existing, and the recent behavior of the valuation ratio is entirely consistent with the risk-premium explanation for low investment and R&D which I have been advancing here (see *Exhibit IV*). In today's markets, the average corporation that sells new securities to buy new capital goods will be creating capital losses for its security holders. "Why invest in real assets?" the corporate treasurer may ask, if he or she can buy claims on those assets in the marketplace at, say, 75 cents on the dollar.

I should note also that the risk-premium explanation is consistent with the structure of investment and R&D in recent periods—that is, the tendency for short-term projects to be favored over long-term investment and for quick-return development projects to be favored over long-term research. The addition of a risk premium to the discount factor, which is typically used by business to appraise any projects whose benefits will be realized some time in the future, will tend to have a much greater effect in reducing the present value of returns expected many years in the future than it does in reducing nearer-term payoffs.

A small final scrap of evidence is a recent McGraw-Hill survey in which about 25% of manufacturing companies said they required that all capital expenditures for modernization and replacement pay for themselves within three years. In a similar survey taken in 1969, only 20% of the companies surveyed had such a policy. The short pay-back criterion is a crude method used by business people to account for risk and gives us more direct evidence for the influence of risk factors on corporate investment decisions. While the increase is small, the movement is consistent with my argument.

If my analysis is correct, the apparent unwillingness of our country to commit resources to the future is not the result of "diminished animal spirits," to use Lord Keynes's term. Nor is there necessarily some basic failing in Yankee ingenuity. Rather the problem seems to involve sharply increased risk premiums demanded by investors and attendant low equity prices. This increases the cost of capital funds to companies and reduces the amounts committed to long-term projects.

Basic research projects, which provide the foundation of technological progress, have the most uncertain and longest-term payoffs of all and thus can be expected to be particularly hurt. Moreover, these effects are likely to be especially acute for small companies, whose stock prices have performed very poorly. Venture capitalists, except for some brief flurries of activity, have tended to become as inactive as Maytag repairmen, and the new Xeroxes and Digital Equipments of the future are not being formed and capitalized on the stock exchange. The problem is in large part that the climate for risk taking has deteriorated.

How to improve productivity

If I have been correct in my diagnosis, the most basic sickness of the U.S. economy is the alarming recent drop in productivity, which in turn puts a ceiling on improvements in living standards and greatly intensifies our inflation problem. While some of the reasons for the productivity slowdown, such as those associated with the age and experience mix of the work force, are unavoidable, the important impediments to productivity growth identified in this article are amenable to change.

Recent low levels of investment and research and development have adversely affected productivity. Moreover, escalating government regulations have affected output both directly, as through required changes in production techniques, and indirectly as through their effect in creating uncertainties and discouraging risk taking.

This analysis suggests the general form of the remedy. We must reorient our economic policies to give high priority to the encouragement of corporate investment and to nurturing of research and development. We must improve the climate for risk taking. While some of the specific prescriptions I offer may seem familiar, they take on even greater urgency in light of our present productivity problem:

1. *Policies to spur investment and R&D.* Corporate tax relief may be usefully employed to offset the increased risk premiums that appear to have hindered business fixed investment and long-term R&D during recent years. A good start was made in the tax bill of 1978, which reduced corporate tax rates and liberalized and extended the investment tax credit. Fortunately, government policy regarding investment incentives has shifted from ennui to enthusiasm. But more needs to be done.

The interaction of inflation and our current tax system makes effective tax rates rise with high inflation. It is well known, for example, that as inflation increases nominal incomes and pushes us into

Exhibit IV
Valuation ratio and business fixed investment

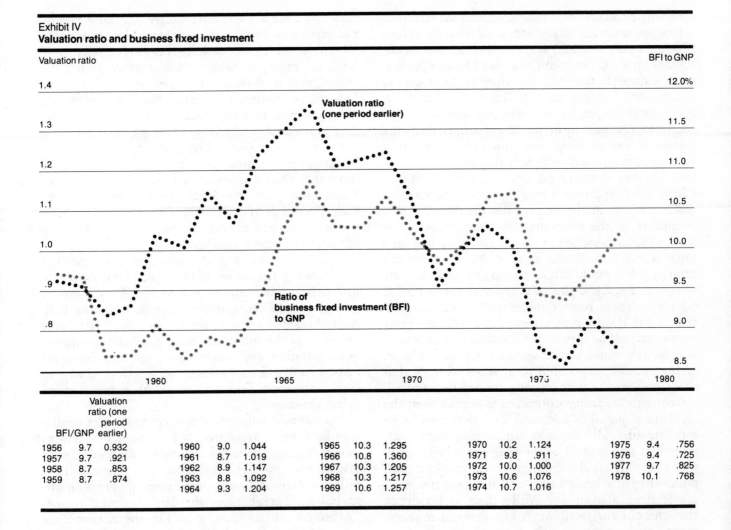

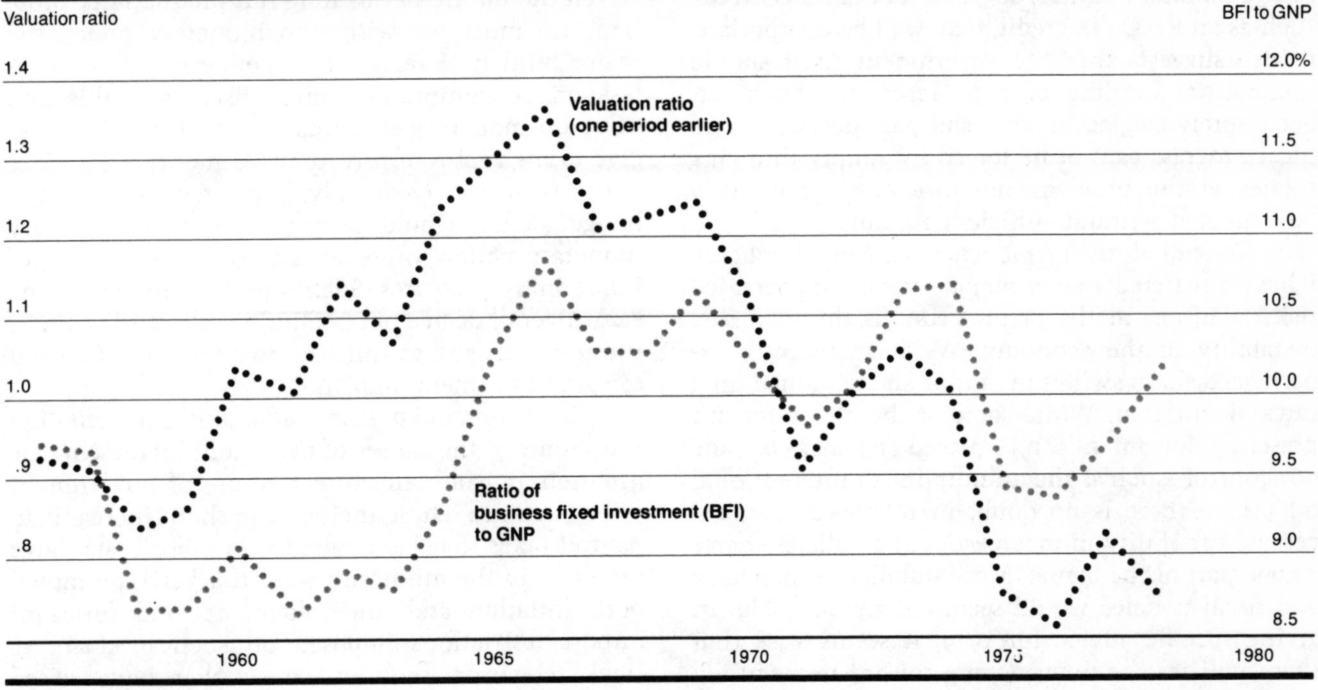

	BFI/GNP	Valuation ratio (one period earlier)												
1956	9.7	0.932	1960	9.0	1.044	1965	10.3	1.295	1970	10.2	1.124	1975	9.4	.756
1957	9.7	.921	1961	8.7	1.019	1966	10.8	1.360	1971	9.8	.911	1976	9.4	.725
1958	8.7	.853	1962	8.9	1.147	1967	10.3	1.205	1972	10.0	1.000	1977	9.7	.825
1959	8.7	.874	1963	8.8	1.092	1968	10.3	1.217	1973	10.6	1.076	1978	10.1	.768
			1964	9.3	1.204	1969	10.6	1.257	1974	10.7	1.016			

higher tax brackets, effective personal tax rates tend to increase over time. To help offset these effects, personal tax rates have periodically been lowered.

What is perhaps not as obvious is that effective tax rates on properly measured corporate income and on returns from financial investments are also subject to similar pressures. For example, real corporate tax burdens will tend to rise since tax-deductible depreciation changes are figured on the basis of lower original costs rather than replacement costs. Similarly, effective tax rates on capital gains tend to rise (quite sharply) with inflation.

The problem is that investors may have to pay heavy taxes on the sale of capital assets even when they actually receive less in real value for their assets than they had originally paid. Thus some form of more accelerated amortization and some inflation adjustment in the method of taxing capital gains can be justified as a means of preventing inflation from systematically damaging the climate for risk taking.

Such changes in tax laws need not be the camel's nose under the tent of full indexation. Discrete tax changes are necessary to prevent inflation from diminishing the incentive of Americans from undertaking long-term risks and to shift the investment incentives that do exist away from real estate shelters and municipal bonds and toward capital formation. Nor should we interpret such policies as an attempt to "soak the poor." On the contrary, we should rather appreciate the beneficial effects of tax policy on the supply side of the economy—effects that are intimately connected with the level and growth of real living standards. Capital is a seven- not a four-letter word.

Because the benefits of research and development expenditures often "spill over" onto all participants in the economy and cannot be limited to the company that has done the original work, there is good reason to believe that the market, left to its own devices, will allocate too few resources to R&D. Such underinvestment in R&D is likely to be greatest at the basic end of the R&D spectrum. This consideration (as well as the increased risk premiums I have discussed earlier) suggests that tax incentives, such as an R&D tax credit, may well be appropriate. It also suggests that the government itself should increase its funding of basic research, which has been sorely neglected over the past decade. Technical progress cannot be forced by simply throwing money at the problem, but innovation can easily be strangled without sufficient funding.

2. *General thrust of monetary and fiscal policies.* I have suggested that a major reason for increased risk premiums at the present time is the increased instability of the economy. We have recently experienced sharp swings in output and sustained high rates of inflation. While some of the blame for our present predicament can be placed on shocks outside our control—such as the quintupling of international oil prices—there is no doubt in retrospect that excessive variability in macroeconomic policies shares a good part of the blame. More stability in monetary and fiscal policies would seem clearly desirable. In giving specific advice for 1979, it seems wise that these policies are now moving toward restraint.

Currently, capacity utilization is not far from the level the Council of Economic Advisers uses as an estimate of "full" capacity utilization; the unemployment rate is close to the range now believed to represent full employment given the present composition of the labor force; and inflation has been accelerating alarmingly. While there is no doubt that the current restraint in our demand management policies runs the risk of a mild recession later in 1979, a slowdown in real growth is clearly appropriate and should help cool the inflationary fever.

Conversely, policies geared toward a continuation of rapid rates of real growth would almost certainly lead to an acceleration of inflation and an even sharper recession in 1980. The latter boom-bust course of events is precisely what must be avoided.

3. *Mix of monetary and fiscal policies.* The preceding recommendation about the durability of restraint in our overall demand management policies is a familiar one—most recently embraced by the Carter administration in the 1979 Economic Report of the President. What has received too little attention, however, is the issue of how macroeconomic policies should be mixed. While I am comfortable with movements in the general thrust of economic policies, I believe the present mix of policies is far from optimal.

Recently, we have relied heavily on fiscal policy to stimulate the economy. A projected budget deficit of even $29 billion is much too large considering how close we are to full capacity and how rapidly the state and local surpluses have already shrunk. Given the nature of our long-run productivity problem, we must not assign to monetary policy the major burden of restraint. A policy mix that relies less on consumption-oriented fiscal stimulus and more on monetary stimulus would be more conducive to high rates of private investment.

For 1979, a considerably larger reduction in the budget deficit would permit a more expansionary monetary policy to be carried out with less risk of inflationary pressures. Such a policy mix, given the same overall degree of restraint, would tend to lower interest rates and to shift the composition of output toward investment and R&D.

4. *Government policies affecting the inflation rate.* Some of the causes of the recent increase in the inflation rate are the direct result of government policy actions. These include the sharp increases in payroll taxes that have raised unit labor costs; large increases in the minimum wage that have promoted both inflation and unemployment; and forms of import restrictions imposed on such products as steel, television sets, and meat that have raised prices directly.

Agricultural policy has also contributed to inflation by turning away from a free market system to one of acreage controls and price supports. Dairy price supports may have cost U.S. consumers a billion dollars annually; sugar price supports another billion. Paraphrasing the late Everett Dirksen, "A billion dollars here, a billion there, sooner or later it adds up to real money."

The Brookings Institute, hardly an organ of the Republican Party, has estimated that these "self-inflicated wounds" have probably added one to two points to the inflation rate. There is insufficient realization of the extent to which the acceleration of inflation was "made in Washington." Reversing these kinds of measures is obviously politically difficult. Indeed, the root causes of our current inflation lie in the attempts of different groups to obtain increases in real income out of a pot that is not filling at the same rate.

Nevertheless, it is clear that the government does have the power to take decisive direct actions on inflation that could be quantitatively quite important. As I have suggested earlier, a decline in the rate of inflation would do much to remove the penumbra of uncertainty responsible for the substantial increase in risk premiums that are now discouraging long-term investments and R&D.

This article is not the place for a full discussion of the new program of price and wage guidelines.

In my view, their greatest danger lies in the widespread fear the guidelines create that they are a prelude to mandatory controls. Price and wage controls can lead to shortages and severe misallocations of resources. Controls have tended to squeeze profit margins, and undoubtedly their effect in the early 1970s was to discourage many long-term investments that would otherwise have been undertaken by industries that were then operating flat out at full capacity. This lack of investment added to our longer-run inflationary problems by holding back aggregate supply. Moreover, such controls make long-run planning even more uncertain and clearly are the wrong medicine for our current disease.

5. *Government regulatory policy.* Without doubt, government regulatory policy has had the undesirable side effect of discouraging innovation. While I applaud the objectives that have led to the establishment of such agencies as that for environmental protection, these agencies have not been sufficiently careful in analyzing the impact of their regulations on investment and R&D. I am pleased that the Carter administration has initiated a massive interagency review of government's own impact on faltering U.S. innovation under the direction of Commerce Secretary Juanita Kreps. Public regulatory and antitrust policies must be made much more consistent and must be redirected toward improving the economic climate for private risk taking and for investment in the future.

The outlook

The future for business fixed investment and R&D in the 1980s could be exceedingly bright. Our low investment and R&D expenditures for the last several years suggest that many potentially profitable projects exist. Our industrial plant is aging. Sharp swings in relative prices, such as the enormous increase in international oil prices, have created a favorable environment for investment and innovation. The fall in the price of the dollar has created potentially favorable movement in our international competitiveness.

If we can create more consistency in macroeconomic and regulatory policies, if we can tilt the thrust and mix of these policies toward the encouragement of long-term investments, if through tax policies we create an environment more conducive to risk taking, then the next decade could well be one of more real growth in living standards, increased employment, and less inflation. ▽

Individual initiative

In a way it is again the problem of individual initiative with which we are confronted. Individual initiative was one of the great stimuli both of the economic system and also of personal development under liberal capitalism. But there are two qualifications: it developed only selected qualities of man, his will and rationality, while leaving him otherwise subordinate to economic goals. It was a principle that functioned best in a highly individualized and competitive phase of capitalism which had room for countless independent economic units. Today this space has narrowed down. Only a small number can exercise individual initiative. If we want to realize this principle today and enlarge it so that the whole personality becomes free, it will be possible only on the basis of the rational and concerted effort of a society as a whole, and by an amount of decentralization which can guarantee real, genuine, active cooperation and control by the smallest units of the system.

From
Erich Fromm, *Escape from Freedom* (New York: Holt, Rinehart & Winston, copyright © 1969 by Erich Fromm). Reprinted with permission of the publisher.

How deadly is the productivity disease?

On the national level we really don't know, but companies can take their own productivity pulse

Reported declines in the nation's productivity have triggered an avalanche of fears, explanations, and cures. But what if the productivity problem does not exist? Or what if it is not as bad as the government tells us? In this intriguing essay, Stanley Henrici argues that the instrument used to monitor the illness, the Productivity Index issued by the Bureau of Labor Statistics of the U.S. Department of Labor, is not necessarily error free.

While the index may not always be wrong, Henrici suggests that the government—and business—be more cautious in drawing conclusions from its readings. If certain directives for national economic policy are based on 1% or 2% movements in the index, and these policies are not in fact called for, then not only will the money put into them be wasted, but the real problems ailing the economy may be ignored—or exacerbated.

In making his plea for caution, however, Henrici does not leave the individual company hanging. He discusses productivity measures that managers will find far more helpful in deciding when, and if, their particular business is in trouble.

Stanley Henrici recently retired as general manager, organizational systems of Heinz U.S.A. A previous contributor to HBR ("Eyeing the ROI" in May-June 1968), he has also written for a number of other publications. His most recent book, Salary Management for the Nonspecialist, *was published by AMACOM in 1980.*

Illustrations by Richard A. Goldberg.

Stanley B. Henrici

The diagnosis is in from our governmental doctors. The thermometer of our productive health—the Productivity Index (PI) issued by the Bureau of Labor Statistics—tells them the economy is sick; the United States suffers from "productivity disease."

Any of us feeling this productivity pulse would have to agree it is faltering. The PI rose steeply through the sixties and most of the seventies, except for the recessionary period of 1974—something like the heart rate of a jogger setting out on the morning trot. By 1976 it was more than 50% higher than in 1960.

But like the pulse of the jogger who soon collapses exhausted on the grass, the PI has been tapering off, beginning at the end of 1977. In moves unprecedented in our history, it fell 0.2% in 1978 and 0.4% in 1979. The vital signs do seem to be failing. But are we dealing with a sick patient or a sick stethoscope?

Let's look at the ailment more carefully. Maybe the index camouflages real problems you as a manager face, thereby concealing the solutions. I propose to take an objective look at it to see whether the government can make useful sense of the flood of unrelated data it requisitions from the business community.

On a more down-to-earth plane, I will suggest some productivity measures that would be far more helpful to most managers than the much overused and highly overrated national index.

Reprint number 81606

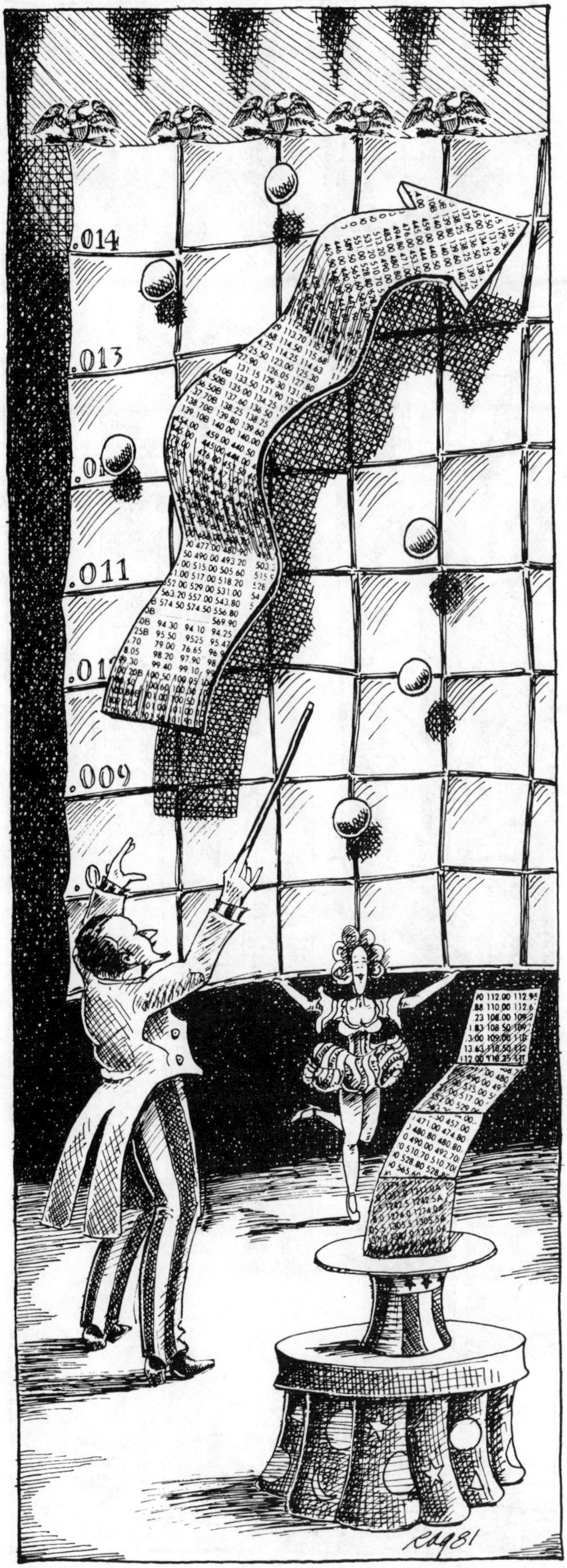

How the instrument works

Nearly everyone, I think it is safe to say, accepts the PI at face value as a starting point for discussion and analysis. It seems easy to understand and has an authoritative ring. But open it up and, instead of a simple stethoscope amplifying a heartbeat, you find a fascinating complex of parts that don't always mesh.

The productivity index is the ratio of national output per employee hour in any year compared with that of the base year. To calculate it, the Bureau of Labor Statistics (BLS) brings together three different kinds of data—how much we produce (output or gross domestic product) in light of how long it takes (input or hours spent producing the output), all adjusted for inflation (using the deflator to reduce GDP to constant dollars). It seems simple enough, but each of the three pools of data suffers from its own peculiarities.

Output

The output numerator, for example, is not what we might take it to be. When thinking of productivity we instinctively visualize a worker on an automobile assembly line, say, or a bricklayer putting up a wall. But for statistical purposes, a nation's output cannot be a physical count. To discover it, you don't add up the number of coal pieces dug up, the amount of toothpaste squeezed into tubes, or the number of Twinkies baked. Nor do you readily add in a count of lawsuits, dental exams, and sessions couples have with marriage counselors.

The statement of output requires a common measure, and for this the BLS uses GDP, which the BLS defines as "the market value of final goods and services produced." It doesn't directly measure the goods produced but instead measures their dollar value.

And how does the BLS measure the value? By definition, it says, "GDP is equal to income received by labor and property for services rendered in the current production of goods and services, in addition to capital consumption allowances, indirect business taxes, and several other minor items." In 1979, for example, out of $2,414 billion worth of GDP, three-fifths, or $1,461 billion, consisted of employee compensation—not the goods and services the employees produced but compensation for their production.

In the case of services, compensation is the only yardstick of output there is. How else do you measure for an index the value of what teachers, lawyers, nurses, and TV repairmen do? The more hours they put in, the more money they get. When the GDP is used to calculate the PI, then, the top and bottom of the ratio—GDP and hours—rise and fall together. Even when deflated, compensation remains compensation and not physical product.

Further, if the other components of GDP (such as corporate profits, proprietors' income, or net interest) go up faster than do employee-hours, the government says we have a productivity increase! And if indirect business taxes (fees and sales, excise and property taxes) rise relative to employee-hours without the sacrifice of some other component, the undeflated output per hour seems to climb.

In a special sense, of course, these things are all part of output. But they are far from the kind of physical production that comes to a commentator's mind when he talks about the work ethic or the impact of minorities on the workplace. Indeed, the kind of output used in the productivity index has little to do with employee effort at all. So even at this early point in our discussion we can safely say that this index, which arouses so much concern, is quite different from what is commonly conceived. But let's move on.

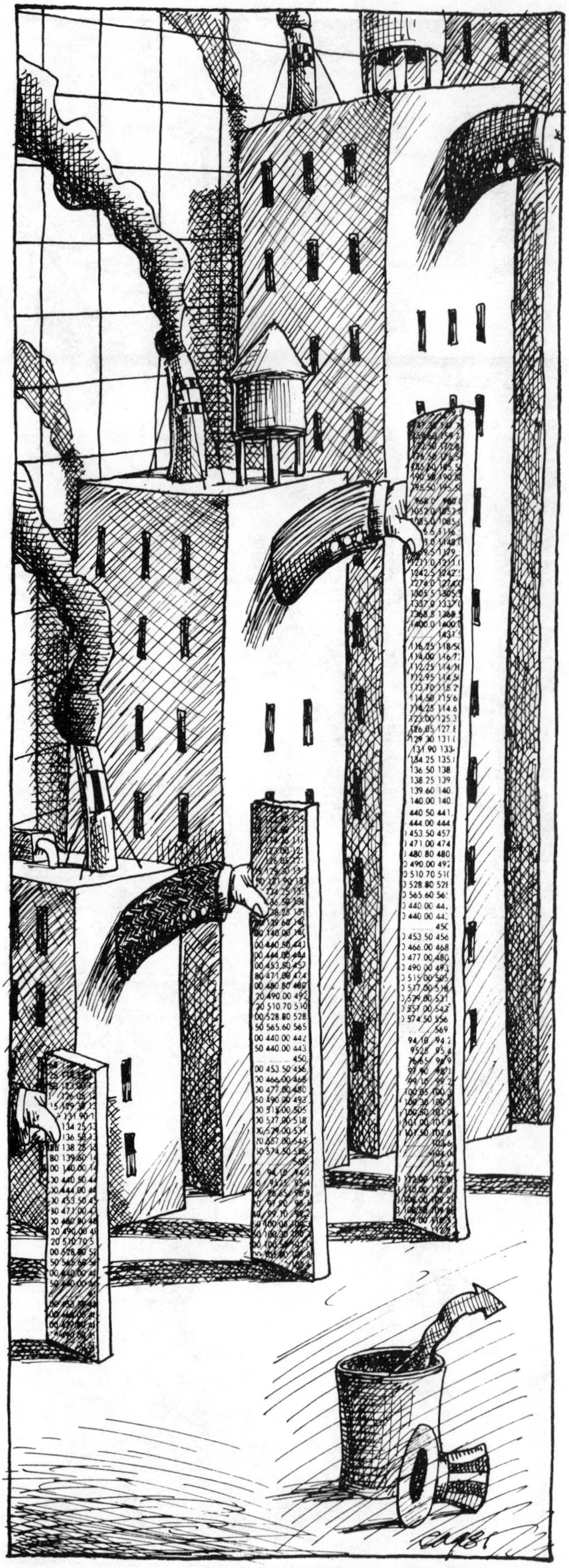

Deflation

Before output (GDP) can realistically be inserted into the productivity calculation, the government economists must compensate for the rise in prices. Otherwise dollar output per employee-hour, though mounting imposingly, would be an empty shell. Accordingly, economists at BLS and its sister organization, the Bureau of Economic Analysis (BEA), keep track of the changing prices of all the outputs and purchases in the United States and shrink them to 1972 dollars.

Arriving at deflators for this bewildering variety of outputs is such an awesome task that you have to wonder whether it can be done realistically. It's no great thing to discover the change in price of a standard commodity like a lathe or a pencil. But what about services like those of an advertising agency or the Fortran teacher at a local computer school? If their price fluctuates, is it due to inflation or to a hidden productivity component (in the case of the teacher, more or fewer students)?

In addition, the nature of some outputs changes over the years. How much of the price changes in automobiles are due to inflation and how much to pollution controls? How do you deflate the price of a home video recorder or a microwave oven when these things scarcely existed in 1972?

Perhaps more important, how do economists allow for changes in quality, as with computers? A draft memorandum of the Bureau of Economic Analysis says, "It is assumed that there is no price change for computers . . . that all price changes are offset exactly by quality changes." That may seem like an offhand approach to the reader, but it is hard to think of a better one. My point here is that these decisions often constitute judicious guessing rather than conclusions derived from hard data.

And the more inflation rages, the tougher such decisions become. Of necessity the economists at BLS and BEA have developed ways of coping with the complexity. But the job is variable and judgmental—something like trying to identify and clock all the animals fleeing a 40-mile-wide forest fire.

Considering the effort that goes into production of the deflators, criticisms about details sometimes seem like idle carping. For example, some critics charge that the deflators are too "heavy" because they are based on list prices rather than the actual transactions. Nit-picking? But what if that extra load of deflation amounts to 1% or 2%? That would fall right through to the PI, holding it down.

It is undeniable that the government's judgment on deflators shapes the PI just as much as the raw output itself—perhaps just as much as the sweat of the laborers whose productivity the index purports to assay.

Input

Looking at the simple productivity equation (output/employee-hours), the average observer might conclude that employee-hours are the easiest to determine. But this input side may also be questionable. And the PI is only as good as the summation of hours the BLS collects.

When we look closer at it, we discover a fundamental statistical difficulty. The PI rests on the hours employees are paid for work, not the actual time they spend at the workplace. So our equation includes not only those hours spent at the office or assembly line but also paid vacations, holidays, and sick leave.

The total number of hours paid could shrink nominal output per hour because it bloats the number of hours tallied compared with those actually worked. Since workers generally produce nothing in a day spent playing quoits at the backyard picnic, the use of hours paid sinks the productivity index by a like amount.

How well the BLS counts employee-hours will certainly affect the accuracy of the total and hence the significance of a PI based on that total. Such is the complexity and geographic spread of American business that learning what all its employees are doing is no easy job.

Because there is no such thing as a national time card, the BLS must draw on a variety of records and estimates. From establishments having more than 250 employees, it receives a monthly report of paid-for hours of production and nonsupervisory employees. These it supplements with a sampling program for smaller businesses. The agency also has access to reports from state unemployment boards, which supply the total number of employees for "covered" employers.

What is missing from these data, however, may be more important: some 13 million workers in areas not covered by unemployment insurance (roughly 14% of the total civilian labor force).

The BLS estimates their number, and you have to marvel at its achievement. Somehow the BLS comes up with a figure representing the hours of practically everyone: the migrant worker sorting tomatoes, the girl helping out in her father's flower store, Norman Mailer, your paperboy, and the line inspectors at the local box factory. Considering the fact that the decennial census, with a massive field force and a $1 billion budget, has been accused of several percentage points of inaccuracy, the BLS estimates are that much more remarkable.

It's like an estimate of the number of herrings in the ocean. There is really no way to be sure of it, but try to prove that it's wrong!

Even if the observer is kindhearted and supports the method, saying that absolute accuracy is of secondary importance as long as the data are gathered consistently, there is a problem. The accumulative effect of a bias can creep in, such as an improvement in estimating procedures. For example, a more accurate count of those employees underestimated in the past because of their "nondocumented" status would amplify the denominator of the output-per-hour ratio and de-escalate the productivity index.

The most important point to be made, however, is that the total hours used in calculating the PI are derived from a blend of reports, surveys, samples, and estimates. If this procedure misstates a trend by as little as one percentage point, the statistical anomaly could produce a 1% year-to-year productivity change. And we all know how much stress economists place on a 1% change in the productivity index.

A serious bias

I hope I haven't belabored the point. My purpose is to show that the data feeding the PI machine are not pure, by any means. They do not accrete, like a crystal; they are constructed, like a cheesecake. The human hand has been at work. And the origins of the outputs and inputs really are unrelated.

It is not surprising, then, to discover odd variabilities in the productivity index. For example, let's look at the change for manufacturing between the third quarter of 1978 and the fourth quarter of 1979:

Quarter	Percent change
III '78 to IV '78	+1.0
IV '78 to I '79	−3.8
I '79 to II '79	+1.7
II '79 to III '79	+2.5
III '79 to IV '79	−1.4

The productivity of the American worker zoomed up 1% in the fourth quarter, sank 3.8% in the very next, then swelled again in the second quarter of 1979. It's as if the surface of Lake Michigan were to rise and fall some 50 feet at a time!

These oscillations suggest a supersensitive indicator. But sensitive to what? I argue that the PI reacts sharply to the statistical and definitional vagaries that the BLS—and its 2,000 employees—must grapple with, and that its oscillations are due to imputed and estimated figures, to misreported hours and prices, to undetected transactions and unidentified workers, to slightly inexact deflators, and most of all, to the simple impossibility of quantifying the unquantifiable.

A U.S. Department of Commerce publication states that, "Productivity series suffer from statistical limitations." And one of the leading productivity specialists, Professor John W. Kendrick of George Washington University, warns, "Productivity measures are subject to unknown and probably not inconsequential margins of error."

Granting such cautions, some economists may argue that there is no better alternative. But George Terborgh, economics consultant to the Machinery and Allied Products Institute, has constructed a different productivity index based primarily on counts of physical units (not dollar values) derived from the Federal Reserve Index of Manufacturers' Production.

The *Exhibit* shows how Terborgh's scale compares with the government's index. His shows a growth rate in productivity some 33% higher than that of the BLS. Terborgh has his own explanation: "The lag of the official productivity index appears to have been affected by inflation. It strongly suggests that there is something about the deflation of current-dollar values that generates a downward bias in a period of inflation." The simple question arises, does inflation influence productivity or the numbers used to measure it?

We could continue to ask such questions, but I think the problems with the system are evident. Individual company managers must remember, however, that what the government can do but roughly on the national level, companies can do with rewarding precision on their own turf. Each organization, even each corporate department, can establish its own index of output per hour to establish the truth about its productivity.

Measuring microproductivity

Companies know whether employee productivity is important to them. The refining, chemical, utilities, and food industries, for example, probably stare hard at output per unit of material input, while much of the financial sector does not regard itself as a converter of employee-hours into a final product. But any company whose economic use of time determines its profit can benefit from an internal PI.

Such an organization must first determine the output measure to be used. Ideally, we would all like to tally units of physical output, but few manufacturing organizations have a limited range of products. (I will comment on the special case of services later on.) Even within a single product line such things as size, color, and differing physical specifications introduce variables that make the physical count wobble year in and year out. A line of disparate products (e.g., toothpaste, brushes, and powder) will further muddy the physical count.

I suggest instead that a company use net revenue dollars as its measure. This approach, not very distant from the well-known Scanlon Plan, would then parallel the government's but would be much easier to verify. Still, there are some problems

Exhibit **Output per employee-hour in manufacturing**
1951-1979

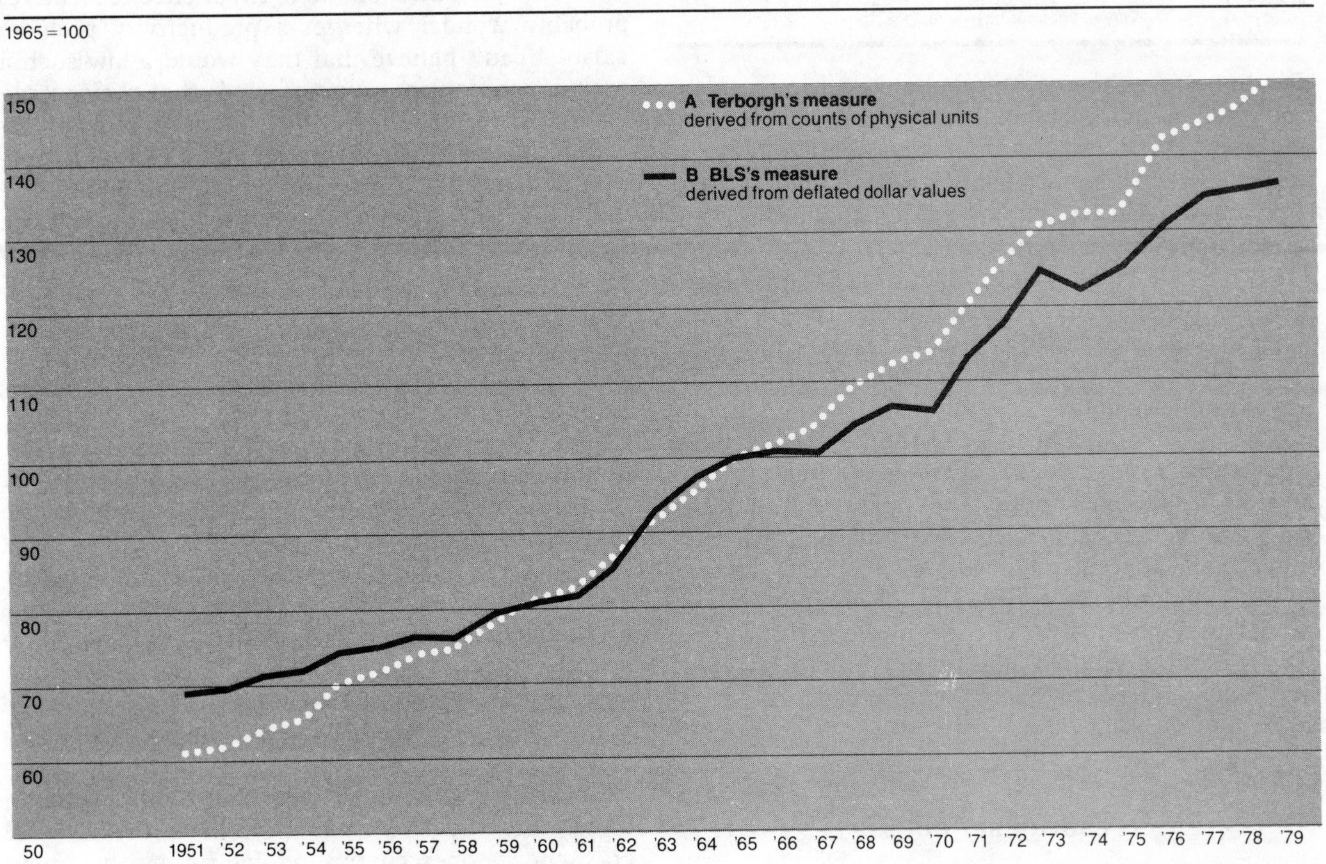

to watch for. Suppose the company subcontracts certain components that it previously made and at the same time lays off employees. The net revenue per hour would rise, which spuriously suggests an increase in productivity. It is preferable to state output, then, in terms of value added by the company. So output would equal revenues minus purchases (extended in some cases to take into account such things as rentals and interest paid).

Profit per employee-hour would be even simpler, but profit is not really what employees are employed to turn out. And marketing, financial, and inventory-control practices can affect profit even more. Management acumen is tied to profit; employee-hours are linked more closely to volume and, of course, general efficiency.

Adjusting for inflation

To compare this year's index with last year's, the company must adjust its value-added indicator for inflation. It selects a base year from which to track the index. Then it deflates sales revenue (less purchases) by the inflationary change of price in each of its products in order to determine equivalent output in base-year dollars. While this calculation twists the national PI index, causing the government innumerable headaches, within one company the interaction of price changes with productivity and quality is better understood. It poses the simple question, "What would this product have sold for in the base year?"

The company also can use total employee-hours worked for the input end of its equation. If the hours counted are a total from top to bottom of the organizational chart, the impact of having too many chiefs per Indian will soon become apparent.

To summarize, our microproductivity measure starts with:

$$\text{Output per hour} = \frac{\Sigma \text{ Deflators} \times (\text{Product revenues} - \text{purchases})}{\text{Total hours worked}}$$

And moves to:

Productivity index =	Output per hour, current year / Output per hour, base year

Further, the company can calculate a separate index for each of its divisions. For example, a sales department could use sales dollars per sales employee-hour. A factory could quantify salable value added per manufacturing employee-hour (including salaried employees as well).

Even nonmanufacturing organizations can test productivity. A retail business might track sales dollars (or possibly transactions) per employee-hour. Or a hotel could examine dollars (or perhaps guest-days) per hour.

Some managers think that having engineered task standards obviates the need for an overall productivity index. They argue that looking at performance against the standard will tell all. But again, that attitude ignores the time factor. Work standards are set for the job as it is today; they ignore year-to-year changes in the nature of the work. Besides, salaried jobs are not usually covered by such standards but only by a company PI.

A cautionary note

Organizations must handle their own productivity indexes with the skepticism the government seems to lack in handling its PI. For employee productivity really is not everything. Retention and growth of market share may depend more on quality and consumer satisfaction than on internal economics. A hotel cutting back on services in order to improve labor productivity might find itself with empty rooms.

Few business managers would trade high sales volume with low productivity for low sales volume with high productivity. But there is a national obsession with output per hour and it can rub off on individuals. There is always the danger that the patient will take unnecessary medicine for an imaginary disease.

Is this hypochondria or the real thing?

Journalists, economists, politicians, and academics harp on our productivity disease. I am suspicious, however, when corporate executives do not join in. They may know something the estimable observers do not.

Based on their experience, executives probably wonder whether a productivity problem exists. I can't believe that they would allow such a problem to continue uncorrected—that they would let their factory and office managers passively watch output per hour shrivel and collapse. Corporate demand for dollars to support marketing expense and inflated inventories is too great to tolerate creeping cost infection. And a company too sluggish to recognize the problem would find that the invisible foot (which Adam Smith was too polite to mention) might kick it right out of the marketplace.

Executives have moved beyond the simplicities of labor control in evaluating their businesses. They look for a good return on investment—not necessarily governed by the precise return on people. If productivity improvement contributes the lion's share to their particular return, then the executives should lean on it. But for many, the broadest avenue to success in today's world is better management of marketing, finance, distribution, and inventory.

I suggest that we abandon the national obsession with the productivity index. The rivers of data that flow into the system are made up as much of judgment as of facts, and their intricacies undermine the PI's credibility. Even the internal cross-checks on accuracy involve human judgment subject to human error.

We should admire the result and the heroic effort of the government economists who produce the PI. But we should not be overly impressed by changes of 1% or 2% in the magnificent instrument they've produced.

If we disregard that fallible instrument, we may find that the United States is not so sick after all. Is the productivity ailment psychosomatic? Perhaps the question should not even be asked. As Molière's imaginary invalid says, "Can I believe my ears? . . . Me? Not ill?" Hypochondria is never a welcome diagnosis. ⛉

2 How can we motivate the work force?

Quality of work life–learning from Tarrytown

At this large GM plant the union and management jointly seek to change the meaning of work itself

Robert H. Guest

Currently, when business people and researchers talk or write about the beginings of the human relations era in management, the name Hawthorne is invariably mentioned. In the future, when they talk about quality of work life, they will refer to Topeka, Kalmar, and Tarrytown. Each plant's experience with a quality of work life effort, essentially a structured program to involve workers in decisions affecting how they work, is unique. Each plant had different problems and different reasons for beginning a quality of work life program. Tarrytown, a GM car assembly plant in New York state, is perhaps the plant with the greatest number of people ever to have undergone such a program and is perhaps one that had the most to gain, for it was in a fairly sad economic state when the program began. This is the story of the developing and ongoing quality of work life program at Tarrytown, accented by quotes from the people involved.

Mr. Guest is professor of organizational behavior at the Amos Tuck School of Business Administration at Dartmouth College. He has published widely on the subject of work life, and is the coauthor, with the late C.R. Walker, of *The Man on the Assembly Line* (Harvard University Press, 1952, republished by Arno Press, Inc., New York, 1979), one of the first books to outline the questions that quality of work life programs attempt to solve.

Drawings by Ernst Aebi.

Reprint number 79402

Imagine that an executive of one of our largest corporations is told that one of his plant managers wants to spend over $1.6 million on a program that has no guarantee of any return in greater efficiency, higher productivity, or lower costs. Then imagine how he would react if he were told that the union is in on the program up to its ears and that the purpose of the program is referred to as "improving the quality of work life."

If the reader imagines that the average top corporate manager would say the plant manager had lost his senses and ought to be fired, the reader is probably in the majority. The striking fact, however, is that one particular executive, the head of what is probably the largest division of any manufacturing company in the world (18 plants and almost 100,000 employees) knew just what was going on and approved the idea enthusiastically.

This is the story of the General Motors car assembly plant at Tarrytown, New York. In 1970, the plant was known as having one of the poorest labor relations and production records in GM. In seven years, the plant turned around to become one of the company's better run sites.

Born out of frustration and desperation, but with a mutual commitment by management and the union to change old ways of dealing with the workers on the shop floor, a quality of work life (QWL) program developed at Tarrytown. "Quality of work life" is a generic phrase that covers a person's feelings about every dimension of work including economic rewards and benefits, security, working conditions, organizational and interpersonal relationships, and its intrinsic meaning in a person's life.

For the moment, I will define QWL more specifically as a *process* by which an organization attempts to unlock the creative potential of its people by involving them in decisions affecting their work lives. A distinguishing characteristic of the process is that its goals are not simply extrinsic, focusing on the improvement of productivity and efficiency per se; they are also intrinsic, regarding what the worker sees as self-fulfilling and self-enhancing ends in themselves.

In recent years, the QWL movement has generated wide-scale interest. Just since 1975, more than 450 articles and books have been written on the subject, and there are at least four national and international study and research centers focusing on quality of work life as such. Scores of industrial enterprises throughout the United States are conducting experiments, usually on a small scale; and in an eight-month world study tour a few years back of more than 50 industrial plants in Japan, Australia, and Europe, I found great interest in "industrial democracy."

So what is special about the Tarrytown story? First, it has the earmarks of success. Second, it illustrates some underlying principles of successful organizational change that can be applied in a variety of work environments. Third, although a number of promising experiments are going on in many General Motors plants and in other companies, this QWL program has involved more human beings—more than 3,800—than any other I know of. Finally, and this is speculative, I believe that Tarrytown represents in microcosm the beginnings of what may become commonplace in the future—a new collaborative approach on the part of management, unions, and workers to improve the quality of life at work in its broadest sense.

Readers interested in the Tarrytown story might want to read the article "Work Innovations in the United States" by Richard E. Walton, HBR July-August 1979. In that article, the author describes other examples of work improvement projects and what we have learned after 10 years of experience with them.
The Editors

Tarrytown—the bad old days

In the late 1960s and early 1970s, the Tarrytown plant suffered from much absenteeism and labor turnover. Operating costs were high. Frustration, fear, and mistrust characterized the relationship between management and labor. At certain times, as many as 2,000 labor grievances were on the docket. As one manager puts it, "Management was always in a defensive posture. We were instructed to go by the book, and we played by the book. The way we solved problems was to use our authority and impose discipline." The plant general superintendent acknowledges in retrospect, "For reasons we thought valid, we were very secretive in letting the union and the workers know about changes to be introduced or new programs coming down the pike."

Union officers and committeemen battled constantly with management. As one union officer describes it, "We were always trying to solve yesterday's problems. There was no trust and everybody was putting out fires. The company's attitude was to employ a stupid robot with hands and no face." The union committee chairman describes the situation the way he saw it: "When I walked in each morning I was out to get the personnel director, the committeeman was shooting for the foreman, and the zone committeeman was shooting for the general foreman. Every time a foreman notified a worker that there would be a job change, it resulted in an instant '78 (work standards grievance). It was not unusual to have a hundred '78s hanging fire, more than 300 discipline cases, and many others."

Another committeeman adds, "My job was purely political. It was to respond instantly to any complaint or grievance regardless of the merits, and just fight the company. I was expected to jump up and down and scream. Every time a grievance came up, it lit a spark, and the spark brought instant combustion."

Workers were mad at everyone. They disliked the job itself and the inexorable movement of the high-speed line—56 cars per hour, a minute and a half per operation per defined space. One worker remembers it well, "Finish one job, and you always had another stare you in the face." Conditions were dirty, crowded, and often noisy. Employees saw their foremen as insensitive dictators, whose operating principle was "If you can't do the job like I tell you, get out."

Warnings, disciplinary layoffs, and firings were commonplace. Not only did the workers view the company as an impersonal bureaucratic machine, "They number the parts and they number you," but also they saw the union itself as a source of frustration, "The committeeman often wrote up a grievance but, because he was so busy putting out fires, he didn't tell the worker how or whether the grievance was settled. In his frustration, the worker would take it out on the foreman, the committeeman, and the job itself."

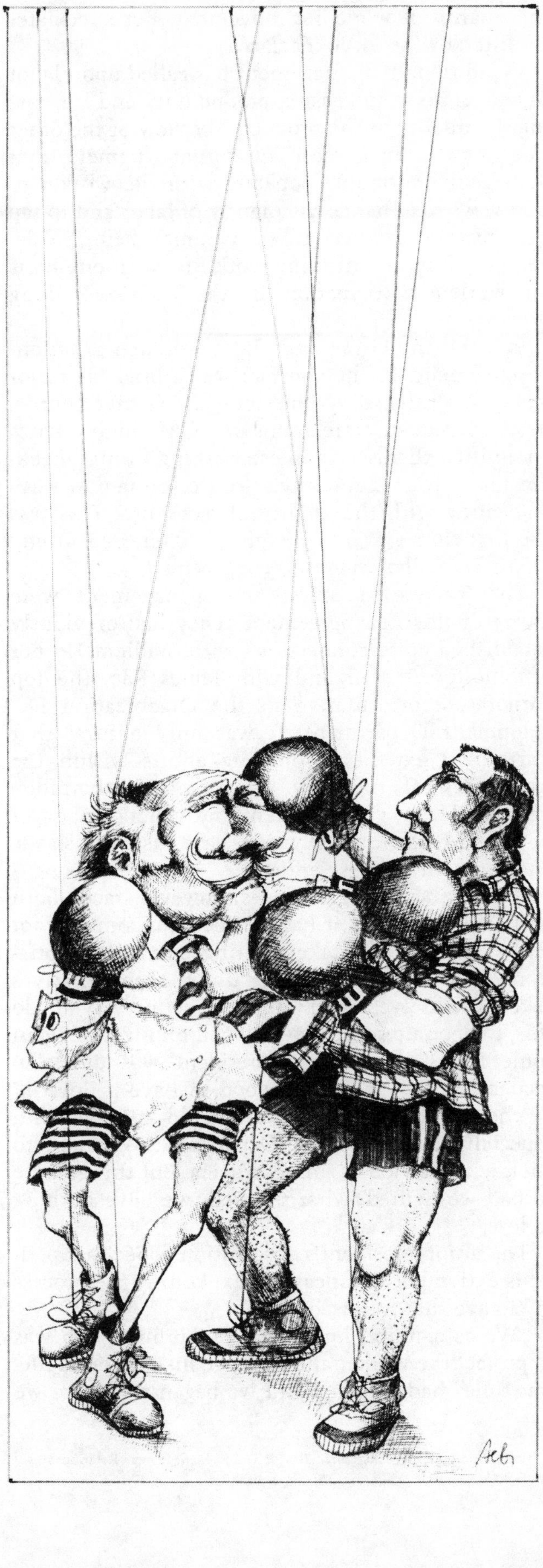

In the words of both union and management representatives, during this period "Tarrytown was a mess."

Beginnings of change

What turned Tarrytown around? How did it start? Who started it and why?

Because of the high labor turnover, the plant was hiring a large number of young people. The late 1960s was the time of the youth counterculture revolution. It was a time when respect for authority was being questioned. According to the plant manager, "It was during this time that the young people in the plant were demanding some kind of change. They didn't want to work in this kind of environment. The union didn't have much control over them, and they certainly were not interested in taking orders from a dictatorial management."

In April 1971, Tarrytown faced a serious threat. The plant manager saw the need for change, and also an opportunity. He approached some of the key union officers who, though traditionally suspicious of management overtures, listened to him. The union officers remember liking what they heard, "This manager indicated that he wanted to create a philosophy of management different from what had gone on before. He felt there was a better way of doing things."

The plant manager suggested that if the union was willing to do its part, he would put pressure on his own management people to change their ways. The tough chairman of the grievance committee observed later that "this guy showed right off he had a quality of work life attitude—we didn't call it that at that time—inside him. He was determined that this attitude should carry right down to the foremen, and allow the men on the line to be men."

The company decided to stop assembling trucks at Tarrytown and to shuffle the entire layout around. Two departments, Hard Trim and Soft Trim, were to be moved to a renovated area of the former truck line.

At first, the changes were introduced in the usual way. Manufacturing and industrial engineers and technical specialists designed the new layout, developed the charts and blueprints, and planned every move. They then presented their proposals to the supervisors. Two of the production supervisors in Hard Trim, sensing that top plant management was looking for new approaches, asked a question that was to have a profound effect on events to follow:

"Why not ask the workers themselves to get involved in the move? They are experts in their own right. They know as much about trim operations as anyone else."

The consensus of the Hard Trim management group was that they would involve the workers. The Soft Trim Department followed suit. The union was brought in on the planning and told that management wanted to ask the workers' advice. Old timers in the union report "wondering about management's motives. We could remember the times management came up with programs only to find there was an ulterior motive and that in the long run the men could get screwed." Many supervisors in other departments also doubted the wisdom of fully disclosing the plans.

Nevertheless, the supervisors of the two trim departments insisted not only that plans *not* be hidden from the workers but also that the latter would have a say in the setup of jobs. Charts and diagrams of the facilities, conveyors, benches, and materials storage areas were drawn up for the workers to look at. Lists were made of the work stations and the personnel to man them. The supervisors were impressed by the outpouring of ideas: "We found they did know a lot about their own operations. They made hundreds of suggestions and we adopted many of them."

Here was a new concept. The training director observes, "Although it affected only one area of the plant, this was the first time management was communicating with the union and the workers on a challenge for solving *future* problems and not the usual situation of doing something, waiting for a reaction, then putting out the fires later." The union echoes the same point: "This demonstrated how important it is to solve problems before they explode. If not solved, then you get the men riled up against everything and everybody."

Moving the two departments was carried out successfully with remarkably few grievances. The plant easily made its production schedule deadlines. The next year saw the involvement of employees in the complete rearrangement of another major area of the plant, the Chassis Department. The following year a new car model was introduced at Tarrytown.

Labor-management agreement

In 1972, Irving Bluestone, the vice president for the General Motors Department of the United Automobile Workers Union (UAW), made what many consider to be the kick-off speech for the future of the quality of work life movement. Repeated later in different forms, he declared:

"Traditionally management has called upon labor to cooperate in increasing productivity and improving the quality of the product. My view of the other side of the coin is more appropriate; namely, that management should cooperate with the worker to find ways to enhance the dignity of labor and to tap the creative resources in each human being in developing a more satisfying work life, with emphasis on worker participation in the decision-making process." [1]

In 1973, the UAW and GM negotiated a national agreement. In the contract was a brief "letter of agreement" signed by Bluestone and George Morris, head of industrial relations for GM. Both parties committed themselves to establishing formal mechanisms, at least at top levels, for exploring new ways of dealing with the quality of work life. *This was the first time QWL was explicitly addressed in any major U.S. labor-management contract.*

The Tarrytown union and management were aware of this new agreement. They had previously established close connections with William Horner of Bluestone's staff and with James Rae, the top corporate representative in the Organization Development Department. It was only natural that Tarrytown extend its ongoing efforts within the framework of the new agreement. Furthermore, Charles Katko, vice president and general manager of the GM Assembly Division, gave his enthusiastic endorsement to these efforts.

Local issues and grievances, however, faced both parties. In the past, it had not been uncommon for strike action to be taken during contract negotiations. The manager and the union representatives asked themselves, "Isn't there a better way to do this, to open up some two-way communication, gain some trust?" The union president was quick to recognize "that it was no good to have a 'love-in' at the top between the union and management, especially the Personnel Department. We had to stick with our job as union officers. But things were so bad we figured 'what the hell, we have nothing to lose.' "

The union president's observation about that period is extremely significant in explaining the process of change that followed:

"We as a union knew that our primary job was to protect the worker and improve his economic life. But times had changed and we began to realize we

1. Irving Bluestone, "A Changing View of Union-Management Relationships," *Vital Speeches*, December 11, 1976.

had a broader obligation, which was to help the workers become more involved in decisions affecting their own jobs, to get their ideas, and to help them to improve the whole quality of life at work beyond the paycheck."

The negotiations were carried out in the background of another effort on management's part. Delmar Landen, director of organizational research and development at General Motors, had been independently promoting an organizational development effort for a number of years. These efforts were being carried out in many plants. Professionally trained communication facilitators had been meeting with supervisors and even some work groups to solve problems of interpersonal communication.

What General Motors was attempting to do was like the OD programs that were being started up in many industries and businesses in the United States. But, as with many such programs, there was virtually no union involvement. As the training director put it, "Under the influence of our plant manager, the OD program was having some influence among our managers and supervisors, but still this OD stuff was looked upon by many as a gimmick. It was called the 'happy people' program by those who did not understand it." And, of course, because it was not involved, the union was suspicious.

Nevertheless, a new atmosphere of trust between the union and the plant manager was beginning to emerge. Local negotiations were settled without a strike. There was at least a spark of hope that the Tarrytown mess could be cleaned up. Thus the informal efforts at Tarrytown to improve union-management relations and to seek greater involvement of workers in problem solving became "legitimatized" through the national agreement and top level support. Other plants would follow.

The testing period

In April 1974, a professional consultant was brought in to involve supervisors and workers in joint training programs for problem solving. Management paid his fees. He talked at length with most of the union officers and committeemen, who report that "we were skeptical at first but we came to trust him. We realized that if we were going to break through the communications barrier on a large scale, we needed a third party."

The local union officials were somewhat suspicious about "another management trick." But after talking with Solidarity House (UAW's headquarters), they agreed to go along. Both parties at the local level discussed what should be done. Both knew it would be a critical test of the previous year's preliminary attempts to communicate with one another on a different plane. Also, as one union person says, "We came to realize the experiment would not happen overnight."

Management and the union each selected a coordinator to work with the consultant and with the supervisors, the union, and the workers. The consultant, with the union and the management coordinators, proposed a series of problem-solving training sessions to be held on Saturdays, for eight hours each day. Two supervisors and the committeemen in the Soft Trim Department talked it over with the workers, of whom 34 from two shifts volunteered for the training sessions that were to begin in late September 1974. Management agreed to pay for six hours of the training, and the men volunteered their own time for the remaining two hours.

Top management was very impressed by the ideas being generated from the sessions and by the cooperation from the union. The regular repairmen were especially helpful. Not long after the program began, the workers began developing solutions to problems of water leaks, glass breakage, and molding damage.

Layoff crisis

In November 1974, at the height of the OPEC oil crisis, disaster struck. General Motors shut down Tarrytown's second shift, and laid off half the work force—2,000 workers. Men on the second shift with high seniority "bumped" hundreds of workers on the first shift. To accommodate the new schedule, management had to rearrange jobs and work loads the entire length of the two miles of main conveyors, feeder conveyors, and work stations. A shock wave reverberated throughout the plant, not just among workers but supervisors as well. Some feared the convulsion would bring on an avalanche of '78s—work standards grievances—and all feared that the cutback was an early signal that Tarrytown was being targeted for permanent shutdown. After all, it was one of the oldest plants in General Motors and its past record of performance was not good.

However, the newly developing trust between management and the union had its effects. As the union president puts it, "Everyone got a decent transfer and there were surprisingly few grievances. We didn't get behind. We didn't have to catch up on a huge backlog."

What did suffer was the modest and fragile quality of work life experiment. It was all but abandoned. Many workers who had been part of it were laid off, and new workers "bumping in" had not been exposed to it. Also, a number of persons in the plant were not too disappointed to see it go. Some supervisors, seeing worker participation as a threat to their authority, made wisecracks such as "All they are doing is turning these jobs over to the union." Some committeemen felt threatened because the workers were going outside the regular political system and joining with representatives of management in solving problems.

In spite of the disruption of plant operations, the quality of work life team, the plant manager, and the union officials were determined not to give up. Reduced to a small group of 12 people during 1975, the team continued to work on water leaks and glass breakage problems. This group's success as well as that of some others convinced both parties that quality of work life had to continue despite a September 1975 deadline, after which management would no longer foot the bill on overtime.

During this period all parties had time to reflect on past successes as well as failures. The coordinators (one from the union and one from management) had learned a lesson. They had expected too much too soon: "We were frustrated at not seeing things move fast enough. We got in the trap of expecting 'instant QWL.' We thought that all you had to do was to design a package and sell it as you would sell a product."

Also, during this period, the grapevine was carrying a powerful message around the plant that something unusual was going on. The idea of involving workers in decisions spread and by midyear the molding groups were redesigning and setting up their own jobs. Other departments followed later.

At this time everyone agreed that if this program were to be expanded on a larger scale, it would require more careful planning. In 1975, a policy group made up of the plant manager, the production manager, the personnel manager, the union's top officers, and the two QWL coordinators was formed. The program was structured so that both the union and management could have an advisory group to administer the system and to evaluate the ideas coming up from the problem-solving teams. Everyone agreed that participation was to be entirely voluntary. No one was to be ordered or assigned to

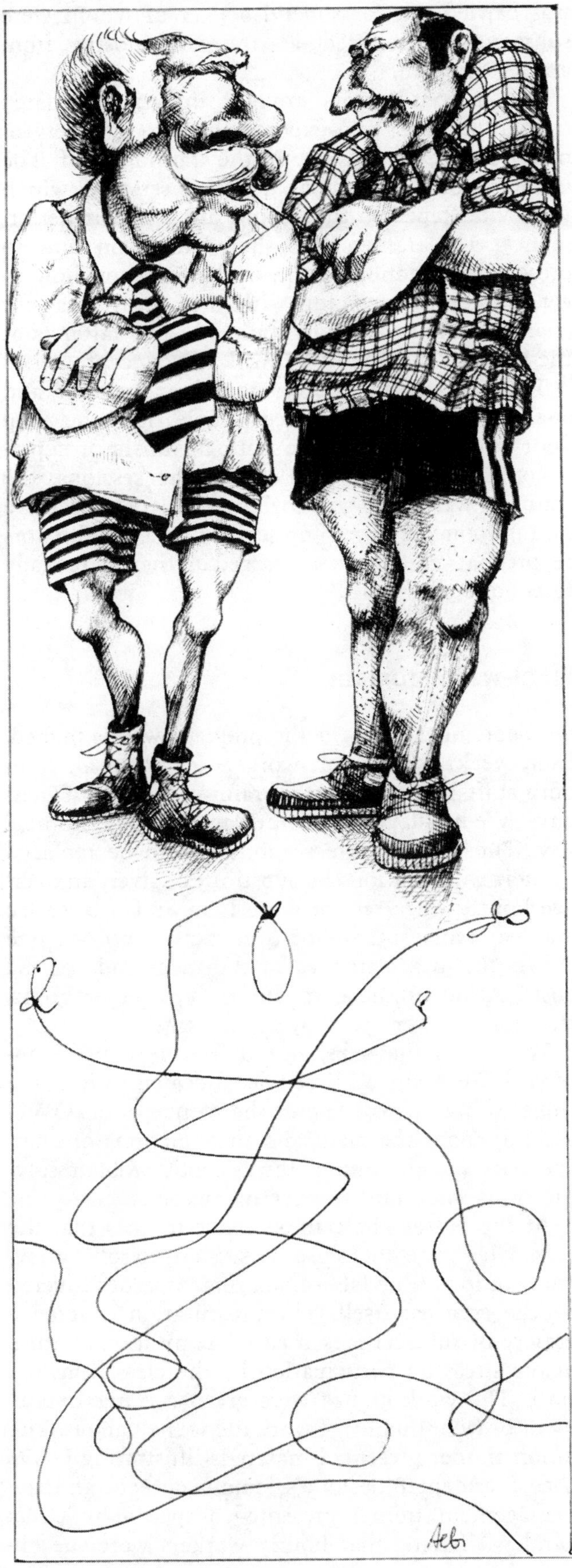

any group. Coordinators and others talked with all of the workers in the two departments.

A survey of interest was taken among the 600 workers in the two volunteering departments; 95% of these workers said they wanted in. Because of the large number that wanted to attend, pairs of volunteers from the ranks of the union and management had to be trained as trainers. Toward the middle of the year, a modified program was set up involving 27 off-time hours of instructional work for the 570 people. Four trainers were selected and trained to conduct this program, two from the union and two from management.

A second crisis occurred when the production schedule was increased to a line speed of 60 cars per hour. Total daily output would not be enough to require a second shift to bring back all the laid-off workers. Instead, the company asked that 300 laid-off workers be brought in and that the plant operate on an overtime schedule. Ordinarily the union would object strongly to working overtime when there were still well over 1,000 members out on the street. "But," as the union president puts it, "we sold the membership on the idea of agreeing to overtime and the criticism was minimal. We told them the survival of the plant was at stake."

Full capacity

Despite the upheavals at the plant, it seemed that the quality of work life program would survive. Then, a third blow was delivered. Just as 60 workers were completing their sessions, the company announced that Tarrytown was to return to a two-shift operation. For hundreds of those recalled to work, this was good news. Internally, however, it meant the line would have to go through the same musical chair game it had experienced 14 months earlier when the second shift was dropped.

Workers were shuffled around according to seniority and job classification. Shift preferences were granted according to length of service. With a faster line speed than before, the average worker had fewer operations to perform but those he did perform he had to do at a faster pace. In short, because of possible inequities in work loads, conditions were ripe for another wave of work standards grievances. Happily, the union and management were able to work out the work-load problems with a minimum of formal grievances.

But again the small, partially developed QWL program had to be put on ice. The number of recalled workers and newly hired employees was too great, and turnover was too high among the latter for the program to continue as it had been. Capitalizing on the mutual trust that had been slowly building up between them, management and the union agreed to set up an orientation program for newly hired employees—and there were hundreds of them. Such a program was seen as an opportunity to expose new workers to some of the information about plant operations, management functions, the union's role, and so forth. At one point, the union even suggested that the orientation be done at the union hall, but the idea was dropped.

The orientation program was successful. Some reduction in the ratio of "quits" among the "new hires" was observed. The union president did feel that "we had set a new tone for the new employee and created a better atmosphere in the plant."

Brave new world

Early the next year, 1977, Tarrytown made the "big commitment." The QWL effort was to be launched on a plant-wide scale involving approximately 3,800 workers and supervisors. Charles Katko, vice president for the division and UAW's top official, Irving Bluestone, gave strong signals of support. The plant manager retired in April and was replaced by the production manager. The transition was an easy one because the new manager not only knew every dimension of the program but also had become convinced of its importance.

The policy committee and the quality of work life coordinators went to work. In the spring of 1977, all the top staff personnel, department heads, and production superintendents went through a series of orientation sessions with the coordinators. By June, all middle managers and first-line supervisors (general foreman and foremen) were involved. Thus by the summer of 1977 more than 300 members of Tarrytown management knew about the QWL approach and about the plans for including 3,500 hourly employees. All union committeemen also went through the orientation sessions.

Also, during mid-1977, plans were underway to select and train those people who would eventually conduct the training sessions for the hourly employees. More than 250 workers expressed an interest in becoming trainers. After careful screening and interviewing, 11 were chosen. A similar process was carried out for supervisors, 11 of whom were subsequently selected as trainers, mostly from among foremen.

The 2 coordinators brought the 22 designated trainers together and exposed them to a variety of materials they would use in the training itself. The trainers conducted mock practice sessions which were videotaped so they could discuss their performance. The trainers also shared ideas on how to present information to the workers and on how to get workers to open up with their own ideas for changing their work environment. The latter is at the heart of the quality of work life concept.

The trainers themselves found excitement and challenge in the experience. People from the shop floor worked side by side with members of supervision as equals. At the end of the sessions, the trainers were brought together in the executive dining room for a wrap-up session. The coordinators report that "they were so charged up they were ready to conquer the world!"

Plant-wide program

On September 13, 1977 the program was launched. Each week, 25 different workers (or 50 in all from both shifts) reported to the training rooms on Tuesdays, Wednesdays, and Thursdays, for nine hours a day. Those taking the sessions had to be replaced at their work stations by substitutes. Given an average hourly wage rate of more than $7 per attendee and per replacement (for over 3,000 persons), one can begin to get an idea of the magnitude of the costs. Also, for the extra hour above eight hours, the trainees were paid overtime wages.

What was the substance of the sessions themselves? The trainee's time was allocated to learning three things: first, about the concept of QWL; second, about the plant and the functions of management and the union; third, about problem-solving skills important in effective involvement.

At the outset, the trainers made it clear that the employees were not to use the sessions to solve grievances or to take up labor-management issues covered by the contract itself. The presentation covered a variety of subjects presented in many forms with a heavy stress on participation by the class from the start. The work groups were given a general statement of what quality of work life was all about. The union trainer presented materials illustrating UAW Vice President Bluestone's famous speech, and the management trainer presented a speech by GM's Landen stressing that hourly workers were the experts about their own jobs and had much to contribute.

The trainers used printed materials, diagrams, charts, and slides to describe products and model changes, how the plant was laid out, how the production system worked, and what the organizational structures of management and the union are. Time was spent covering safety matters, methods used to measure quality performance, efficiency, and so forth. The work groups were shown how and where they could get any information they wanted about their plant. Special films showed all parts of the plant with a particular worker "conducting the tour" for his part of the operation.

To develop effective problem-solving skills, the trainers presented simulated problems and then asked employees to go through a variety of some experiential exercises. The training content enabled the workers to diagnose themselves, their own behavior, how they appeared in competitive situations, how they handled two-way communications, and how they solved problems. By the final day "the groups themselves are carrying the ball," as the trainers put it, "with a minimum of guidance and direction from the two trainers."

Trainers took notes on the ideas generated in the sessions and at the end handed out a questionnaire to each participant. The notes and questionnaires were systematically fed back to the union and management coordinators, who in turn brought the recommendations to the policy committee. The primary mode of feedback to their foremen and fellow workers was by the workers themselves out on the shop floor.

Continuing effort

Seven weeks after the program began in September 1977, just over 350 workers (or 10% of the work force) had been through the training sessions. The program continued through 1978, and by mid-December more than 3,300 workers had taken part.

When all the employees had completed their sessions, the union and management immediately agreed to keep the system on a continuing basis. From late December 1978 through early February 1979, production operations at Tarrytown were closed down to prepare for the introduction of the all-new 1980X model. During the shutdown, a large number of workers were kept on to continue the process.

In preparation for the shift, managers and hourly personnel together evaluated hundreds of anticipated assembly processes. Workers made use of the enthusiasm and skills developed in the earlier problem sessions and talked directly with supervisors and technical people about the best ways of setting up various jobs on the line. What had been stimulated through a formal organized system of training and communication (for workers and supervisors alike) was now being "folded in" to the ongoing planning and implementation process on the floor itself.

In evaluating the formal program, the trainers repeatedly emphasized the difficulties they faced as well as the rewards. Many of the men and women from the shop floor were highly suspicious at the start of the sessions. Some old-timers harbored grudges against management going back for years. Young workers were skeptical. Some of the participants were confused at seeing a union trainer in front of the class with someone from management.

In the early period, the trainers were also nervous in their new roles. Few of them had ever had such an experience before. Many agreed that their impulse was to throw a lot of information at the worker trainee. The trainers found, however, that once the participants opened up, they "threw a lot at us." Although they understood intellectually that participation is the basic purpose of the QWL program, the trainers had to experience directly the outpouring of ideas, perceptions, and feelings of the participants to comprehend emotionally the dynamics of the involvement process.

But the trainers felt rewarded too. They describe example after example of the workers' reactions once they let down their guard. One skeptical worker, for example, burst out after the second day, "Jesus Christ! You mean all this information about what's going on in the plant was available to us? Well, I'm going to use it." Another worker who had been scrapping with his foreman for years went directly to him after the sessions and said, "Listen, you and I have been butting our heads together for a long time. From now on I just want to be able to talk to you and have you talk to me." Another worker used his free relief time to drop in on new class sessions.

Other regular activities to keep management and the union informed about new developments parallel the training sessions. Currently, following the plant manager's regular staff meetings, the personnel director passes on critical information to the shop committee. The safety director meets weekly with each zone committeeman. Top union officials have monthly "rap sessions" with top management staff to discuss future developments, facility alterations, schedule changes, model changes, and other matters requiring advance planning. The chairman of Local 664 and his zone committeemen check in with the personnel director each morning at 7:00 A.M. and go over current or anticipated problems.

After the dust settles

What are the measurable results of quality of work life at Tarrytown? Neither the managers nor union representatives want to say much. They argue that to focus on production records or grievance counts "gets to be a numbers game" and is contrary to the original purpose or philosophy of the quality of work life efforts. After all, in launching the program, the Tarrytown plant made no firm promises of "bottom line" results to division executives or anyone else. *Getting the process of worker involvement going was a primary goal with its own intrinsic rewards. The organizational benefits followed.*

There are, however, some substantial results from the $1.6 million QWL program. The production manager says, for example, "From a strictly production point of view—efficiency and costs—this entire experience has been absolutely positive, and we can't begin to measure the savings that have taken place because of the hundreds of small problems that were solved on the shop floor before they accumulated into big problems."

Although not confirmed by management, the union claims that Tarrytown went from one of the poorest plants in its quality performance (inspection counts or dealer complaints) to one of the best among the 18 plants in the division. It reports that absenteeism went from 7¼% to between 2% and 3%. In December 1978, at the end of the training sessions, there were only 32 grievances on the docket. Seven years earlier there had been upward of 2,000 grievances filed. Such substantial changes can hardly be explained by chance.

Does this report on Tarrytown sound unreal or euphoric? Here are the comments of the most powerful union officer in the plant, the chairman of Local 664:

"I'm still skeptical of the whole thing but at least I no longer believe that what's going on is a 'love-in' at Tarrytown. It's not a fancy gimmick to make people happy. And even though we have barely scratched the surface, I'm absolutely convinced we are on to something. We have a real and very different future. Those guys in the plant are beginning to participate and I mean really participate!"

By May 1979 the Tarrytown plant, with the production of a radically new line of cars, had come through one of the most difficult times in its history. Considering all the complex technical difficulties, the changeover was successful. Production was up to projected line speed. The relationship among management, union, and the workers remained positive in spite of unusual stress conditions generated by such a change.

As the production manager puts it, "Under these conditions, we used to fight the union, the worker, and the car itself. Now we've all joined together to fight the car." Not only were the hourly employees substantially involved in working out thousands of "bugs" in the operations, but plans were already under way to start up QWL orientation sessions with more than 400 new workers hired to meet increased production requirements.

Tarrytown, in short, has proved to itself at least that QWL works.

Learning from Tarrytown

Although the Tarrytown story is, of course, unique, persons responsible for bringing about change in an organization might derive some useful generalizations and important messages from it. (See the ruled insert on page 41 for a list of general observations on quality of work life.)

Bringing about change—any kind of change—is extraordinarily difficult in our modern organizations. It is challenge enough to introduce new machines, computers, management information systems, new organizational structures, and all the bureaucratic paraphernalia required to support our complex production systems. It is even more difficult to organize and stimulate people to accept innovations directed at greater efficiency. Perhaps most difficult of all, as one looks at the quality of work life process and Tarrytown as an example, is for managers, union officials, and even workers themselves to adjust to the idea that certain kinds of changes should be directed toward making life at work more meaningful and not necessarily toward some immediate objective measures of results.

Even when people become committed to this idea, starting the process is not easy. Witness, for example, how long it took to turn the Tarrytown ship around. Look at the roadblocks its people had

Quality of work life – things to consider

What generalizations or principles might one derive from the Tarrytown story? The list below combines those of the participants themselves with my own observations about quality of work life experiments here and abroad. The list is not exhaustive. The first six are limited in general to organizations with collective bargaining agreements. The others have more universal applications.

1. For quality of work life to succeed, management must be wholly competent in running the business as a profit-making enterprise. When management lacks organizational competence and adequate technical expertise, no amount of good intentions to improve worker-union-management communication will succeed. Workers will not be willing to become involved knowing management lacks the competence to do anything about their ideas.

2. The union must be strong. The members must trust their leadership, and this trust must exist within the framework of a democratic "political" process.

3. In most instances, management has to be the first party to initiate change, to "hold out the olive branch."

4. Quality of work life should never be used by either party to circumvent the labor-management agreement. The rights, privileges, and obligations of both parties should remain inviolate. Dealing with grievances and disputes can be made easier through quality of work life efforts, but at no time should management give up its right to manage nor the union its right to protect its members on matters related to wages, hours, benefits, and general conditions of employment.

5. Top management and top union officials must make an explicit commitment to support quality of work life.

6. Even with agreement at high levels and a demonstrated concern on the part of rank-and-file employees, it is essential that middle management and front-line supervisors (and shop stewards) not only know what is taking place but also feel they have a say in the change process. Supervisors naturally feel threatened by any moves to give subordinates greater power in determining how work is to be performed. Union representatives can perceive unilateral work participation as a threat to their political position.

7. A quality of work life program is unlikely to succeed if management's intention is to increase productivity by speeding up the individual worker's work pace or, if it uses the program *as such,* to reduce the work force through layoffs. Workers will quickly see such actions as unfair exploitation. This is not to say that cost savings from better quality performance, lower absenteeism and turnover, and better production methods should not be an expected consequence of the effort.

8. A program should be voluntary for the participants.

9. Quality of work life should not be initiated with a detailed master plan. It should start on a limited scale focused on the solution of specific problems, however small. It should be flexible.

10. At each step in developing a program, all small bottlenecks or misunderstandings must be talked out and solved on the spot. If set aside simply to get on with the "important" plans, the little misunderstandings can later explode with enough force to destroy the entire program.

11. It is not enough to expose employees to the principles of effective interpersonal communication and problem-solving skills. There must be immediate opportunities available for them to use these skills in practical ways right in the job situation itself. Further follow-up action of some kind is necessary to serve as positive reenforcement to the employees.

12. Quality of work life efforts should not be thought of as a "program" with a finite ending. There must be a built-in momentum that is dynamic, on-going, and that can continue regardless of changes in the personnel in the organization. Once employees come to believe that they can participate and do in fact become involved in solving problems, the process gains a momentum of its own.

There is an implied warning here. Management may have the *formal* power to drop quality of work life efforts summarily. Union officers may have the *political* power to scuttle such efforts. Both would be acting at their peril for, under quality of work life, the workers will have gained a unique power to influence substantially the quality of their own lives at work. To them there is no turning back.

to overcome; deep-seated antagonisms between management and labor and the impact of changes beyond the control of the organization itself—new facilities, new products, and personnel changes at all levels, especially among hourly workers. Just when the quality of work life efforts gained some momentum, an unanticipated event intervened and the program was stopped dead in its tracks—almost. Indeed, one gets the impression that the only constant was change itself.

Some observations are in order. Developing this climate for change takes extraordinary patience. It takes time. It calls for sustained commitment at all levels. In most of the efforts to change human behavior that I have observed directly, these characteristics are lacking. Managers and leaders are under pressure to change things overnight. They draw up a program, package it, press the authority button, set deadlines, then move. It all sounds so easy, so efficient, so American.

In changing the way Americans work, we have, as the chairman of Local 664 said, "barely scratched the surface." What went on at Tarrytown was only a beginning. The intrinsic nature of repetitive conveyor-paced jobs has not substantially changed. The commitment to quality of work life is strong at the local level and among some people at division and corporate levels, but it is not universal. Changes in management or new crises could threaten further developments. Nevertheless, a new atmosphere about change and the worker's role in it is clearly emerging. People feel they have some "say," some control over their work environment now and in the future.

The Tarrytown story may, however, reflect something important about quality of work life efforts springing up in many other places in the United States. Studies are showing that workers in our large, rationalized industries and businesses are seeking more control over and involvement in the forces affecting their work lives. Due in part to the rising levels of education, changing aspirations, and shifts in values, especially among young people, I believe we are witnessing a quiet revolution in what people expect from work, an expectation that goes beyond the economic and job security issues that led to labor unrest in an earlier day.[2]

In parts of Europe, the response to this quiet revolution is manifest in broad-scale political efforts on the part of labor and government to gain greater control over the management of the enterprise itself. In the United States, the response is different.[3] Workers or their unions have given no indications that they wish to take over basic management prerogatives. As the Tarrytown story illustrates, what they want is more pragmatic, more immediate, more localized—but no less important.

The challenge to those in positions of power is to become aware of the quiet revolution at the workplace and to find the means to respond intelligently to these forces for change. What management did at Tarrytown is but one example of the beginnings of an intelligent response.∇

2. For recent confirmation based on survey data over a period of 25 years, see M.R. Cooper, B.S. Morgan, P.M. Foley, and L.B. Kaplan, "Changing Employee Values: Deepening Discontent," HBR January-February 1979, p. 117.

3. For a fuller discussion of the differences between American and European responses to labor today, see Ted Mills's "Europe's Industrial Democracy: An American Response," HBR November-December 1978, p. 143.

Quality of work life 27 years ago!

"If a man spends at least a third of his life in direct contact with a mass production environment, why shouldn't we consider as important (to him and to society) the hours of living time he spends inside the factory—as important and valuable, for example, as the product he produces which is consumed outside the factory? We talk of a high standard of living, but frequently mean a high standard of consumption. Man consumes in his leisure, but fulfills himself not only in his leisure but in his work. Is our mass production work environment making such fulfillment impossible?"

"We suggest that the sense of becoming *de*-personalized, of becoming anonymous as against remaining one's self, is for those who feel it a psychologically more disturbing result of the work environment than either the boredom or tension that arise from repetitive or mechanically paced work.—If we are to 'do something about' de-personalization, the first step is to understand it."

"Throughout this study both union and management agreed with the authors that the basic problems to be explored were not those connected with a particular plant, industry or corporation. Rather they were problems related to basic technological and organizational trends in modern industry. *Since these problems exist, let's get all the facts we can. In time we shall be able to solve them*" [Original italics].

"[Worker] suggestions, direct or implied, were within the framework of their own personal plant experience.—One of the most striking findings of the study is the psychological importance of even minute changes in his job experience."

"If it were recognized by both groups (management and labor) that they had much of a mutual interest to tell each other about the assembly of automobiles and about Plant X as a production team, something of great value to human relations might accrue."

Excerpts from:
Charles R. Walker and Robert H. Guest, *The Man on the Assembly Line* (Cambridge: Harvard University Press, 1952, republished by Arno Press, Inc., New York, 1979).

Fred K. Foulkes

How top nonunion companies manage employees

A study of 26 corporations suggests nine factors that can improve employee relations and aid productivity

Among America's largest industrial corporations, only a few remain entirely nonunion. It is no coincidence that the personnel policies of many of these unorganized companies are widely recognized as progressive and equitable. Why do these corporations try to create an attractive work environment? Because, the author contends, their managements recognize sound business reasons for paying close attention to personnel policies. On the basis of a study he conducted of 26 large companies which are predominantly or entirely nonunion, Mr. Foulkes concludes that effective personnel management can be conducive to an organizational climate that aids profitability and growth.

Fred Foulkes is professor of management policy at Boston University's Graduate School of Management. He is also director of the school's Human Resources Policy Institute. This article is based in part on his recent book, Personnel Policies in Large Nonunion Companies *(Prentice-Hall, 1980).*

Reprint number 81505

What is the primary advantage large corporations gain from operating without unions? Many might answer that the biggest advantage is lower costs for pay and benefits.

I would strenuously dispute that answer, however, on the basis of a study I recently carried out of 26 large corporations that are either predominantly or entirely nonunion. My study suggests that such companies benefit most from the flexibility they have to improve productivity in both the short and the long run.

I should add right away that these 26 companies were not chosen randomly. Rather, they were picked because they are respected leaders in their fields and, in many cases, are recognized for their innovative personnel policies. The corporations studied include Black & Decker, Eli Lilly, Gillette, Grumman, IBM, and Polaroid. (For details on the study, see the ruled insert on page 46.)

The experiences of these companies are especially instructive for companies without unions, because these experiences suggest that companies willing to take creative approaches to employee relations can improve productivity. The experiences are also potentially useful for unionized companies, since innovative approaches to employee relations are possible for them too.

Executives of the 26 companies studied believe they achieve higher productivity than they would if they were organized. Their companies, they say, have achieved a high degree of employee loyalty, a low rate of turnover and absenteeism, and a low degree of worker resistance to technological change. One of the companies studied, for example, enjoys a turnover rate of .5% monthly, considerably below the average for its industry. The annual turnover rate of another of the companies studied is 3%. A third company employs fewer people per dollar of sales than any other company in its industry. And a fourth has achieved such a reputation as an attractive place to work that it has its pick of job applicants–it receives an average of 8,000 to 10,000 applications annually for its 500 nonexempt job openings.

In the view of many of those interviewed, such benefits accrue from their freedom to experiment with employee relations plans, their opportunity to deal directly with workers, and the absence of an adversary relationship between employees and management.

Not surprisingly, the accomplishments of many of these companies cannot easily be copied or duplicated. My study revealed that strong top management concern for employees becomes institutionalized through implementation of various policies. Also important are the intangibles of leadership, personal example, and use of symbols.

These companies' rich legacies and traditions affect their managers and employees profoundly.

My study disclosed a set of nine common attributes, policies, and attitudes among large nonunion companies against which the managers of nonunion as well as unionized corporations can measure the effectiveness of their own personnel practices.

1 A sense of caring

First and perhaps foremost, many of the founders of the nonunion companies in my sample held fiercely egalitarian views about treatment of employees. Today, many of the customary symbols of corporate rank and status are absent. In many of the companies, everyone from vice president to sweeper has access to the same parking spaces, receives identical medical benefits, and eats in the same cafeteria. Frequently, executive offices are Spartan or even nonexistent. Employees at all levels call each other by their first names.

Moreover, the salaries of some of the top-level executives are modest by *Fortune* "500" standards. Many of these companies eschew such perquisites as company cars and club memberships that symbolize a visible ruling class of management.

Top management's commitment to employees is demonstrated not only symbolically but also through certain policies and practices. Hewlett-Packard, for example, is committed to job security, innovative training programs, promotion from within through job posting, cash profit sharing, an attractive stock purchase plan, widely granted stock options, and flexible working hours.

In most cases, the founders articulated and put in writing top management's commitment to effective personnel practices when the companies were quite small:

□ At IBM, Thomas Watson stated almost half a century ago the personnel principles that still govern the company; respect for the individual was and is one of those principles.

□ Edwin Land, founder of Polaroid, spoke early in the corporation's life of Polaroid's objectives: "We have two basic aims. One is to make products that are genuinely new and useful to the public, products of the highest quality and at reasonable cost. . . . The other is to give everyone working for the company a personal opportunity . . . to make his work here a fully rewarding and important part of his life."

□ At the Eli Lilly Co., J.K. Lilly wrote in 1916 a *Report on the Subject of Employment* that still guides the company. He noted in part, "The employment function is so important to good organizations as well as right relations that the 'Hiring Office' should be looked upon as one of the most important departments of the Company."

□ Some of Hewlett-Packard's corporate objectives with respect to employees are as follows: "To help HP people share in the company's success, which they make possible; to provide job security based on their performance; to recognize their individual achievements; and to help people gain a sense of personal satisfaction and accomplishment from their work."

What is important, of course, is the way Hewlett-Packard or any other similarly committed company achieves its objectives. While philosophy is important, it is action that counts.

2 Carefully considered surroundings

Several situational factors are also important both in fostering an effective personnel program and in encouraging a climate of trust and confidence. These factors include, among others, plant location and size and the handling of "sensitive work" and particular employee groups.

Determining location & size. The companies I studied consider carefully effects on employees and the chances of remaining nonunion when they select sites for new plants. Among the criteria used by one company are the quality of the public schools and the proximity to a university—as well as the area's attitude toward unions.

A personnel vice president at another company reported why a certain city would not be a good place to construct a blue-collar, production-type plant: "That city is sixth among the top 50 cities in the United States in downtime due to strikes, jurisdictional disputes, and other, related union conflicts. Moreover, there are more EEO charges in that city than in all but two other major cities. It is third in the number of fair employment practice cases and unfair labor practice charges. The city has several militant and aggressive unions."

Not only do many of the companies carefully choose rural or suburban plant sites, but they frequently limit the size of their facilities—between 200 and 1,200 employees—to promote personal and responsive employee relations. In the words of one personnel director, "We like to keep our plants small. We don't want them to grow larger than 200 employees. Beyond that size, both management and personnel lose personal contact with the employee."

Taking care with traditionally union work. Many of the companies studied are also careful about how they handle sensitive work—work that unionized employees often do. Some companies subcontract sensitive or strategic jobs. One company, for example, subcontracts its printing work, while many of its unionized competitors do their own printing. Sometimes sensitive jobs are done in-house but by the unionized employees of a subcontractor.

The idea is to make an organizing drive less likely. If a company's own nonunion employees do sensitive work, management usually pays close attention to their working conditions and wages, attempting to ensure that their treatment is equal to or better than that of comparable unionized personnel.

3 High profits, fast growth, & family ties

Certain financial and ownership characteristics seem to have an important bearing on personnel policies. Most of the companies studied are profitable—some, extremely so. Many are high technology growth businesses, have dominant market positions, and are leaders in their industries. Growth enables them to offer many promotion opportunities, provide full employment, and make profit sharing pay off.

Another important company characteristic is close ties between ownership and management. Two of the companies in my sample are privately owned, and members of the founding family are still active in management. In several of the public companies, a significant percentage of the stock is owned by one or more families, whose members remain active in top management. Thus, management is pushed to endorse the ideals of the founders and owners.

I should emphasize that no company studied displays all these attributes. Nor are these factors a sine qua non for achieving the desired organizational climate. They can even get in the way. For instance, while rapid growth provides many promotion opportunities, it also sometimes leads to such problems as communication difficulties and cramped quarters.

4 Employment security

Many of these companies attempt to minimize workers' usual nagging uncertainty regarding future employment. Several of the companies use various techniques to ensure full or nearly full employment.

During its early years, for example, Hewlett-Packard rejected large government contracts that would have created huge fluctuations in work load, forcing the company often to lay off and then rehire people. Moreover, during the 1970 recession, Hewlett-Packard cut everyone's pay and work time 10% for a six-month period rather than lay anybody off. The pay cut applied to everyone, from chairman of the board to assembly-line worker, as did the practice of not working every other Friday.

Other methods of weathering peaks and troughs in the work load include hiring freezes and the use of temporary or retired workers. This latter method, of course, simply transfers unemployment from the permanent labor force to part-time and temporary workers. Some companies prefer to devote periods of overstaffing to building up their inventories. Others encourage employees to take voluntary leaves of absence—thus guaranteeing continued employment.

Permitting employees to bank their vacation time can also ensure some flexibility in lean times. Work sharing is another way in which some companies avoid or minimize layoffs. Some companies that experience seasonal work loads hire their own retired or former workers during the peaks.

To some extent, one company's full-employment practice becomes its subcontractors' unemployment problem. At one company studied, part of the full-employment strategy is to use subcontractors to help absorb necessary production cutbacks. During tight periods, such subcontracting is curtailed or eliminated.[1]

1. See Warren M. Lowry, "Two-Way Contracting," HBR May-June 1967, p. 131.

Costs of full employment

Although companies that provide employment security boast of the flexibility gained from their nonunion status, they of course lose the option to lay workers off in response to changed business conditions.

The *Exhibit* catalogs the costs and benefits of avoiding layoffs. As it indicates, the costs can be significant. Yet the benefits of employment security cannot be overestimated. Eliminating workers' fears about layoffs can be a cornerstone of effective employee relations.

If layoffs become necessary nonetheless, management must implement a system that is perceived as equitable. The companies in my sample that do not practice full employment rely nearly exclusively on the principle of seniority. They also attempt, through a variety of means, to delay layoffs and cushion their impact. Curiously, none of these companies uses a supplemental unemployment plan.

A point to remember about full-employment practices: they always require effectively coordinating manpower planning and business planning. If a company has a policy of no layoffs, personnel people and line managers must cooperate when formulating strategies.

5 Promotion from within

A policy of promoting from within—accompanied by training, education, career counseling, and (frequently) job posting—is most attractive when a company's growth rate opens up many advancement opportunities. When computerized operations were expanded at one company, it chose to train current employees to be programmers instead of hiring qualified applicants. The training opportunities were simply posted, and interested employees who bid and passed the aptitude tests were trained to be computer programmers on company time and at company expense.

Like employment security, such efforts go a long way in building employee loyalty. Indeed, two-thirds of the companies in my sample have institutionalized the principle of promotion from within by routinely posting job openings. Some companies even provide plant workers extensive training and education so they can move into white-collar positions.

How the study was designed

The 26 companies in the study were defined as nonunion based on the fact that all or nearly all of their production and maintenance employees located in the United States were not members of any union. Twenty of the companies in the sample appear on the *Fortune* "500" list of industrials; and five other either privately owned or service companies had sales figures that would have qualified. Half of the companies studied had sales of $1 billion or more at the time of the study.

The companies each employ between 2,200 and 150,000 people in the United States; 60% employ more than 10,000 in this country.

All but three of the companies are engaged in manufacturing, in a range of industries. The three remaining companies are service organizations. No banks or insurance companies were included in the study. Many of the companies studied enjoy leadership positions in their respective fields. The names of most of them are household words. But the names of most are anonymous as a condition for their cooperation in the original study.

This field study used the case-study interview approach. More than 500 key line managers – including chairmen, presidents, operating executives, lower-level management people, and personnel executives – were interviewed.

Promotion of insiders to good jobs gets attention from company employees. Up-from-the-ranks supervisors who have benefited from such a policy have reason to be loyal and enthusiastic. Indeed, their attitude may contribute to the higher rates of productivity that many of these companies claim.

Promotion from within also helps a company maintain a consistent philosophy as the organization grows larger. Homegrown managers know and respect the company's values and traditions. Unlike newcomers, veteran managers know many employees personally and are familiar with several different jobs and operations. They also serve as excellent role models for employees wishing to follow in their tracks. But remember: extensive reliance on promotion from within requires reliable initial hiring practices and good career development programs.

6 Influential personnel departments

Not only are the personnel departments of the companies studied usually extremely centralized, they also have access to and in many cases are part of top management. More than half of the personnel vice presidents I interviewed report directly to the presidents of their companies. At a few of these companies, the head of personnel is a member of the board of directors.

The personnel departments of the companies studied are well staffed. Many have at least one professional person per 100 employees. Many also devote much attention to training and encouraging personnel people. At one predominantly nonunion company, trainees in employee relations get experience in a union plant, a nonunion plant, and finally in a corporate staff assignment. One company employs a staff person whose sole function is to help plan the career paths of the company's personnel people.

One reason for the influence of the personnel departments at the companies I studied is that line managers' competence is measured partly in terms of employee relations. When a department manager is accountable for the results of an employee attitude survey or the number of complaints filed by his or her subordinates, the expert advice of the personnel department suddenly takes on relevance.

7 Competitive pay & benefits

As might be expected, the 26 companies in my sample work hard to ensure that employees perceive their pay and benefits policies as equitable. All of them, therefore, compensate their employees at least as well as their unionized competitors do. The companies studied thus pay well by both industry and community standards. The nonunion companies watch carefully the union settlements of competitors.

Also, the nonunion businesses make careful and thorough attempts to communicate with workers about their pay increases and benefit improvements. Few of the companies studied will likely ever be vulnerable to a union drive on the basis of either benefits or pay.

These companies also give particular attention to making their benefits visible. One company, for example, presents an annual slide show at each local office comparing its benefits with those of its organized competitors. Black & Decker personnel and benefits professionals present all major benefit changes in group meetings. They not only tell managers and supervisors about the changes beforehand, but personnel staffers also provide them with answers to possible questions from employees.

Some nonunion companies argue that what might appear to be very generous provisions are highly cost effective. For instance, the medical facilities for employees at some companies seem lavish. Polaroid, for one, has on call its own orthopedists, dermatologists, and other specialists—in company facilities. Polaroid managers argue that this is much less expensive than medical insurance payments. Furthermore, employees spend less time away from work when medical professionals come to them.

Many nonunion companies also place heavy emphasis on merit increases, which either substitute for or supplement across-the-board pay increases. According to its proponents, such pay systems can serve as an incentive and will encourage greater work effort.

In the same spirit, many of the companies studied pay blue-collar workers salaries instead of hourly wages. About half of the companies have no hourly employees at all. The practice of bestowing the status of a salary on blue-collar workers represents another attempt to eliminate the "we-they" distinction between management and labor or between office and plant personnel.

The allowances for illness or personal business included in salaries impart respect and responsibility to the worker that are absent when labor is rewarded strictly by the time clock. Besides being consistent with the principle of equal treatment, salary plans differentiate the employee in status from his or her friends at other companies in the same industry or community.

Other common forms of supplementary compensation include profit sharing, company-matched savings and investment plans, and employee stock purchase plans. Profit sharing and stock ownership can also help employees to identify with the company, motivate them to work for its success, and further their understanding of the economics of the business.

Such programs often distinguish large nonunion companies from comparable organized corporations in the eyes of employees. For example, unionized employees at AT&T and General Motors were allowed to participate in their companies' savings and investment plans only two years ago, long after workers in many of the 26 companies I studied were offered that perquisite.

8 Managements that listen

The companies studied use a variety of mechanisms to learn employees' views on various matters. Attitude surveys "take the temperature" of the organization and expose developing employee concerns. Some companies regularly conduct "sensing sessions," or random interviews to understand employees' sentiments.

A number of these companies exclude supervisors from the upward communication process, so employees feel freer to speak out. For example, one company keeps its local managers out of its annual benefits presentations, which include a suggestion, complaint, and discussion session.

These managers now conduct their own regular meetings with employees, in turn excluding the foremen and supervisors. In this way, management believes, it can forestall serious labor problems on the local level. Supervisors are also encouraged by this system to resolve employee problems quickly, because they may fear higher-level investigations or complaints to higher management that reflect negatively on them.

Speak-out programs, which allow employees' anonymously written inquiries to be answered by management, are another common communication device. According to executives of companies that use speak-out programs, 5% to 10% of their employees submit a question at least once a year.

Like other communication programs, speak-outs can backfire if handled gracelessly. At one company, a hardworking technician wrote to inquire why parking at the plant was not on a first-come, first-served basis. This man arrived early every morning, parked his car, and then walked one-quarter of a mile across an empty management parking lot. His letter was answered by a low-level official, who suggested that managers have a divine right to convenient parking. The president of the company later learned of this gaffe, so now a top officer at each location reviews and signs the answers.

The dominant grievance procedure in the companies studied is the open-door policy. However, two companies have (and pay for) formal arbitration programs for certain grievances that can't be otherwise resolved. Two other corporations have appeals boards to which employees can take their grievances. One of the boards includes hourly employees and makes recommendations to the president. The other, which consists of managers, is a decision-making body.

Discussions with representatives of several nonunion companies have convinced me that open-door policies whose reviews and investigations are formal and rigorous can be effective. The office of the chairman of one company usually receives several hundred open-door complaints a year. Investigators working out of the chairman's office follow up on these complaints under an exacting timetable. Because managers usually settle in advance those cases in which the employee is obviously right, the cases that reach the chairman's office tend to be those in which management is right; thus, about three-fourths of the decisions support managers and about one-fourth back employees.

Exhibit **Costs and benefits of a full-employment policy**

Costs	Benefits
Extra payroll and payroll-related expenses:	Flexibility to reassign workers
• training costs	Productivity advantages because of high employee morale
• extra overtime because of reluctance to hire	Greater acceptance of changes in methods and technology
• possible temporary red circle rates	
• extra costs of any special early retirement plans	Lower unemployment insurance costs
Extra employment costs associated with extreme selectivity in hiring	Savings of training costs due to layoffs
Productivity losses associated with people assigned to different jobs	Favorable image in the community and recruiting advantages
Moving expenses	
Extra financial charges because of larger-than-necessary inventories	
Possible slower delivery schedule	
Possible slower rate of change in methods or technology due to need to avoid displacing permanent employees	

Top management's reactions to complaints demonstrate to lower-level management and employees alike whether the higher echelons care about the way employees are treated. When top management wants the decisions to be fair and is willing to investigate and review lower-level decisions, its credibility is enhanced.

The principal value of the formal complaint procedure seems to be the encouragement it gives to managers and supervisors to resolve employee problems before they become formal complaints. Management in a nonunion environment should not expect a formal grievance procedure to be used frequently; nor should such a procedure be relied on as a primary feedback device.

However, in my view, a nonunion company today should not be without some kind of formal complaint procedure. This is especially so in today's environment because employees who feel discriminated against because of race, sex, or age or who think their work area is unsafe can take complaints to an outside agency for investigation. Wise executives prefer to respond to complaints through their own mechanisms rather than deal with requirements set by a government agency.

9 Careful grooming of managers

Managers in these companies know that effective management of people is an important part of their jobs. Many of the companies studied avoid bonuses that reward short-term performance. Instead, they emphasize long-term results, including successful employee relations. They use stock options or other incentives associated with longer-term company success.

Thus, the selection of managers is a carefully considered procedure. Some nonunion companies use a series of panel interviews to evaluate potential managers instead of the traditional process whereby the boss picks his or her favorite for a promotion. Other companies send managerial candidates to "assessment centers" for a series of rigorous and imaginative tests that assess their ability to identify priorities and subdue crises in the managerial ranks.

At the lower levels of the organization, considerable resources are devoted to supervisory training. The supervisors, after all, deal with employees on a day-to-day basis, while top management has only occasional contact with them.

As a consequence of such training and reward systems, managers at all levels are keenly aware of the importance of good employee relations. Results of surveys are viewed as indicators of managerial competence. In many companies, managers believed that a stigma would be attached to their careers if their units had union-organizing drives or major personnel problems.

"People who demonstrate that they can manage well within the ethic of the organization are promoted," said a general manager of one company. At another company, performance is evaluated in terms of both "competence" and "relationships."

Because top management's personnel concerns often focus on the lowest-level employees, the supervisor may have the most difficult role of all in these nonunion companies. In some cases, the preoccupation of the founder with the welfare and security of the hourly workers appears to have depreciated the role of the supervisors, who may feel less secure than those they supervise. If supervisors come to feel insecure and experience too much anxiety, of course, the long-run health of the organization can suffer. Some of the nonunion companies have therefore begun tracking the feelings of supervisors through attitude surveys and other means.

Pride & profits

The 26 companies studied clearly try to create a climate of cooperation between employees and management. However, skeptics may still wonder if the rewards of positive employee relations are financially significant. I noted at the beginning of this article that the top managers of many large nonunion companies have expressed the belief that they can justify their personnel policies as providing great economic incentive. However, it may be impossible to determine precisely by what amounts the personnel practices previously outlined actually alter the bottom line. It certainly is costly to hire your own doctors, conduct attitude surveys, train your own employees for promotion, and offer profit sharing.

But in the view of many of those interviewed, the freedom to experiment with employee relations plans, the opportunity to deal directly with employees, and the absence of adversary relationships between employees and management result in a more profitable enterprise in the long run. Many of the managers take obvious pride in their personnel philosophies and accomplishments and are convinced that their efforts contribute directly and positively to productivity and profits.

Thus, I would argue that, for a large company to remain nonunion, top management needs to be personally involved in personnel management and to constantly demonstrate to nonexempt workers and managers alike its interest and concern for employees. ▽

Horse-collar blue-collar blues

Will what happened to the horse collar, when tractors took the horse's job, happen to the blue collar, when robots do the blue-collar job?

Robert Schrank

The only horse collars you see nowadays hang on old rusty pegs in barns. Some probably reside in museums of the West; the rest, unused, have been thrown away. Because horses no longer do farm work, farmers don't need horse collars. What will happen to blue-collar workers when robots take over their jobs? Will there be nothing left but some old clothes on a peg and a few mementos kept around in museums of the industrial era? The author of this article may be fanciful in his recreation of history, but the questions he poses are serious and very real.

Mr. Schrank is program officer at the Ford Foundation, where he monitors and evaluates employment training and related programs. This is his third article for HBR, the last being "Are Unions an Anachronism?" (September-October 1979). He is also the author of *Ten Thousand Working Days* (Cambridge: MIT Press, 1978).

Illustrations based on original photographs supplied by Bettmann Archive, Inc.

Reprint number 81312

Old MacDonald had a farm and some workhorses, too—and a real concern over their appetites. Working or not, they consumed 25 pounds of feed a day including Thanksgiving, Christmas, and Easter. When his Belgian took sick, MacDonald had to call the vet; and when the horse reached old age, MacDonald, a nice farmer, would have to put him out to pasture, where he could just hang out—eating. None of the farmers around MacDonald's place was happy with this cradle-to-grave horse security arrangement.

Sometime in 1905, a group of farmers gathered at dawn in the middle of a wheat field by a sick MacDonald workhorse. Lying on his side and bucking his head, the poor thing tried to raise his one-ton hulk. Farmer Wheatseed asked MacDonald what had happened to the horse. MacDonald did not know what had caused his big old trusted Belgian to collapse, but he said the horse had been failing for some time now. MacDonald shook his head and said he was not sure whether he should go on feeding the bum or just shoot him. Farmer Pitchfork suggested they get the collar and harness off. "You'll need that for your other horses, unless you decide to trade 'em in for mules—they eat less."

The meeting in the wheat field proved to be a good time for all the farmers to join in deploring the cost of feeding the damn horses and mules. Sometimes, they lamented, the horses did nothing but stand in the stalls all day eating those beautiful oats, rye, bran, and hay—25 pounds worth. "It takes about three acres of pasture to feed each workhorse for a year," Farmer Hoedown said. And this acreage has to be worked by the farmer, observed Wheatseed, a thinking man among farmers: "The horse may eat the pasturage, but he can't plant and harvest the oats. So we end up working for him." Pitchfork,

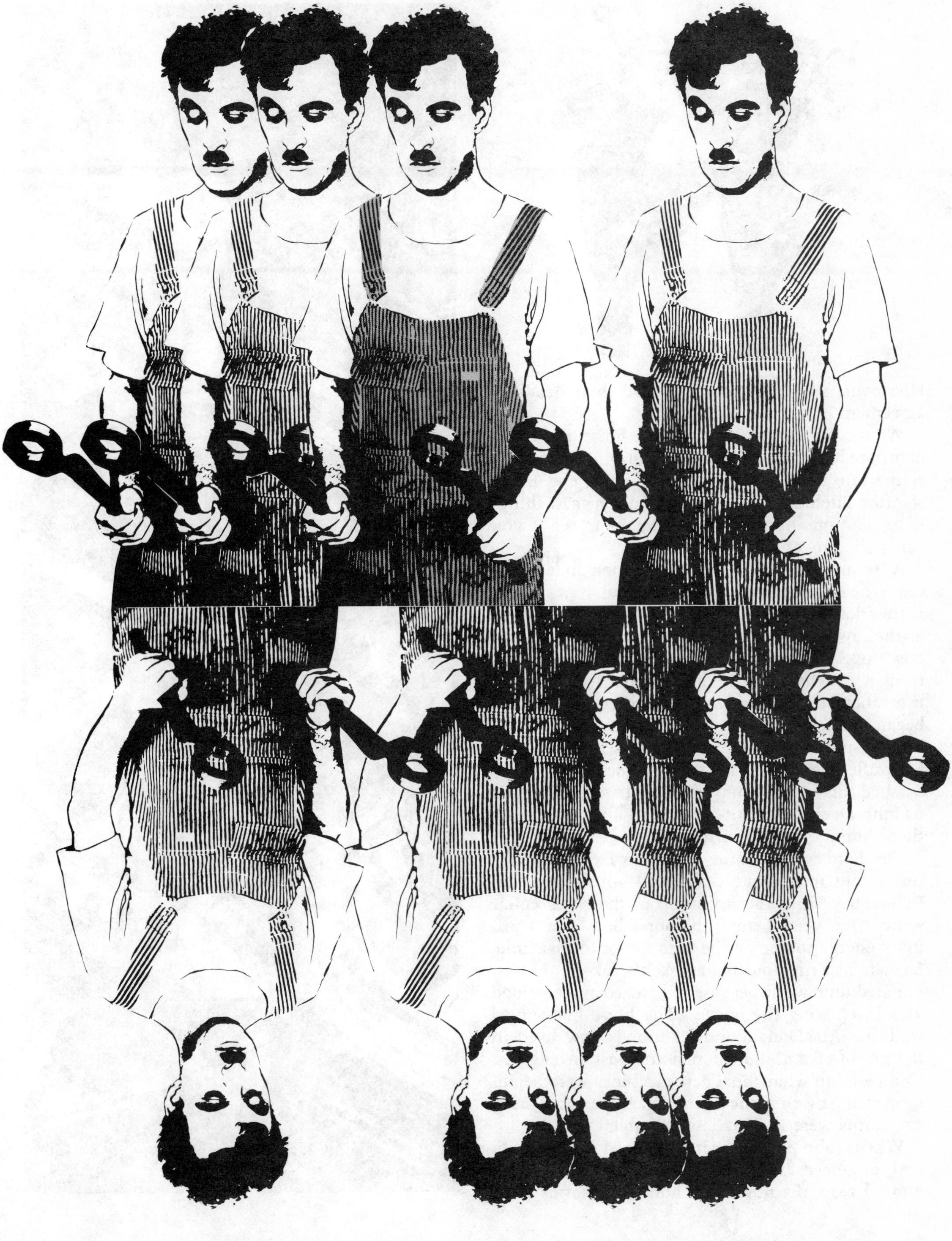

Hoedown, and MacDonald nodded their heads in agreement.

Wondering what to do about the horse, the group continued to stand around the stricken Belgian, who stared into the sky with his one exposed eye. Every so often Pitchfork or Hoedown would suggest things like, "Get one of your other Belgians to see if you can pull him up."

As so many before it, the conversation ended with old Wheatseed saying how wonderful it would be if they had a machine like the steam engine down at the sawmill to do the work of these troublesome creatures. "We could run it when we need it, shut it off when the work is done, and not worry all the time about these damn beasts." While the buzzards began to circle over the stricken animal, Hoedown—his foot now resting on the Belgian's rump and his hat pulled down over his eyes to block out the sun—issued this farmer's prayer: "Dear Lord, please send us John Deere to invent a tractor to liberate us from these hungry old hayburners."

The Lord was listening, and John Deere's tractor turned out to be more than Hoedown dreamed of. Remember, since the invention of the horse collar some 1,200 years before, the horse had been a primary energy source on the farm. (Prior to that time, farmers had tried putting an oxen's yoke on horses, but it didn't work because it blocked major blood vessels, choking the horses.) The horse had served well, but MacDonald and his friends now lived in the era of steam and internal combustion engines. Compared to what these new machines were beginning to do, by 1910 the 26 million horses on America's farms were looking less desirable every day.

When John Deere heard of Hoedown's prayer and produced the first commercial farm tractor around 1910, the number of horses and farms start-

ed dropping faster than tractors could come off the assembly lines. The number of farms declined from 6.4 million in 1910 to 2.3 million in 1979, while the tractor population went from 1,000 to about 4.5 million. These tractors do 3 times the work of 26 million horses.

While joy and celebration at the solution of the horse problem still sang in the hearts of the farmers, the tractor engineers were experiencing difficulties of their own. The unpredictable, undisciplined, unmechanical, fun-loving humans who worked on the tractor assembly line were presenting problems. Not only did they need to eat regularly and have adequate clothing and shelter, but they also showed an increasing appetite for leisure time to watch TV, fool around with cars, campers, snowmobiles, stereos, boats, fishing tackle, bowling balls, hunting gear, and so forth.

In 1981, a group of engineers stood around a partially assembled chassis in the Ford assembly plant in Mahwah, New Jersey. The car had no doors and its interior was unfinished. The plant had been shut down, and the engineers were part of a company task force trying to figure out how to reopen the place profitably.

It was engineer Rod Piston, with his foot up on the unassembled car's trunk space, who first said that the problem with making cars and tractors was the blue-collar people. "They're just not dependable," he said. "They regularly get sick, and you can never be sure if they'll show up on Friday or Monday. Even if they do show, they're off smoking in the john or having coffee or lunch and always take longer than they should. Besides, these blue-collar people need to eat every day of the year and they need clothes and homes, which means demands for more pay plus health, welfare, and pension benefits—and all this social security stuff goes on whether they're producing or not."

Axel Gear, an industrial engineer, gloomily agreed. "It's impossible to build cars or tractors and pay $15 an hour with all those benefits." Letting his thoughts run, he ruminated, "We've made a lot of progress in cutting manpower on these lines. In 1930, it took about 400 man-hours of labor to assemble a car. It only takes about 115 to do it in 1981. But now we need to eliminate the food, clothing, rent, and benefits altogether so we can just get on with our business of building cars."

Chief Engineer Bolthead was moved by what he heard. He looked down the stilled line with its unassembled cars and said, "If we could run this line with robots only, we could make money here." (The company had placed a six-million-dollar order for robots for its Detroit and Wilmington assembly plants.) "A robot can now be purchased for around $40,000. Spread out over eight years of life, that's about $4.80 an hour. We can run them only when we need to, and we won't have to worry about rates, benefits, sick leaves, pensions, and Blue Cross." He was really getting enthusiastic now. "Robots aren't eligible for seniority, are they?"

Axel Gear assured him, "No, they're not. But what about all the people who will be laid off?"

Bolthead answered, "Look, robots don't eat, don't take off on Fridays, don't suffer hangovers on Mondays. As far as eliminating these jobs is concerned, you can look at it like this—it's neither an antiunion nor an antihuman act because this work is universally deplored as monotonous, boring, meaningless, repetitive, dumb, and unhealthy. Remember Charlie Chaplin in *Modern Times*? We can now do away with all that dumbness. From our engineering viewpoint, we need to remember that our whole effort

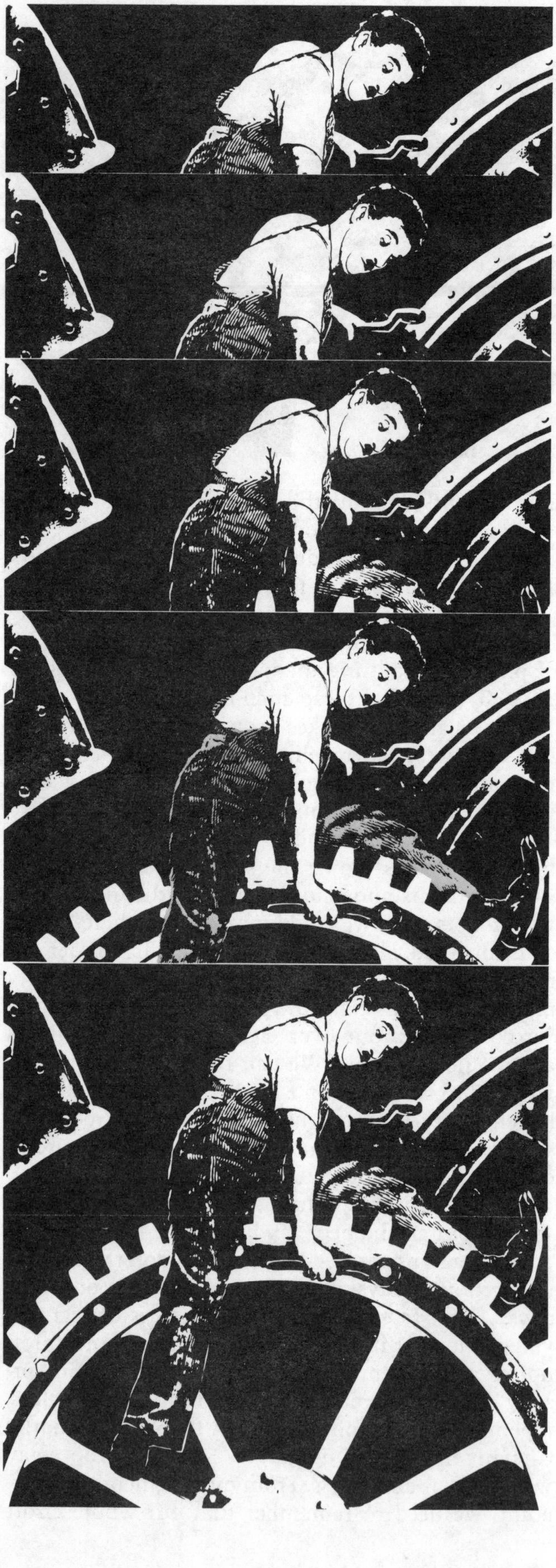

toward an efficient factory has been to eliminate these unpredictable, uncertain, demanding, and inefficient humans."

Axel Gear said, "Yeah, what we need are machines–they're always on time and they don't eat lunch. Maybe they need some maintenance once in a while, but with 10 years amortization over, you can then send them to the junkyard with no pension, no health care, no social security. Machines are clearly superior." His voice rose to a crescendo. Bolthead broke in, "Take it easy, Axel. You're getting carried away."

As it happened, Rod Piston was himself the son of an old farmer who had dreamed of a farm without horses and had seen it all come true. "When I was a kid," Piston said, "I saw the tractor replace the horse on my father's farm. We may be on the verge of the same thing in manufacturing. It's this new cheap microcircuitry technology that makes it all possible. Anyhow, we've got to do it or the Japanese will manufacture us right out of this business altogether. If the present trend continues, the cheapest stuff in Japan will all be stamped, 'Made in U.S.A.' "

Axel Gear tried to reassure Piston. "Look at it this way," he said. "There's a general clamor afoot in the land for increased productivity. Now, you'll notice that whenever this productivity issue comes up, it almost inevitably ends with the manufacturing sector as the problem." Gear wanted to know if the others thought this strange: "Only about one-third of the 100 million of us who work are in manufacturing. What about the productivity of the rest of us working at things called service or communications or professions?"

Bolthead reminded the group that his father was a machinist who, like his buddies, traditionally re-

sisted increasing production because it was a sure way to work your way out of a job. So the only thing industry could do was mechanize and automate the factories.

Axel Gear observed, "To solve the economic problem of foreign competition, we've got to displace humans with robots. We could have more leisure by sharing the jobs that are left. This would give us all more time for fun and games. Or blue-collar people could buy their own robots, and the robots would work for them. Somewhat like a New York taxi medallion."

"Look, this is how it might go," Piston said. "A blue collar—BC—is laid off by General Motors. He or she buys a robot and rents it to Buick to weld door frames. Buick pays the robot owner a piece rate for the robot's output. BC maintains the robot by going into the plant between shifts to keep it in grease, oil, cotter pins, and felt pads and to make sure it hasn't been mistreated. To purchase the robot, the laid-off blue-collar people could use all or part of their severance pay or obtain a low-interest loan from the Small Business Administration. This could be a fine solution for the unemployed. To paraphrase a French queen, 'If they have no jobs, let 'em own a robot.' "

Gear agreed. "Employees could find this advantageous," he said. "They wouldn't have to maintain an army of robots when they didn't need them—during model changeovers, layoffs, and so forth. During plant shutdowns or layoffs, as he or she waited for the old spot to open up again, a BC could rent the robot to another employer on a daily or weekly basis."

Bolthead was enthusiastic again. "Look, as owners learn to reprogram their own robots, a whole new spirit of free enterprise and entrepreneurship could emerge—for instance, programming the robot so it could be rented out to a bridge toll collector who needed the night off for the bowling league's final match. Or the robot could cut the neighbor's grass, do baggage inspection at airports, or take people on tours of museums."

By now Gear was practically jumping up and down with excitement. "No robot," he said, "would be programmed to slip around with a neighbor's wife or pick peaches off his peach tree. What we would have is a corps of robot inspectors who could check out the programming to ensure that robots would do only boring and monotonous jobs and wouldn't start fooling around with industrial engineering or plant management—stuff like that."

Piston said, "Look, we'll have to keep those robots in their place before we have another uppity bunch on our hands."

At that moment Peter President and Sam Senior, who were on a catwalk above the shop floor, paused in their inspection of the closed plant and leaned over the railing.

"Do you suppose those guys down there are really worth what we pay them?" asked Sam. "They've been hanging around talking for hours."

Creativity by the numbers

Intel measures 'absolutely everything'– and innovation flourishes

An interview with Robert N. Noyce

In an inflationary era, the tiny computer on a chip that Intel makes is a dream product–as it becomes more efficient and more powerful, it becomes cheaper. With the cost falling by 30% a year, applications for microcomputers have cropped up everywhere, and the limits to their usefulness are nowhere in sight. Because of their small size and reliability, they have not only enhanced all the major functions of the computer but they have invaded the consumer market in digital watches and electronic games, to name only a few of their myriad uses.

It was at Intel Corporation, of Santa Clara, in the heart of California's "Silicon Valley," that the microprocessor, the specialized semiconductor chip that contains the "brain" of a computer, was invented in 1971. While maintaining its lead in the technology of microprocessors, Intel has developed more than 20 highly innovative products that have made the company an acknowledged leader in the semiconductor industry. By putting as much as 10% of all revenue into R&D every year, Intel has managed consistently to keep ahead of the competition with new products, and, as others have tried to catch up, it has enjoyed profit margins over 20%, twice those of the rest of the industry.

Intel's revenues increased each year from 1976 to 1978 by 43% compounded. In the next couple of years, it expects to reach $1 billion in sales.

Robert N. Noyce is vice chairman of Intel. He attended Grinnell College, where he was elected to Phi Beta Kappa, and Massachusetts Institute of Technology, from which he received his Ph.D. in physics. He was on the research staff of the Shockley Semiconductor Laboratory, where he was involved in the design and development of silicon transistors. In 1959, with eight defectors from the Shockley Laboratory, he started a semiconductor division for Fairchild Camera and Instrument. While at Fairchild, as director of research, he helped develop the integrated circuit which was the precursor and prerequisite to the microprocessor. With Gordon Moore, another scientist-executive, Noyce left Fairchild in 1968 to start Intel. They were joined within a year by Andrew Grove, who had been associate director of research at Fairchild. Moore is now chairman and chief executive officer of Intel, and Grove is president and chief operating officer. President Carter presented the National Medal of Science to Noyce in January of this year for his work on semiconductor devices, especially on integrated circuits.

In this interview, conducted and edited by Lynn M. Salerno, assistant editor, HBR wanted to find out from Robert Noyce what it is like always to be the front runner in a fast-moving industry (it is "working on the edge of disaster"); his views on management of scientists ("they love to be measured"); and whether Intel experiments with flexible workweeks ("very hesitatingly"); about Intel's highly successful strategy ("we build on strength and try to stay out of competition where we're weak"). Finally, in a setting where even the president often wears a gold chain instead of a tie, Noyce described the environment as "confident, but not relaxed."

Photographs by Mason Morfit.

Reprint number 80308

HBR: From its beginning, Intel has had a spectacular record. What's the secret of your success? Did you have a specific management philosophy from the start?

Robert N. Noyce: No, you didn't have to then. In a small organization there's enough communication so that the objectives are very clearly defined to begin with. If you can't communicate with only 25 people, your communication skills are pretty awful. So our organization was very sharply focused. We knew what product we were going after; everybody understood that very well. That was almost enough of a statement of objectives to last through the first couple of years.

What is the management style now?

Now we've run out of the collective experience of everyone. There's only one member of the board who has ever worked for a company larger than Intel—as Intel is today. And consequently, we feel that we're plowing new ground in terms of how we organize, how we do things, how we keep focus.

How do you keep focus?

Well, the thing that we've been concentrating on recently is the culture. What makes Intel *Intel*? A lot of it is what has evolved because of the personalities of the people around. It is MBO practiced all the way through. I think there's a lot of lip service given to MBO, and it's not practiced. But here everybody writes down what they are going to do and reviews how they did it, how they did against those objectives, not to management, but to a peer group *and* management. So that's also a communication mechanism between various groups, various divisions, et cetera.

Do you have a formal way to do that, then?

Yes, and it's pretty well built into the system. There is an openness, a willingness to discuss problems, identify them, which is not confrontational but rather, "Hey, I've got a problem. Here's how it's going." The executive staff, which basically consists of all the division managers, is truly an executive staff. They worry about the whole business, not just their own business, although they have the primary responsibility for their own business. There is very little in the way of staffers, as such. Staff work is done by line management as a secondary assignment. If we have a recruiting problem or a special project that needs to be done, we take a division general manager and say, "Okay, that's your secondary assignment for now."

How long have you had this kind of arrangement?

We just never have built a staff. We've always used line management for that kind of a function. I think that the way the business planning is done may be unique in terms of breaking the business into what we call strategic business segments. A committee is formed of the people, usually middle managers and below and a few senior managers, who make strategies, operate, identify trends, and identify the resources needed for operating that business segment. So that's a great training ground for oncoming management.

You don't have a separate planning function, then?

No, strategic planning is imbedded in the organization. It is one of the primary functions of line managers. They buy into the program; they carry it out. They're determining their own future, so I think the motivation for doing it well is high. Now that is not to say that we won't call on other resources. If we have a product area that we don't know much about, we certainly will call in a market research organization or whatever to give us more information to work on. But it is not a planning function that reports to the president, and it has no interaction with the organization.

Are there other important features of the culture?

The other essential aspect of the culture is that we expect people to work hard. We expect them to be here when they are committed to be here; we measure absolutely everything that we can in terms of performance.

Don't you find that approach difficult with the management of scientists?

I don't think it's difficult at all, because they're used to it. You know the old story about the scientist is that if you can't put a number to it, you don't know what the hell you're talking about. Well, as an example, customer service is poor—how poor? Let's measure what the response time is when a letter comes in, and we'll plot that versus time. Let's measure how many of the commitments on delivery schedules are met, how many are met in a week, how many are more than a month late.

What kind of people do you look for to work at Intel?

I think that the people we want to attract are, in general, high achievers. High achievers love to be measured, when you really come down to it, because otherwise they can't prove to themselves that they're achieving.

Or that anybody cares whether they are or not?

Yes, the fact that you are measuring them says that you do care. Then they're willing to work—they're not only willing but eager to work in that kind of environment. We've had people come in who have never had an honest review of their work. We get senior managers who come in, and we say, "Okay, in your six-month review, or your annual review, here are the things that you did poorly, here are the things you did well." A lot of these people have never heard that they ever did anything poorly. It's the new culture of our schools, you know, no grades. Everybody passes. We just don't happen to believe in that. We believe that people do want to be praised. So we try to do that.

That's an interesting outlook.

Even schools are beginning to move back to giving grades again. It was an aberration, I think, that occurred during the Vietnam War that was a very poor trend in our educational environment and was very poor training for people who wanted to go out into competitive society.

How do you keep making this a challenging place to work?

I think it's because people have the control of their own destiny, and they get measured on it. They get their M&M candies for every job, as one of our business instructors always said. It's now getting to be a real challenge because the billion-dollar company is clearly in view in the next year or so. The question is whether we can do it right. A great deal of effort goes into thinking about how we plan it, how we operate it, and how we build incentives into it. Where are we going? Are we going where we want to go? How do we win at this game called business? And, as I say, I think that our team is made of high achievers who really want to do that. They still see plenty of challenges.

Is there a lot of internal competition?

Well, there isn't the political infighting that you often see in companies. The direction is very carefully and definitely set, and everybody understands that. It's partly because of the way it's set—for both the MBO system and the strategic planning system. There just isn't any room for politics in the organization. It is very quickly rooted out. Someone who's crawling over someone else's body just doesn't get very far.

How does it get weeded out, though? The culture's strong enough?

No, I think the information is open enough so that what the individual manager is doing is put under a microscope once every six months by all his peers. His peers know all those games, too, so politics just doesn't work. He doesn't get any support from his peers if he's doing that. It's an interactive company. Most of the divisions are heavily dependent on another organization that will let them get their job done.

You tried a three-day workweek some time back and that didn't work out. What is the situation today?

We still have a three-day week in Portland. If you have a capital-intensive activity, how many hours a week can you use it? What we do is run four 12-hour shifts on three days; so, 36 times 4 equals 144 hours a week, instead of three 40-hours, or 120 hours per week use of the equipment. It is simply a question of efficient use of the capital equipment.

So it wasn't a plan for trying a flexible workweek. Do you experiment with that kind of thing at all here?

Very hesitatingly. There are too many other parts of our society that are geared around the five-day week. The kids are in school five days a week. How does mama arrange to go to work? What happens to the family life if you take those work patterns and make them different from the rest of the family? In general, it doesn't work very well. It's sort of like a graveyard shift; there's a different group of people than on the day shift.

There seems to be a lot of control here. Is that a correct impression?

Oh, it's a very disciplined organization. *Very* disciplined. And we pride ourselves on our discipline. Did you see the little graph as you came in the door there, the Late List? It gives the percentage of people who come in after 8:10.

Doesn't that bother the people working here?

Yes, it bothers a lot of people. But they get used to it. And it becomes a point of pride after a while. It's another way of saying to people that they're valuable to us. How can we do our work if they're not here? Intel is the only place I've ever worked where an 8:00 a.m. meeting starts at 8:00 a.m.

Do you have any way for employees to get their gripes up the pipeline?

Well, initially, when the company was smaller, Gordon [Moore, Intel chairman] and I would have lunch every Thursday with a random group of employees. Now, that has broken down. You can't be very effective when you have 10,000 employees in the United States alone. Our total employment is over 15,000. But the lunch discussions are held at smaller group levels, and you'll find that if you walk around here at noon nearly every conference room has some sort of a lunch going on in it.

Are the employees expected to come?

No. Originally, my secretary would take an employee list and just invite the first 10 names and then the next 10 names, so it was alphabetical. Sometimes if we had a particular thing we wanted to probe, we'd take an interest group—people with common interests, all the personnel people, all of the college kids who had come in six months ago, or something like that—to get a different view on it. But usually it was a random selection. So if they were busy that day, they'd be invited next week, and so forth, down the list. We used to get through all employees in those days. They were invited at least twice a year. It did, I think, give you a sensitivity to what people were thinking out there. We heard a lot of bitches, and we got a lot of suggestions. We still do.

You have a rather spartan office. Is it typical of executive offices here?

Yes, I'd say so, for the older ones. The newer ones? There are none.

What do you have instead of offices?

The typical office landscaping sort of thing; no solid walls, open plan. Modular units that you can shift around as needed. In all the new buildings there are loads of conference rooms, so if you have to chew something you go in the conference rooms.

What if you have a private telephone call? Should you wait until lunchtime?

What kind of a private phone call would you have? I think that's part of the open communication. There are no secrets. I know the first time I started to think about it, it was shocking, but I had no hesitation to sit in any of those open offices and call nearly anyone. Occasionally I will use a conference room in one of the other buildings to make a phone call, but there really are just very few things when you stop to think about it that need to be handled that way. It's a habit to think that your phone calls are all confidential. But they aren't. Most people aren't interested. If the guy that's sitting next to you is somebody you trust and he overhears what you're saying, it doesn't matter very often.

Do most people like the open arrangement?

Yes, and there's a reason for it. We're social characters. Being locked in a box all day is not a very happy kind of situation when you get right down to it. Also, we try studiously to avoid the appurtenances of power. When we redo an office area we upgrade it a little bit. Part of it is an antisnob kind of a feeling.

Is there any kind of dress code?

You'll notice walking around here that less than 10% of the executives have a tie on. In fact, a lot of males here wear gold chains instead.

Was dress ever important here?

Yes. Ten years ago certainly I wouldn't have thought of coming into the office without a tie except on Saturday or Sunday or off hours, or something like that. It's much looser now. And if I'm not visiting

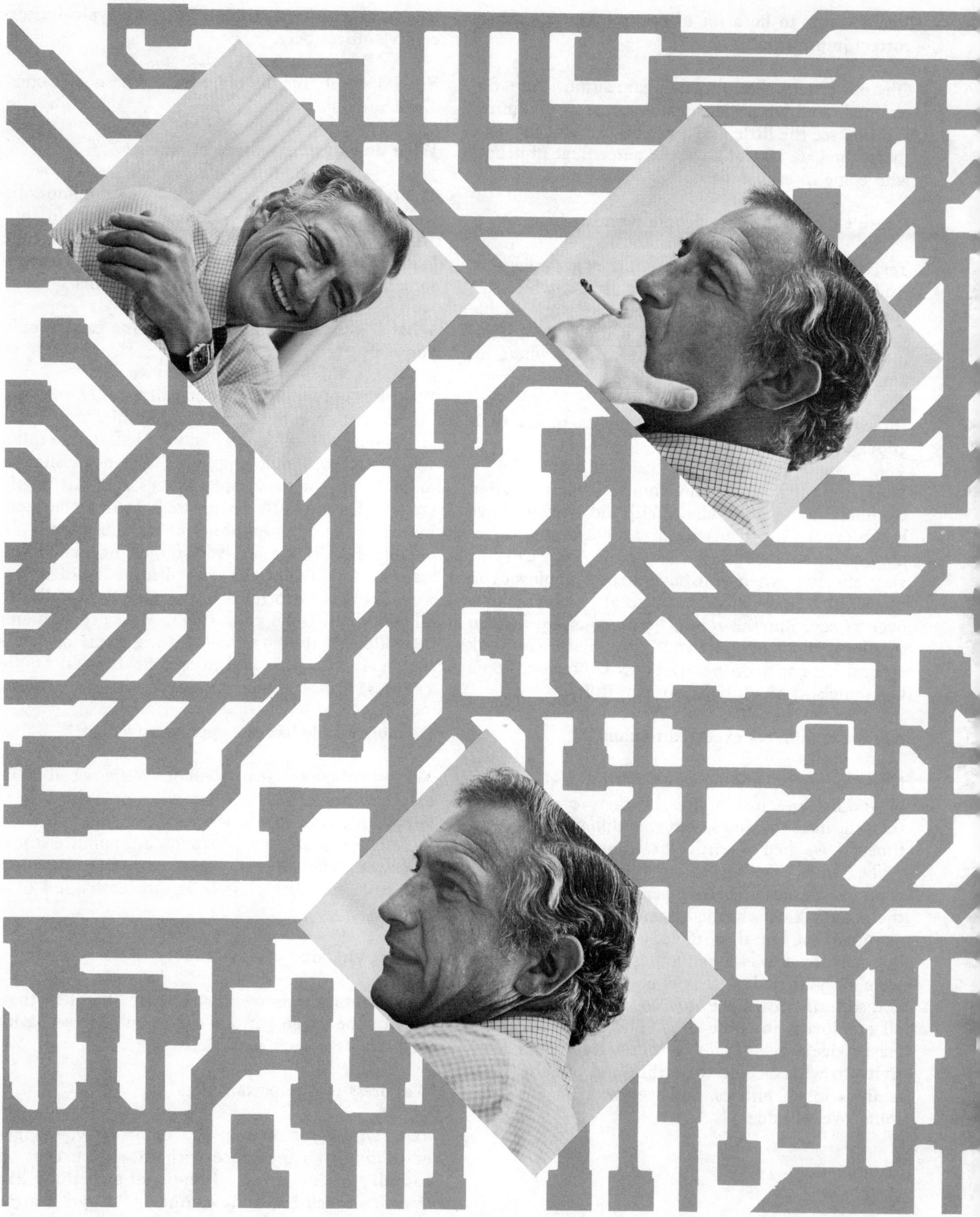

somebody from outside the company, I will probably not wear a tie, probably not even wear a jacket. I will put on a sport shirt. It's sometimes shocking to people who come from the East Coast, although they're getting acclimated to it. They meet the president, and he's wearing a sport shirt and a gold chain.

Would you call this a relaxed atmosphere?

I don't think you could call it relaxed. A confident environment, but not a relaxed one. One of the problems we have when people come in from other companies is that they just don't believe the intensity of Intel. They're not used to it. We're in an intensely competitive industry where change is very rapid, and there is no resting on your laurels because you'll get wiped out next year if you just sit back.

Doesn't that take an awful toll on people?

It does on some.

Do you have a company psychiatrist?

No, but we have lost some people. In particular, during both the recessions of 1971 and 1975, a lot of people left the industry and just never came back, feeling that it was not a relaxed place. But then we go back to the high achievers, the people who want to be where the action is. The crew is very young. The average age of the population around here is far younger than in the old established businesses, partially because Intel is only 12 years old. But also it's because we are very actively recruiting straight out of school.

When you started your bubble memory capacity, Intel Magnetics, you got three people who came from Hewlett-Packard to start it. Why did you do that instead of starting the project with people here?

It's a different technology. We had no particular expertise in it. We felt that the entrepreneurial start-up in a new field like that was the best way to get ivory tower types to focus on the real problem. That's an unfair characterization of those guys because they're certainly interested in the commercialization of bubble memories, but it was a separable entity that you could do on an entrepreneurial basis. I think it's been effective.

You think that's a good way to expand your capabilities?

Oh, yes. It's a question whether it's related to your current activities. When it's not an evolution of your current activities I think it's extremely dangerous to do it that way. We try to keep the incentives, in terms of options and so forth, pretty consistent with the outside start-up and with people who are already here, so that it's equitable. And if the outsiders are enormously successful, they'll do better than the people here; if they are not as successful, people who are already here will do better, so it's a good incentive.

Do you try to find future markets by making the product yourself, or do you have people here who just study it without making it?

I'd say that in terms of the market areas that we're carving out, they're sort of the natural extension of the technology that we're doing. The only significant acquisition we've ever made was a Texas company, MRI, which is a software company. We did buy a watch company when digital watches were first coming along, but it was, in a sense, an entrepreneurial situation. It had 13 employees in it.

That didn't really work out?

It didn't work for us. We thought it was a technology game, and it turned out to be a merchandising game. That's just not our game. What we're doing is what we see as the logical next step of what we have to do. For instance, in selling the microcomputer chips, we had to provide instrumentation to let the designer design with those chips because it wasn't available somewhere else. But that was an essential part of getting the microcomputer established in the market. If we are going to do a good job of designing microcomputers, we have to know more about software. So the software company was a major acquisition in terms of buying a capability that we didn't have, but that we saw as a necessary layer of capability on top of the ones we already had.

Are some companies dipping into your field so they can find out more about your business?

Sure, Hewlett-Packard is getting significantly into the semiconductor business. Burroughs is, and so on. And it's important that they know more about this business because it's an essential tool for them. It's also important that we know more about their business because it's an essential market for us.

Are the lines starting to blur, moving up and also moving down?

Yes. Making semiconductors is becoming an essential technology to the computer industry, so they are participating in it. The computer is, you know, essentially where the semiconductor industry is going, so we're moving into some fringes of their business. The technology is driving us there, simply because if you're going to make ever more complex things, you are going to be making computers. That's the major complex thing that is being built with the semiconductor. It might turn out to be a calculator or a controller for the tape recorder or the engine controller for an automobile, but it's still a computer in one sense or another.

What's going to be the end of all this?

Oh, I don't know. I think it's that people do well what they do well, and they succeed at what they do well.

There's not going to be a lot of bumping of heads?

There hasn't been particularly, no. The high-volume products are purchased in the so-called merchant market for semiconductors. The highly specialized ones, for which there is very little volume, have been made by computer companies for themselves because we wouldn't. We have no interest in making them. Computer companies are not interested in manufacturing the design aids to help build microcomputer systems, so we do that. You can define as many businesses as there are companies in the business, because each has defined a different market that it's going after. Certainly IBM and DEC are both in the computer business, but you don't think of them as the same. There's a little segment where there's an area of competition, but in the main they're in different businesses. And I think that that's true here.

It's a good idea to know where your strength lies. Would you say that's one of the key things?

Yes, and certainly in strategic planning, the analysis of where our strengths and weaknesses lie is an essential part. We build on strength and try to stay out of competition where we're weak. Our strength is clearly in the components manufacture, in the design capabilities there, so that's where we want to compete. That's where we want to do battle with our competition. We certainly don't want to compete with IBM, anymore than we want to compete with General Motors. Just because we make an engine control, we don't want to make an automobile.

You don't want to be another IBM?

We'd like to be another IBM. I'd love to have 70% of the market. But getting into throwing rocks at each other is not nearly as productive as going on and building our own businesses.

When people like you and Kenneth Olsen and Edson deCastro, men who have been among the prime movers in electronics, are gone, do you think Intel and DEC and Data General will be different?

Hewlett-Packard hasn't changed a great deal with the changing of the guard over there, and I think it's because it was a well-conceived, well-built organization. IBM hasn't changed a great deal since Tom Watson left. If you think of the character of IBM now compared to 20 years ago, it's a little different, but you can't say that there were any major changes in the thrust of the business. And again I think it's because it was a well-conceived, well-executed management style that works, so there was no need to change it.

Would Intel change, then, without you and Grove and Moore?

I believe that Intel has been a very successful company, that we have innovated in terms of how things are done, in terms of management styles, and in terms of culture as well as product; and I think the momentum is there that will keep it moving in that direction.

How would you say Intel differs from other companies in your industry?

I used to characterize our business as compared to others in the industry as working on the edge of disaster. We are absolutely trying to do those things which nobody else could do from a technical point of view. We measure everything that we do so that when something goes wrong we have some idea of what it was that went wrong—a very complex process. We've tried to extend that same philosophy to the running of the whole organization. You don't do something unless you know what you're doing. You don't change something unless you know that it's been done on a pilot basis, that it won't louse up something else. And our industry's unique in that because it is very, very complex in terms of the technology that goes into it.

And it's very easy to make a mistake?

Very, very easy to make a mistake. We're working where a speck of dust ruins everything–that kind of an environment as far as the actual production is concerned.

You probably couldn't start an Intel today, could you?

I think you could start an Intel. It wouldn't be in this field. I think that there are still plenty of opportunities.

But it would take a tremendous amount of money, wouldn't it?

This field would. But there are significant companies that were started with relatively little. One of my favorites is called Apple Computer. And the guy started it by selling a car, and that was the capital. He started it in his garage, literally.

And he and his partner were only in their twenties, too, weren't they?

That's right. So it's like the start-up of Hewlett-Packard, which was done in a garage with $5,000. That was a lot more money when Hewlett and Packard started than when these guys started recently on $5,000. So, we're talking about those opportunities that are brain-intensive rather than capital-intensive.

But mergers and acquisitions are still cutting down the number of companies. How long will Apple Computer or a company like that be what it is today?

I don't know. A similar question is whether the acquisitions of the semiconductor companies have really decreased the number of competitors or not. They're still in business. Fairchild is still selling whether it's part of Schlumberger or not. Mostek will exist whether it's part of United Technologies Corporation or not. I was sad to see Fairchild merged quite as early as it was, in the sense that this last quarter we finally beat it in volume.

You weren't sad because of sentimental feelings about your beginnings there?

No. Just straight competition.

When you started Intel, did you have trouble getting capital?

No, we never really had any trouble getting money. It may shock a lot of people to find this out, but we never wrote a business plan, never wrote a prospectus. We just said, "We're going into business; would you like to support it?"

But you did have the experience and the expertise?

We had a track record. There was clearly a great demand for semiconductors. It was still a rapid growth environment during that time.

Howard Head once said that, when he started Head Ski, if there was a sales meeting to attend he'd attend it, if there was an ad to write he'd write it, if there was a floor to sweep he'd sweep it. That can be a problem for a lot of entrepreneurs. Did you ever have to do everything?

I've scrubbed the floors, I've done the glassblowing, I've run diffusion furnaces, and so on, in the past; I've done the customer calls, and I've talked at sales meetings.

Did you ever feel that you had to?

No, those were the things to be done, so I did them. I guess if there is a frustration in a larger organization, it is that it takes longer to see the results of what you're doing. There's a massive inertia. So that you push on one thing and a year later you can see the movement. A small organization can turn on a dime and change direction. You suggest another way to do things and you can get it implemented in a week or two. When you have 10,000 people to change the direction of, it just doesn't happen that way. What you hope you do, or can do, is to break the organization down into small manageable units so that you can change the direction of one unit at a time. And I think that has been done effectively.

So being effective in the organization is the way you find a challenge?

There's an enormous satisfaction in seeing that you've really affected the society, and I have no doubt in my mind that Intel has really affected our society. If nothing else, the microcomputer revolution is an Intel-induced change that has occurred in our society. And we're just beginning to see some changes that are going on in the society because of it. It is much less necessary to be in the city for communicating now than it was 20 years ago. As a matter of fact, the necessity of going to work is much less now because you can have communication facilities at home so that you can work at home. We have several engineers who have their terminals at home. They can work just as well there as they can here.

In your role as vice chairman, do you personally have more time to spend at home?

No. I intended to, but it doesn't work out that way.

How many hours a week do you work?

Oh, I usually get in here by 7:45 to 8:00 and usually go home about 6:00 or 6:30. I don't work weekends, at least, not in the office.

Do you take work home with you?

Reading. There are such voluminous amounts to try to get through to keep up with what's going on. I am willing to take more vacation time than I used to be able to.

Were you able to before but you just wouldn't?

Precisely. And actually that is one of the reasons why Intel was a two-headed monster when we started it. In the Fairchild situation, I simply felt that I couldn't leave and relax, which is a stupid way to run your life. One of the primary objectives in getting Intel going was to have it arranged so that I could leave and relax, and I started out with a partner that I could trust, whose judgment I trusted. Beyond that the energy goes into organizational building and team building, so that the team can carry on the job.

Now that you've removed yourself more or less from day-to-day operations, do you miss that?

Yes. How should I put this? I wanted to remove myself from the day-to-day operations so there would be more time to think about some other things, but that's a difficult thing to do, too. Some of the time you wonder about what you are doing. I mean, the complexity of the organization is such that it's an absolutely full-time job just to keep up with what is going on. It's several full-time jobs, as a matter of fact.

So it becomes dangerous to try to do something else as well as be involved in daily operations, because you don't have enough knowledge about what's going on and you make some horrible mistakes. Too many people depend on you to be right to take that risk. If you're going to try to do other things beyond that, then you'd better be sure that somebody is watching the store. But it is so habitual to watch the store that it becomes somewhat of a role crisis doing something else. I think that there are broader issues, however, that need to be thought about anyway.

Do you mean that there are broader national issues that you'd like to think about?

Maybe that's the motivation. Where's American capitalism going? Is it going down the tubes or is it going to survive? Where is the American standard of living going? Is it going to bread and circuses as it has been for the last decade or is it going to do what we did in the 1960s, that is, continually increase the standard of living for the population? Where's our international competitive situation going? Are we going to have the discipline to solve the energy problem in the United States? It's those kinds of questions that I think are important.

What is your major concern right now?

My major concern right now for all U.S. business is how we are going to compete with Japan. Because they're doing it right, and we're doing it wrong.

Well, we must be doing some things right. You are; this industry is.

But if you look at what gave Americans strength, it was the high level of motivation in innovation, the high availability of venture capital; and you look at the industry now, it's capital intensive. Now suddenly you have a major shift in the advantages and disadvantages.

What can be done about it?

As a nation we can't let Japan win this competitive battle because of complacency. I think we're much more alert to the situation than the automobile industry was—or the steel industry, the TV industry, the tape recorder industry, the ball-bearing industry, the bicycle industry, or the motorcycle industry. Just list them all as they disappear out of American society because of Japanese competition. It's a little frightening to think that this is happening in this industry right now. Yes, the semiconductor industry is healthy right now, but if we are to remain healthy, some changes will have to be made.

What kinds of changes are you thinking of?

In America, there's so little investment capital available that it's come to a situation where you pick the low hanging fruit and you don't worry about planting the new trees. You don't have the resources available to do both. And I think that's the thing that's likely to damage American industry. If there isn't a change in that, this industry, which is a centerpiece of American technology, could all be lost to the Japanese.∇

Ideas for Action

Edited by Timothy B. Blodgett

Developments, trends & useful proposals for the attention of managers

Stanley D. Nollen is associate professor of business economics, School of Business Administration, Georgetown University. A teacher of managerial economics and of social policy for business, he has coauthored a book on flexible working hours and has also written Permanent Part-time Employment: The Manager's Perspective *(Praeger, 1978).*

Reprint number 79559

Does flexitime improve productivity?

Stanley D. Nollen

Flexitime is one of the major developments in employment policy of the 1970s. This work scheduling innovation, introduced in Germany in 1967, was first used in this country in the early 1970s. It has spread rapidly; by 1977 an estimated 13% of all U.S. organizations were using this approach, or roughly 6% of the work force (not counting professionals, managers, sales people, and self-employed persons who customarily set their own hours).

Under flexible work hours (flexitime for short), employees choose their arrival and departure times at and from work within limits set by management. Usually the organization establishes core hours—a midday period when all employees must be present—with a flexible band at both ends of the working day. Sometimes employees can even "borrow" time off from one workweek and make up for the lost time another week.

Flexitime is highly regarded as an employee benefit and morale builder. "It seems like a very innovative way to increase employee dignity and satisfaction at no real cost to the company," according to a midwestern manufacturer.

Now comes the news, based on employers' experience, that flexitime may yield a hard dollars-and-cents productivity gain to the enterprise. It gives promise of helping solve the serious nationwide problem of lagging productivity growth.

The indications of the effectiveness of this technique come from 8 surveys and 30 case studies conducted in the last few years by many researchers. The surveys covered some 445 organizations using flexitime, and the case studies obtained opinion data from more than 10,000 workers and more than 500 supervisors. Their employers included drug companies, banks, insurance companies, electronics manufacturers, transportation enterprises, utilities, and government agencies. Although not of the highest quality, the evidence does indicate certain trends and patterns. These provide our first tentative answers. Here are the key results:

☐ In 8 surveys of companies using flexitime, the median proportion that subjectively reported increased productivity was 48%.

☐ In 14 case studies, the median proportion of employees who claimed that their productivity had improved was 45%.

The range in these studies was wide—from a low of 20% of companies reporting productivity gains in one survey to a high of 71% in another, and in the employees' reports, 13% to 79%. (In all the findings I report, the aver-

Exhibit I
Reported productivity effects in case studies

Median percent reporting increases

	Employees	Supervisors
Individual productivity	45	22
Quantity of work	37	38
Quality of work	46	23

Exhibit II
Productivity effects attributed to flexitime (selected studies)

A. Surveys

Study	Measure	Percent and characteristics of organizations subjectively reporting increases
Administrative management society, 1978	Production	31% Mainly finance, insurance firms (n = 56)
Elbing, Gadon, and Gordon, 1974	Individual productivity	57 German companies (n = 30)
Martin, 1975	Productivity	55 Most industries, many small companies, average length of use = 1.3 years (n = 55)
Nollen and Martin, 1978	Productivity	48 All industries, sizes of firm; average length of use = 2.3 years (n = 196)
U.S. Comptroller General, 1976	Productivity	44 Diverse private sector companies (n = 9)
Weinstein, 1975	Productivity	29 One-third manufacturing and small companies (n = 33)

B. Case studies–opinion reports

Study	Measure	Percent and characteristics of employees subjectively reporting increases
Golembiewski, Hilles, and Kagno, 1974	Own productivity	43% SmithKline Corp. employees after 6 months (n = 274)
Gomez-Mejia, 1978	Productivity	66 Nonexempt production, engineering, marketing employees of Control Data Corp. (n = 286) 51 Managers at Control Data Corp. (n = 100)
Holley, Armenakis, and Feild, 1976	Work accomplished	95 Accounting department employees at mid-sized airline after 10 months (n = 58)
Magoon and Schnicker, 1976	Productivity	47 State Street Bank of Boston employees after 8 weeks (n = 127)
Morgan, 1977	Work performance	28 Salaried employees of Berol Corp. after 2 months (n = 127)
Mueller and Cole, 1977	Work accomplished Work quality Productivity Work quality	37 } Clerical employees after 1 year (n = 1912) 36 } 27 } Supervisors' opinions after 1 year (n = 318) 32 } U.S. Geological Survey
Port Authority of New York, 1975	Work effectiveness	45 Headquarters staff after 8 months (n = 850)
Schein, Maurer, and Novak, 1978	Production Work accomplished	57 } Supervisors at Metropolitan Life Insurance Co. after 14 weeks (n = 63) 49 }
Swart, 1978	Complete work requirements Work quality Daily work output Individual productivity Work group productivity Production	31 Qantas Airways employees (n = 1950) 21 Qantas Airways supervisors (n = 100) 22 Headquarters office, Firestone of Canada (n = 91) 79 Headquarters staff, Pacific Gas & Electric (n = 458) 72 Supervisors' report at Pacific Gas & Electric 38 Supervisors' report at Sandoz Inc.
U.S. Social Security Administration, 1975	Work quantity Work accuracy	51 } Data processing employees of SSA after 6 months or more 46 }
Zawacki and Johnson, 1976; Robison, 1978	Productivity	58 Hewlett-Packard employees after 1 year (n = 114)

ages were somewhat higher than medians. In the case of split medians, I report the higher result.)

Potential of flexitime

Before I go into detail about the research, let me list ways that flexitime can boost productivity:

1. Reductions in paid absences (personal business, sick leave) and idle time on the job (less chatting on arrival at work and departure from work because fewer employees are arriving and departing at once) produce more actual labor from the same number of hours.

Of course, this is not strictly a productivity increase; it is an output gain due to an increase in effective labor input. It is a clear gain to the organization, however, since it incurs no additional cost of labor input. (One caution: unions may be justifiably concerned that workers share in productivity gains.)

2. Productivity may rise because of better organization of work. Tasks can be more efficiently allocated over the day because of concentration of meetings, telephone calls, and visits into core hours, leaving work that requires thinking and concentration to be done at the beginning and end of the working day when there is more quiet and fewer distractions. Workers are freer to finish jobs they have started and thus avoid inefficient start-ups and shut-downs.

These efficiencies apply to many jobs (professional, technical, managerial, administrative, craft, and job shop production) but perhaps not to machine operators and laborers.

3. People have different biological clocks. There are "morning people" and "night people." Some people function better early in the day while others function better later on. Flexi-

C. Case studies – Hard data on size of productivity increase

Study	Measure	Percent increase after flexitime and characteristics of study
Fields, 1974	Productivity – transactions per day	8% Clerical employees of Mutual of New York; 6-month post-test average versus prior month (n = 22)
Morgan, 1977	Work performance – 9-point self report scale	12 Salaried flexitime versus nonflexitime employees of Berol Corp. after 2 months
Schein, Maurer, and Novak, 1977	Productivity:	Clerical employees of Metropolitan Life Insurance Co.: 4-month post-test average versus:
	Records handled	0 Prior 8 weeks (n = 46)
	Claims processed per employee	46 Same period previous year (n = 65); 28 Annual average previous year (n = 65)
	Checks written	13 Prior 8 weeks (n = 100)
Swart, 1978	Productivity – cards punched per hour	17 Keypunching unit at Gulf Oil of Canada
	Productivity	2-3 Estimate of Pacific Gas & Electric
U.S. Congress, House, 1977	Productivity per employee	6 Secretarial services department, First National Bank of Boston
U.S. Geological Survey, 1977	Output	14 Maps produced; 13 Vouchers processed; 6 Technical reports (U.S. Geological Survey)
U.S. Information Agency, 1975	Ratio of vouchers processed to vouchers received	5 U.S.I.A. clerical employees after 6 months (n = 33)
	Accounts payable (decrease)	16
U.S. Social Security Administration, 1975	Productivity – work units per hour	12 Low-graded data processing and claims; 40 Handling workers (mostly young mothers); 21 In 3 work units; 3-month post-test average versus same period prior year (n = 353)

Note: This exhibit focuses on U.S. private sector studies; for additional European and public sector studies, see the list of references. The summary of results in the text includes all studies, only some of which are included in this exhibit.

time permits workers to accommodate to their biological patterns.

4. The greater employee morale and job satisfaction that flexitime usually produces may bring about increases in productivity. This is the "happy worker is a productive worker" theory in action. Of course, the link between job satisfaction and productivity is filled with contingencies, only some of which are known. Because no stable linear or invariant relationship exists between them, productivity gains flowing from job satisfaction gains should occur in some work settings but perhaps not in all.

5. Flexitime may bring about better managerial practices and thereby further productivity in many levels of the organization. At the supervisory level, successful flexitime programs require a change from a negative, controlling style to a positive, facilitating style. A shift in supervisory style toward more self-management may eventually foster productivity gains in some work settings. "Flexitime gets rid of redundant supervisory practices," said a personnel executive at AT&T. Obviously, eliminating excess supervision means lower costs and more output.

6. Flexitime may induce further organizational improvements—better labor-management relations, greater worker participation in management, programs enhancing the quality of work life, more training, and new organizational development strategies. These in turn will stimulate productivity. Whether it is more output from the same labor input or the same output from fewer total inputs, the results are lower costs.

Empirical evidence

Of course, there are many ways to look at productivity. In some organizations studied, the question employees were asked did not strictly concern productivity, but rather daily work output or completion of the daily work requirements. Here the responses were less positive than the 45% median overall: the median proportion of employees who claimed increased work output (from eight case studies) was 37%, with a range of 22% to 95%.

It is harder to point to a greater quantity of physical output than it is to higher productivity, which is a more elusive (and more glamourous) notion. In one sense, work output is a better gauge; in another sense, it misses some very real but hard-to-see effects. For example, daily work output might be unchanged but annual output could still be greater due to less absenteeism.

Work quality is another measure of productivity. From five case studies, the median proportion of employees reporting quality increases was 46%.

Supervisors—who are critical links in flexitime programs—were a little less likely than their subordinates to regard flexitime as effective. Where responses were obtained from both employees and supervisors in the same company, the proportion of supervisors reporting productivity gains was 7 to 15 percentage points below the proportion for workers. The supervisors also reported quality increases somewhat less frequently.

Exhibit I summarizes the opinions of workers and supervisors derived in studies of 22 corporations. Also see *Exhibit II* for details of some of these studies.

How big were the productivity gains achieved? Based on 19 estimates from 12 studies in which researchers took measurements of output per worker, the median size of productivity increases (most of them in the private sector) was 12%—the range was 0% to 45%. A recent review of federal agencies' experiences concluded that 2% to 5% gains were most common there (see "Flexitime" bibliography on facing page).

All these studies measured fairly homogeneous work groups after two to six months' use of flexitime. The employees were mostly white-collar workers whose jobs required a range of skills. There was one productivity measurement from a multishift, continuous-process operation; it showed "no adverse effect" on production.

Is the evidence believable?

These results, if taken at face value, imply that flexitime holds considerable promise as a productivity improver. They suggest that the chances of perceived productivity gains are one-third to one-half, and that the size of the gain—in the range of 5% to 14%—is substantial. But there are several reasons to doubt these results or their applicability.

First, only successful flexitime programs are reported in the literature. How many cases are there of productivity losses or zero gains? Failures of flexitime are usually not studied. While this fact does not inflate the results obtained from surveys (if they are free of response bias), it does overstate the favorable impression we get from case studies.

However, we also know that the failure rate of flextime is remarkably low—8% is estimated in one study.[1] Thus the degree of overstatement of productivity effects is surely small.

Second, the self-reports from companies whose executives noted productivity increases due to flexitime may be biased upward if they expected those results and hence "found" them partly to fulfill their expectations. A test of this source of bias is the comparison between the number of organizations listing productivity gains as a reason to use flexitime (or as an expected advantage) with the number who reported them as an effect.

The evidence here shows that the frequency of productivity gains exceeded expectations and that there is no bias on this account. For example, in one survey only 16% of all the flexitime users volunteered that increased productivity was a reason to use flexitime, but 48% thought productivity did rise. In another study, 14% of users listed productivity improvement as a reason for adopting flexitime, while 29% reported that it had such an effect.

Third, the scientific quality of "hard" productivity measurements is questionable. The technique used in all measurements of the effects was a before-after comparison of average output per worker (with individuals as the unit of analysis), or total work unit output related to the number of workers in the unit. Few studies used control groups. Other inputs aside from labor may have changed. So we cannot say with certainty how much of the productivity effect attributed to flexitime was in fact caused by it.

Even if flexitime does bring productivity gains, do they last? In several telephone interviews I conducted at companies studied by the researchers, managers said yes. For example, continuous monitoring of routinely collected hard data at Berol Corporation shows that even after five years of experience with flexitime, absences and paid leave have remained lower than before. At SmithKline Corporation, where flexitime has been used for seven years, good productivity results have lasted because, I was told, flexitime lets workers continuously vary their schedules as work and personal needs change over time.

And when I compared statistically the opinions of 61 managers whose experience with flexitime extends more than three years with the opinions of 31 users for less than one year, I found no difference. Longitudinally tracking the same companies over time similarly turns up no fall-off in their impressions of productivity gains.

Managing flexitime

What matters most to prospective users of flexitime is, of course, the answer to the question, "Will I get better productivity if I convert to flexitime?" or, "How do I increase the chances of reaping a productivity dividend when I go to flexitime?" The answers depend on prior knowledge of the mechanism by which flexitime increases productivity. And here we are on the frontiers of knowledge; we are just not sure.

We do know from reliable data that effective labor input often increases after flexitime is adopted. Absenteeism, tardiness, and paid leaves often drop and stay low, and that translates directly into higher productivity.

But the key to productivity gains from flexitime may be how it is managed, according to current reports from managers themselves. Flexitime says to employees, "We are paying you to get the job done, not to put in your time." Faced with this positive challenge, they respond. The manager's job is to get this message delivered.

But often supervisors are skeptical. Won't chaos result? How do you control flexitime? As one manager said, "If you treat workers as adults, they will act as adults." Flexitime forces managers to invest more responsibility in their workers. Control Data Corporation has found that managers are

1. Stanley D. Nollen and Virginia H. Martin, *Alternative Work Schedules, Part I: Flexitime* (New York, AMACOM, 1978), p. 44.

more effective under flexitime because they have to plan in order to make it work. So managers themselves are part of the productivity gain. ▽

'Flexitime' bibliography

This list of publications provides an opportunity for interested readers to learn more about experience with flexible working hours, or flexitime. It supplements this article. The author compiled the list.

Administrative Management Society, *Flexitime Programs* (Willow Grove, Pa.: Administrative Management Society, 1978).

Thomas F. Cowley and Barbara Fiss, "Federal Employees See Increase in Productivity," *Monthly Labor Review*, February 1977.

Alvar D. Elbing, Herman Gadon, and John R.M. Gordon, "Flexible Working Hours: It's About Time," HBR January-February 1974.

Cynthia Fields, "Variable Work Hours—the MONY Experience," *Personnel Journal*, September 1974.

Robert T. Golembiewski, Rick Hilles, and Munro S. Kagno, "A Longitudinal Study of Flexi-time Effects: Some Consequences of an OD Structural Intervention," *Journal of Applied Behavioural Science*, vol. 10, no. 4, 1974.

Luis R. Gomez-Mejia, Michael A. Hopp, and C. Richard Somerstad, "Implementation and Evaluation of Flexible Work Hours: A Case Study," *Personnel Administrator*, January 1978.

William H. Holley, Jr., Archilles A. Armenakis, and Hubert S. Feild, Jr., "Employee Reactions to a Flexitime Program: An Attitudinal Survey," *Human Resource Management*, Winter 1976.

Warren Magoon and Larry Schnicker, "Flexible Hours at State Street Bank of Boston: A Case Study," *Personnel Administrator*, October 1976.

Virginia H. Martin, *Hours of Work When Workers Can Choose* (Washington, D.C.: Business and Professional Women's Foundation, 1975).

Campbell R. McConnell, "Why Is U.S. Productivity Slowing Down?" HBR March-April 1979.

Frank T. Morgan, "Your (Flexi) Time May Come," *Personnel Journal*, February 1977.

Oscar Mueller and Muriel Cole, "Concept Wins Converts at Federal Agency," *Monthly Labor Review*, February 1977.

Stanley D. Nollen and Virginia H. Martin, *Alternative Work Schedules, Part I: Flexitime* (New York: AMACOM, 1978).

Stanley D. Nollen, *New Work Patterns* (Scarsdale, N.Y.: Work in America Institute, 1979).

John D. Owen, "The Traditional Workweek and its Alternatives," in *Employment and Training Report of the President 1979* (Washington, D.C.: U.S. Government Printing Office, 1979).

Port Authority of New York and New Jersey, *Flexible Work Hours Experiment* (New York: Port Authority, 1975).

B.C. Partridge, "Notes on the Impact of Flexitime in a Large Insurance Company: II. Reactions of Supervisors and Managers," *Journal of Occupational Psychology*, vol. 47, no. 4, 1973.

David Robison, "Hewlett-Packard Tries Flexitime: White-Collar, Production Workers Endorse Flexible Work Schedules," *World of Work Report*, November 1978.

Simcha Ronen, Sophia B. Primps, and John Cloonan, "Testimony," in *Flexitime and Part-Time Legislation*, hearing before the Senate Committee on Governmental Affairs (Washington, D.C.: U.S. Government Printing Office, 1978).

Sally Rousham, *Flexible Working Hours Today: Practices and Experiences of Over Fifty British Organisations*, Management Survey Report No. 17 (London: British Institute of Management, 1973).

Virginia E. Schein, Elizabeth H. Maurer, and Jan F. Novak, "Impact of Flexible Working Hours on Productivity," *Journal of Applied Psychology*, August 1977.

Virginia E. Schein, Elizabeth H. Maurer, and Jan F. Novak, "Supervisors' Reactions to Flexible Work Hours," *Journal of Occupational Psychology*, vol. 51, no. 4, 1978.

J. Carroll Swart, *A Flexible Approach to Working Hours* (New York: AMACOM, 1978).

J. Carroll Swart, "Flexitime's Debit and Credit Option," HBR January-February 1979.

U.S. Comptroller General, *Benefits from Flexible Work Schedules—Legal Limitations Remain* (Washington, D.C.: U.S. General Accounting Office, 1977).

U.S. Comptroller General, *Contractors' Use of Altered Work Schedules for Their Employees—How Is It Working?* (Washington, D.C.: U.S. General Accounting Office, 1976).

U.S. Congress, House of Representatives, Subcommittee on Employee Ethics and Utilization of the Committee on Post Office and Civil Service, *Part-Time Employment and Flexible Work Hours* (Washington, D.C.: U.S. Government Printing Office, 1977).

U.S. Geological Survey, *Flexitime: Evaluation of a One-Year Experiment* (Reston, Va.: U.S. Geological Survey, Branch of Management Analysis, 1977).

James Walker, Clive Fletcher, and Donald McLeod, "Flexible Working Hours in Two British Government Offices," *Public Personnel Management*, July-August 1975.

Harriet Goldberg Weinstein, *A Comparison of Three Alternative Work Schedules: Flexible Work Hours, Compact Work Week, and Staggered Work Hours* (Philadelphia, Pa.: University of Pennsylvania, The Wharton School, Industrial Research Unit, 1975).

William McEwan Young, "Application of Flexible Working Hours to Continuous Shift Production," *Personnel Review*, Summer 1978.

Robert A. Zawacki and Jason S. Johnson, "Alternative Workweek Schedules: One Company's Experience with Flexitime," *Supervisory Management*, June 1976. ▽

'By days I make the cars'

To an assembly line worker quality of work life means good stock, fair treatment, and recognition as an individual

John F. Runcie

Arriving at a final assembly plant early in the morning, workers spend time in undefined activities such as talking and setting up concession stands. Once the line starts, the workers start; when it stops, they stop. During that eight-hour day, workers adapt to the endless sameness of their jobs in numbers of innocent ways—playing games, working slowly to force themselves to catch up, trading jobs—and some not so innocent ways—dope, liquor, sabotage, and theft. The quality of work life solutions that sociologists and human relations experts proffer pale beside the workers' need for conditions that enable them to perform their jobs well. When these conditions are satisfied, writes the author—a sociologist who spent five months working on the line—workers might become more interested in how decisions are made. Although the author had tried to maintain his objectivity, life on the line became as real and as inexorable for him as it is for people who work on it day after day. He feels the real problem in the plant stems not from bad stock or favoritism but from the view that people ought to be as identical as the cars they make.

Mr. Runcie is director of social research for Development Analysis Associates Inc., a consulting firm in Cambridge, Massachusetts. Previously on the faculty of the University of Michigan, he has concentrated his research on occupational cultures and, more recently, on cultures in underdeveloped countries. His latest publication is *Experiencing Social Research*, rev. ed. (Homewood, Ill.: Dorsey Press, 1980).

Reprint number 80309

The automobile assembly line has been the subject of songs, movies, and, more recently, articles in the business press that describe and decry the alienation of the worker in a job that causes "blue collar blues." The singer of a popular country and western song laments, "By days I make the cars and by night I make the bars."[1] Is working on the line as bad as it is made out to be? The answer is yes—and no.

A large percentage of the workers on the line today use drugs or alcohol or both. To put up with the stresses and problems of the line, many workers take unauthorized absences; others resort to sabotage and theft. On the other hand, if you ask workers how long they intend to work in the plant, most will tell you that they expect to remain there until they retire. Many workers told me that they like to work on the line, and many remain on the line even though they have enough seniority to move into other jobs. Some even return to the line after trying out other jobs in the plant because they like line work better than the alternatives.

Clearly, the line can be many things to many people, but for the assembly line worker in an automobile plant, the line is the central focus of the day. It is the reason he or she is working; *it* governs the day. When the line starts, the worker starts; when the line stops, the worker stops. The line is a fact of life.

In this article, I present a picture of the life of the assembly line worker from two points of view—that of the people who work and live on the line and my

Author's note: This research was supported in part by funds from the C.S. Mott Foundation and the Chancellor's Special Fund of the University of Michigan—Flint.

1. Mel Tillis and Danny Dill, "Detroit City," Cedarwood Publishing Co., Inc., copyright © 1962, 1977.

2. Robert Schrank, *Ten Thousand Working Days* (Cambridge, Mass.: MIT Press, 1978).

own. For five months I worked on the line as an "objective" researcher, trying not to be so involved in the subject of the research as to distort it. (For a description of the research methodology, see the accompanying ruled insert.) But I often found myself responding to situations as any other worker in the plant might and, for all intents and purposes, I was a worker first and a researcher second. While I may not completely go along with all the other workers' opinions, I am in general agreement with their overall tone and implications.

The job

Arriving in the early morning darkness, workers must pass a protection checkpoint at the plant gate. Some days the guard will stop you and ask you to show your plant pass; on other days you can just walk past, flashing the card as you enter. It always seemed to me that the guards chose the coldest or rainiest days to stop us, which didn't endear the plant guards to anyone.

Once inside the plant, the early arriver finds many workers already waiting for the start of the shift. Some arrive well before the line starts and stand around talking with the others who arrive early. These same workers may well be the ones who hang around after work talking with others in the parking lots. As Robert Schrank found in his time in a plant, "schmoozing" with other workers is an important part of any worker's day.[2] Several workers arrive early for a different purpose: to set up their small concessions to sell coffee, doughnuts, or other items. These on-the-job moonlighters have adapted to assembly line work by becoming entrepreneurs, subsidized in their pursuits by the unknowing auto companies.

Shortly before the scheduled start of the line, workers begin to congregate near their work stations—putting on aprons, getting their materials ready for the day, and building up reserves of their "stock," the assembled pieces they build into cars. By building stock ahead of time, you can make the day a bit easier for yourself.

For example, in my first job on the line I was responsible for installing the stabilizer bars, which give the car additional stability in cornering, on the underside of the front end of the car's chassis. To do the stabilizer bar job, I had to build two pieces of stock for each car, take one of three possible stabilizer bar models, move to the line as the chassis came by upside down, place the bar on it so it would not slip, put down one of the pieces of stock, and, finally, install the other piece on the chassis to secure the bar.

Each piece of stock was composed of a bolt approximately eight inches long on which I had to place, in order, a metal ring much like a washer, two rubber bushings that had to face each other, another ring, a bar to keep the sections separate, a third ring, two more rubber bushings facing each other, one more metal ring, and, finally, a nut to keep the whole assembly together. To install the piece of stock, I had to disassemble it so that only one rubber bushing and one metal ring remained on the bolt.

While holding the rest of the pieces, I'd insert the bolt through a hole in the chassis, replace the parts on the bolt, insert the bolt through a hole in the stabilizer bar, and finger-tighten the nut. Unless I did it just right, my carefully constructed piece of stock would come apart and fall on the floor, and I'd have to start over. By the time I'd finish, I could see the next chassis arriving, so I'd go back to the bench and start the whole process again.

The entire process—build stock, select bar, install bar—was supposed to be completed in 75 to 80 seconds. Because it was impossible to do the job in the time allotted, I would often arrive early and build up a backlog of stock in case I got behind, which I did regularly. If there was any stock left at the end of a shift, I'd hide it to use the next day. (The job was so hard that workers from one shift would not leave their extra stock for workers on the next shift. It was every man for himself.)

The people in the area generally acknowledged that the stabilizer bar job was the most difficult of all. In fact, one of the workers whose job it was to fill in for me during rest periods did not want to do it. That reliefman offered to pay me $10 if I would not take a rest period because he didn't want the foreman to know that he couldn't do the stabilizer bar job.

After I had complained to the foreman about the difficulty of the job, and after other workers had also complained to both the foreman and the union committeeman, the company clocked the job. When the time study was completed, the company seemed surprised to discover what we had known all along—that the job required 150% of the time the engineers had allotted to it. No wonder I was always behind! The company then removed some of the tasks from the job, which made it slightly easier. The job was

Research methodology

Using three separate methods, I gathered the data for this study from the workers in an automobile assembly plant in a medium-sized city in the Midwest.

First, I spent five months as an employee on the line, working on numerous different assembly operations. Although certain persons in both the management and the union hierarchy knew who I was and the general purpose of my research, no one in the plant itself knew. Once my observation period was completed, I interviewed 22 workers. These were extensive interviews, taking on the average two hours. Finally, I distributed a questionnaire to all workers in the final assembly complex of the plant on both shifts of a particular day. I received 209 usable responses, which represents a return rate of approximately 24%.

Such a three-pronged approach, while often seen as "methodological overkill," allows us to compare findings from one approach with findings from another to see if they are similar. If the findings differ, the complementary approaches allow for a greater probability of discovering why there is a difference and also for reconciling the difference.

still difficult, however, and required building stock ahead of time each day. In terms of the number of tasks required and the amount of time necessary to do them, the stabilizer bar job was the most difficult of all my jobs in the plant.

It is hard to imagine doing the stabilizer bar job over and over each day, each week, but until I was moved to another part of the plant, I did: 368 times in an eight-hour day. The first few days on the job I even found myself dreaming about it at night and doing the job in my sleep. One man told me that his job bothered him so much that his wife woke him up one night and told him that in his sleep he had imagined he was still doing the job, but he was doing it on her forehead.

In the course of my stay, I worked on approximately 20 different jobs in the plant. I worked on so many jobs because (1) I was of low seniority and got moved around as needed and (2) I wanted as wide experience as possible, and those persons in upper management who knew of my research obliged me by helping to move me to as many new and different jobs and shifts as possible without revealing my true purpose in the plant. Some of the jobs lasted only a few minutes as the foreman tried to decide where best to use me; others lasted two to three weeks—long enough to discover that illusive sense of rhythm that allows a worker to do the job and still have time to rest in between cars. I found that the easiest jobs are not always that easy, the most difficult jobs not always that hard.

My most boring, monotonous, and, therefore, hard job was as a driver in the repair section. In this job, along with two others I was expected to ferry cars from one section of the repair floor to another. Although three of us were assigned to the task, most of the time two were sufficient; we were only needed if a car had to be moved. We worked out a schedule so that two of us were available at any one time, with the third hiding out of sight, reading a newspaper, napping, or eating lunch.

If you subtract the relief time given to each worker during a normal eight-hour day (a total of 46 minutes according to the union contract), as well as the other official and unofficial time off from my paid eight hours, I actually worked a total of about two and one-half hours. Most workers I talked to wanted this type of job and looked forward to the time when their seniority would give them access to such a position.

One of my easiest jobs in the plant was one that no one else wanted because it was "so hard." On this job I had to kneel down next to the car and ride along with it as it moved down the assembly line. From this position I had to reach in through the open door and carefully place a small clip on the emergency brake cable up under the dashboard. This job was difficult because it was impossible to see what you were doing. Once I had the rhythm, I could do the job in about 30 seconds, leaving me almost a minute in between cars to rest, read the paper, look out the window, or talk to the workers around me. In fact, I often let myself fall behind so that I then had to work fast to catch up. On other occasions I would stay with a car longer than necessary so that the foreman would not realize how easy the job really was.

By the end of that particular job, I could work an entire shift and not make a mistake, whereas I never was able to master some other jobs and, to this day, do not know how the regular operators handle them.

Once the worker has the rhythm of the job, it is not nearly as hard to do as it is to describe. You become adapted to the flow of the job and begin to find other things to do with your mind. Some workers try to find shortcuts to make the jobs even easier. Others read books, magazines, or newspapers in between cars. Still others (I was one of these) try to calculate how many cars have already been completed and how many more are still to come.

Counting cars was one conscious method I used to pass the time; other methods came unconsciously. One time I realized that I was doing my job to the rhythm of an aria from an opera I had heard the last weekend. Another time I found myself a thousand miles away, driving an imaginary automobile down a highway I had not been on for years. How many chassis went by during my mental lapses—and whether I even did my job—I don't know and never found out.

Adapting to the line

Workers generally adapt to boredom and monotony in one of two ways: remain in the plant and find a way to get along or take off. Absenteeism is an extremely big problem. As one utilityman said, "People take time off because they're bored. They get tired of the same old routine." During hunting season, for instance, so many take off that other workers are often asked to "work a double," that is, to work two shifts back to back. Even during the rest of the year, on many mornings the line could not start due to the shortage of workers. Often we would stand around waiting for the company to find people to fill the holes in the line.

For those who remain on the job, adaptation takes many and often ingenious forms. While not all workers became bored with their jobs, enough do so that shutting one's mind to the surroundings becomes common. I remember one day when I was inadvertently in another worker's way, the other worker walked into me, backed up, walked into me again, and did the same a third time, until he realized that there was something or someone in his path.

One worker said: "I'm pretty good at blocking things out. I sing songs. One day I recited my multiplication tables. You get like a computer, you do the job automatically." What workers do about the monotony and boredom is as individual as the workers themselves.

Another worker told me: "I throw stock, I throw gloves, I bullshit about everything. I lie about how many hours we're working. I daydream a lot."

A third said: "[There's] not much you can do, I guess. You just do the work. Daydream, that's the best. [*What do you dream about?*] Gettin' out of this place. Gettin' off the line for about six hours. Just put your mind in a different place, say you're not here. I daydream about when I was a kid. Then you sit and laugh, and people look at you like you're crazy or something."

Talking, gossiping, or becoming an entrepreneur are only some of the techniques workers use to overcome the boredom of the line. We also played numerous games to make the time pass more quickly. We played "football" with a ball made out of foam rubber wrapped in electrical tape; in "basketball" we threw screws, bolts, nuts, or washers into a styrofoam cup taped to a girder. Another game we played was "hooting": when a worker hoots at the top of his or her lungs, others pick up the cry and the hooting goes up and down the line until it dies out sometime later.

Other means for decreasing the boredom and monotony are trading jobs (where two people agree to trade jobs for some specified period of time); doubling or tripling up (where one worker does the work of two or three workers for some period of time, after which he or she rests and another person does the jobs for a while); alternating jobs (where two people agree that one will do both jobs on cars no. 1,3,5, and 7 and the other will cover for cars no. 2,4,6, and 8); and working up the line (where workers work as fast as possible to get ahead and actually work "up the line" from their assigned work stations); or, as mentioned earlier, letting work fall far behind so that extraordinary effort is required to catch up.

Not all of the techniques the workers use to decrease the boredom and monotony are quite so benign, of course. Workers often block out monotony and boredom with alcohol or drugs. When I asked one young worker why he used drugs, particularly marijuana (which tends to be the drug of choice in the plant), he answered, "If I smoke [marijuana], I can stare at a spot on the floor all day long and not get bored." Another worker said: "I know a few guys that get completely messed up and they can run their job as good as when they're straight. There's a lot who couldn't. On second shift I've seen them take a guy and hide him 'cause he was so messed up. I don't like to get stoned when I'm working 'cause I don't know if I've done the whole car or not."

While the incidences of outright sabotage and theft are not great, a number of workers told me that they occasionally let a car go by without doing their jobs. Sometimes they take their frustrations out on the car or the tools themselves—breaking tools, banging tools against the bench, or causing air wrenches to emit high-pitched shrieks.

Exhibit
Workers' feelings about work in the plant*

	Yes	No	Uncertain
Do you have to take a day off every once in a while?	54.3%	43.3%	2.4%
Is absenteeism a big problem in the plant?	86.1	9.1	4.8
Do you ever drink at lunchtime?	40.4	59.6	–
Have you ever gotten high while working on the line?	32.7	66.3	–
Have you seen others in the plant get high while working on the line?	50.9	49.1	–
Do you think it's not important how much you know but whom you know that counts?	78.4	12.0	9.6
Does your supervisor treat everyone fairly?	43.8	48.1	8.2
Would the company be better off without a union?	2.9	88.0	9.1

*These are only some of the attitudinal questions used in the larger research project. In the questionnaire, attitudes were measured on a five-point scale rather than on the three-point scale shown here, and the percentages represent only those workers who actually answered each question.

Note: Several of the statements presented to the workers have been edited into question form for this article, but the substance remains the same.

Feelings about work

Most of the workers I met had strong feelings about their work. These feelings centered mainly around the job itself and the company, as well as the union. (See the *Exhibit* for a summary of workers' feelings about work in the plant.)

The company

Although the benefits and wages are high in the plants, if the quality of work life were not okay, one would expect that workers would want to leave. When I asked one 22-year-old woman how long she planned to remain with the company, she said, "I plan to put in my time and be a retiree." A 22-year-old man said: "Till I retire. I think that the company is the best place for me to work in [this town]. There is a lot of potential here if you want to make it. There's a lot of things I can do here to make me happy. I like to be able to say I accomplished something."

Another man said: "Thirty years and then I'm gonna retire. I hate it, but what else are you gonna do for a living? What else is there to do? Thirty years in the shop is enough for anybody." (At which point his wife added, "It's better than anything he's done before.") Most workers believe that, while work in the plant is not everything one might want, it presents better opportunities, better pay, and better fringe benefits than other jobs in the area.

If one assumes that workers would not remain long if the job were not agreeable, then you would expect the seniority levels of the workers in the final assembly plant to be below the minimum needed to transfer. (This indirect measure of their relative feelings toward working for the company has to be qualified, though, because the workers I talked to were in the final assembly plant, where the lower seniority workers predominate.)

In fact, the average seniority of the workers in the plant is quite a bit above the minimum needed to transfer out to the easier jobs, where the workers make "easy money." (The average for the entire plant is a little under eight and one-half years on the job; the minimum to transfer is two years.) Of course, other departments may well have high seniority levels, and it may be that the workers in the final assembly plant are waiting until they have even higher seniority so they can get a job in a particular plant.

While many prefer them, not all workers want to move to the easier jobs. One reliefman who had nine and one-half years of seniority and who still worked in the same area of final assembly told me: "That's the only zone I ever worked in. I could go anywhere I want to with my service, but I like that zone. I was in [another and easier job] for five years, but I couldn't hack it. The doctor told me to get off it 'cause I wasn't active enough, always [feeling sick]." This same repairman said "a lot of people go in there and they don't want to work. I want to work."

While the majority of the workers think the company is a good place to work, some feel ambivalent: "The company wants cars. If you drop dead, they'll pull you out of the way and somebody else will be there the next day. That line has to run no matter what. As for our benefits, they're hard to beat—medical insurance, time off, and they're trying to get more time off. [*Is the company a good place to work?*] To me it could be better. I think it's a good place to work, but I want better than where I'm at right now."

Or, as another worker said: "The shop can be anything you make it. I'm looking forward to a future there. You can climb the ladder there higher than any other place I could go with my education. I think the biggest plus in the shop is security. There're layoffs and stuff, but compared to the outside, there's a lot of security."

The union

For the workers, the union exists and is there when you need it. But, as in the old joke, many of them would "not want my son or daughter to marry a union official."

Very few of the workers feel they would be better off without a union in the plant. At the same time few had much good to say about the union. One reliefman summed up his feelings about the union this way:

"I don't have a lot to say about the union. I think they charge way too much money for what we get out of it. Unions are good but you don't see what you pay for. When you get penalized, it just seems management and the union get together on it. The committeeman we have is too buddy-buddy with all the foremen and G-Fs [general foremen]. A lot of the guys have to settle with what the foreman and committeeman come up with."

Workers generally see the union as they see the company: large, impersonal, and probably all right. The committeeman, like the supervisor, is someone with whom you must work all the time, and he (or she) is either good or bad.

One worker said his committeeman is "... excellent.... Some people say he's been there so long he's slacking off and that we need another one. He's friends with all the uppers at the union, and he knows a lot of people. He is the best one I've ever seen. He never forgets it if you ask him something." Another committeeman was considered "... worthless as tits on a piece of bacon" by one worker but held in high regard by others.

Most workers do not know what the union has done for them in the recent past. Thinking that nothing important occurs there, most union members do not attend union meetings. Between 2% and 4% of the total membership attended union meetings in the local of which I was a member. Attendance at union meetings is sufficiently unusual that once, when I attended a meeting and a picture of me sitting next to one of the union officers was taken and published in the union newspaper, I was rumored to be a union spy sent to see what my fellow workers were up to. Even meetings called to discuss new and important contract developments aren't attended. A recent meeting of my local to discuss the latest contract with the automobile manufacturer, which contained some important changes over the previous version, managed to draw less than 1% of its membership.

The workers I knew viewed union officials much the way most people see other elected officials, as suspicious but necessary. Because union officials are privy to secret material and socialize with the top managers of the company, the workers don't completely trust them. At the same time workers are quite adamant that they need a union in the plant, and they are quick to call for the committeeman to intercede for them when they are in trouble.

Quality of work life

While sociologists, psychologists, and human relations specialists may make suggestions on how assembly lines could be made more humane and less boring, the workers probably know best what it will take to make them happier, more contented, and, most important perhaps, more productive. When discussing the possibility for change, most workers I talked to commented either on management or supervisory style in the plant or on other general modifications the company could make. Workers see only a few places where changes they could make would be effective.

One thing that bothers most workers about their jobs is what they call "bad stock," material that does not meet specifications or is in some way defective, which causes the worker to fall behind. In the stabilizer bar job, for example, it was maddening to open a box of rubber bushings and find them useless because the majority didn't have holes drilled through them. Others agreed with me:

"Any repair I send is because of defective parts. The screws would strip out [early in the model year], but they are getting that straightened around finally."

"As long as I get good stock, there's no hassle with the job."

"Half the time the parts don't fit right."

"One day the stock is good, the next day it's bad, and you got to fight it. That's poor economy, the rejected stock. The stuff gets cheaper every day, the stock does. A guy's gonna pay so much money for the car, it ought to have real good stock on the car."

Whether the concern about stock is sincere or manifests a deeper feeling that something else is wrong, I don't know. I do know, however, how frustrating it is continually to have parts that do not fit, especially when it makes the job move more

slowly and makes you fall farther and farther behind, getting more in the hole with every passing chassis.

Another distinct problem in the plant is the favoritism supervisors show toward certain workers. My own experience confirms that it's really destructive. While the official policy of the plant is nondiscriminatory, discrimination does in fact exist. Thus although women are supposed to be given the same jobs as men, it does not usually happen that way. Almost universally, women are given easier jobs than are given to the men in the same plant. In some situations, it seemed that the easier jobs were given to women in exchange for sexual favors. One worker told me about the girlfriend of one of the general supervisors who had a meteoric rise in the job hierarchy. The girlfriend may well have been a good worker but having good connections did her no harm.

Workers who have relatives in "high places" can also get away with behavior for which other workers would be disciplined. In one section of the plant where I was, two workers had higher-up relatives in the company. One worker had been disciplined so many times that, were it not for his connections, he would have been fired long ago. I saw this worker openly drinking liquor on the job, sharing a drink with the supervisor, smoking marijuana, coming in late, leaving early, and so forth. The other workers knew of his connections and resented them.

For his part the supervisor did not seem in the least concerned about the morale problems the favoritism he showed the worker was generating. Rather, the supervisor seemed more concerned about the long-term consequences for his own career than the effect the favoritism was having on the other workers in that area.

I responded to the other case of favoritism in that department as a worker, not as a dispassionate observer. One of the young workers apparently felt that he should be a supervisor, even though he worked on the line. Apparently, he felt this way because his father had an important position in the company. This young man did what he wished, when he wished. Often at the expense of the job he was supposed to be doing, he "supervised" other workers. He would leave his work station and move to another part of the area when he thought something was going wrong that needed his immediate attention.

One day this young man and I almost came to blows over his assertion that he could do what he wanted, when he wanted, even if it meant that I could not do my job. Knowing that I would be fired for physically removing this worker, I told the foreman that the young man was in imminent danger of being placed upside down in a large parts bin if he did not get out of my way. The foreman realized that I was quite upset and caused him to stay out of my way for the remainder of the shift.

I think the young worker was quite nonplussed at my reaction. Other workers later told me that no one else had ever spoken to him quite so strongly and that he was somewhat put off by my not realizing that I should defer to him. I suspect that the foreman had had to screw up his courage to tell the young worker to be careful, because this was also the first time I had ever seen the supervisor stand up to him.

Above and beyond the more general problem of favoritism, the workers I talked to generally felt that supervisors do not treat all workers fairly. For example, at one point I was asked to learn a new job, was given one-half day of training, and was then told to "run" it by myself. The other workers told me that you are normally given three days of training to learn a job, during which time an experienced worker works alongside the trainee showing him or her the tricks of the trade.

During my first day alone on the job, one of the supervisors criticized me rather severely. When I informed him that I had not been given three days to learn the job and that I thought the union representative should be present to hear his criticism, he apologized and said I would be given some help. The assistance I received was from another worker who had little more idea of what the job was than I had, and this "training" lasted for only another half day.

Shortly after my run-in with the foreman, I was told that a rumor was going around that I was an undercover operative for the plant security forces sent to spy on the workers to see if they were engaging in sabotage or using drugs on company property. I later found out that the rumor was started by the foreman who had criticized my work.

My experience was common. Many workers told me similar stories: "I can't say I've had any problems with any of the foremen in there except one. He doesn't like me 'cause he doesn't like women. He came up to me one day when I was bent over a car and said my jeans were too tight. I said 'stop looking at my ass, and you won't have any problems. Nobody else is complaining.' "

"I would say the supervisors are just like any other employee, 95% of them; 3% are the overreactive type, and the other 2% are the hard-core—the ones who laugh about penalizing people. Never showing a guy when he's wrong . . . just stickin' it to him. . . ." (Some supervisors are proud of such reputations. The supervisor who started the rumor about me often referred to himself as a "gold-plated bastard" who would send workers home for the smallest rule violation.)

"As a whole they're pretty good. The general foreman on second shift is great. He goes out of his way to be friendly. Some of them would go out of their way to fire their mothers. Some of them, if they get down on you, will go after you. If you're a good worker, they'll go out of their way for you. If there's a clash of personalities with them, you could be in trouble."

"You're gonna have a few that are real assholes here and there. [He] is the lowest thing that walks as far as I'm concerned. He and I never see eye-to-eye or get along very good. I think some do a pretty good job. There's too many things that have to be changed for him to be effective. He catches too much shit from both directions to be any good. I don't think I personally dislike anyone. I dislike their methods of handling their management relationships."

One of my supervisors had a unique attitude toward working with his people—he was known to tell new hires (as he told me in our first discussion) that he did not care if they smoked (marijuana) or if they drank, all that concerned him was that there be no fighting in his area. He may have been one of the few supervisors who realized that the workers used drugs or alcohol and accepted that fact. How useful such an attitude is I can't say, except that it's extremely realistic.

Practically all workers are confronted with impersonality. When a new worker enters some departments, the first question the supervisor asks is, "What's the social?"—meaning the worker's social security number. It seems that no one cares what your name is, only your number. Workers are often referred to as "heads," not people, as when one supervisor calls another and asks if there are any extra heads that can be sent over to help out.

Management also tends to ignore workers' suggestions about jobs. I have seen engineers ignore comments from workers that could improve the productivity of an individual job. At one point I noticed that two air hoses were crossed, creating a potentially dangerous situation. When I suggested they be uncrossed, the foreman said they had been designed that way by the engineers, who clearly knew better than I how the plant works.

On another occasion I submitted a suggestion concerning means for alleviating the bad stock problem. It was not until a year later, after I had left the company, that I received a check and a notification that my suggestion had been accepted. During the time my suggestion was under consideration, I never received even a postcard telling me that my comments had reached them.

Impersonality, favoritism, and bad stock are all problems that management might do something about. In addition, workers noted a number of more general conditions they thought should be corrected, such as trash and dirt: "An assembly plant is going to be greasy. But I mean the overall conditions, the housekeeping. If there was some color in the plant. You go in and you have to kick the trash out of the way. General housecleaning. I can't accept the fact, the conditions, like it is now as far as paper all over. Half the time it looks like hell. If the floor was clean around where you work, I get a better attitude."

I certainly agree about the conditions in the plant. Some of us were occasionally asked to stay after the rest had left for the night to sweep up around our production area. As some people's sole responsibility in the plant was to sweep, you might think that the assembly line workers shouldn't have to. The cafeteria and restrooms also received their share of justified criticism for dull food and lack of cleanliness, respectively. Many workers told me that they do not come to work to be entertained, but they do feel they should be given at least minimal amenities.

What do workers really want?

The workers want changes in the plant, but they are not certain what the mechanisms for the changes should be. Not long before I began my work at the plant, the company and the union had agreed that they should jointly attempt to improve the quality of work life (QWL). To accomplish the stated goals, a number of joint management and labor committees were set up to monitor quality of work life and to solicit suggestions for improving the situation in the plant.

At one membership meeting of the local union to discuss the cooperation, the union representatives said they felt they should be paid from the union treasury for their attendance. A number of other union members at the meeting questioned the attendance payments but, more significant, challenged the entire concept of the QWL meetings and raised questions as to whether the union should involve itself in joint meetings with the management to try to solve the problems.

3. F.J. Roethlisberger and William J. Dickson, *Management and the Worker* (Cambridge, Mass.: Harvard University Press, 1939), p. 553.

Ultimately, the experiment met with only limited success at best. Workers in the plant distrusted the committees. Workers felt that improvements in the quality of work life on the line would simply bring with them what other improvements had brought in the past–a faster line speed. A number of first-line supervisors thought that, by attempting to improve the quality of work life, the company was simply "mollycoddling" workers who needed a good kick in the pants rather than lace curtains in the windows.

By far the greatest majority of the workers I talked to had not heard of the committees and, once they were acquainted with the work of the committees, were not convinced that they would help anyway. To workers quality of work life is not an abstraction; it affects their jobs. If a workbench is too close to a pillar, if a hose connection is loose, if the work area is too cold, if a pair of gloves is not available in the morning, the quality of work life is diminished. Once these problems are eliminated, workers would be able to enjoy the luxury of deciding the degree to which they really want to be involved in either overall company decision making or in simply choosing the color for the walls.

Accompanying the individual nature of the QWL problems is the fact that, while many workers know what it is they do and what their own job title is, most do not really know how their jobs fit into the whole. Some additional orientation for all workers—new and old—might increase their feelings of belonging to the company.

Workers do care about the company well beyond the paycheck they bring home each week. Workers may say that all they care about is the paycheck, but they know that the quality of the automobiles they build determines largely what they take home. While intrinsic work satisfaction is important, it is also important to know that you are making enough money to live comfortably, are covered by extremely comprehensive medical and dental insurance, and can leave the job and not worry about it.

What is extremely important for the company, the union, and the workers to understand (and it has become more obvious to me the more I have thought about the situation) is the need to deal with workers as human beings. Workers do not want something for nothing. Most people are interested in making a living; they want to come to work and be treated with the respect normally accorded to adults. F.J. Roethlisberger and William Dickson made the same point more than 40 years ago.[3] They concluded that each worker:

"... is bringing to the work situation a different background of personal and social experiences. No two individuals are making the same demands of their job. The demands a particular employee makes depend not only upon his physical needs but upon his social needs as well."

Many years, many studies, and many people later, industrial relations still has not become human relations.

The technology of the assembly line fosters the idea that the people should be like the products rolling off the line. All workers should think the same, act the same, do the same things. When a person comes along who does not play by the rules and wants simply to be seen as an individual, the members of the system react to bring the person back to the norm. But no one person totally fits the mold. Everyone is different, and people can only adapt so far. Maybe how they are treated has to change. Some supervisors, union officials, and workers realize this —but, sadly, not enough do.

It's not lonely upstairs

Seeing the company leader need not be an event, and company survival can become a mutual effort

An interview with Renn Zaphiropoulos

In 1969 Renn Zaphiropoulos and four other engineers founded Versatec, Inc. in Santa Clara, California to manufacture electrostatic printers, plotters, and dual-function printer-plotters for computers. Although the fledgling company was a latecomer in its field, it prospered and grew rapidly. In fact, today it outsells all competitors combined. It employs about 900 people in Santa Clara and abroad, and it maintains field services in more than 50 countries. In 1975 Xerox Corporation acquired the company.

In this interview Mr. Zaphiropoulos, president and chief executive officer of Versatec and vice president of advanced product development, Information Products Group, at Xerox, talks about the management philosophy that has worked so well at his company. He describes the organization as a series of concentric circles rather than as the conventional pyramid. He also discusses the value of celebration after achievement, the encouragement of creativity in problem solving, and the emphasis Versatec places on closeness and openness in relationships.

In four succeeding interviews, other employees show how this philosophy works. In the first two, William Lloyd, a vice president and founder, and Ian Turner, director of development and engineering, focus on innovation. In the last two, Bobbette Johnson, manager of employee relations and training, Cynthia Trainer, an assembler, and Vitória Cardoza, a quality assurance inspector, talk about the ambience of the company.

The interviews were conducted and edited by Pamela M. Banks, manuscript editor at HBR, and by David W. Ewing, executive editor–planning at HBR. The photographs were taken by John Marriott.

Reprint number 80612

HBR: What made you and the others want to start this company?

Renn Zaphiropoulos: In our previous company the environment was frustrating. We were not in the command positions. We had to ask too many questions before we could get going on anything new, so we left to do our own thing.

When we started out, we had two objectives, and the company has grown around them. They are still our objectives. One is to make money because that is a condition for survival. The other is to arrange a situation in which people look forward to coming to work. These two things have to go together. If you are too one-sided about making money, it becomes a sweatshop and people hate your guts. If you are too one-sided the other way, it becomes a country club. You cannot have either objective without the other.

Is it hard to keep this balance as you add new departments and layers of management?

When the general idea is that people should be put in an environment that encourages free communication, there is a de-emphasis of levels and status. We do this here merely by being the kind of people who are comfortable being close to others. These are not the kinds of things that anyone can do by following any sort of formula. You cannot say, "Now it is really important for me to communicate the problem; therefore, I'm going to go out and communicate."

I think what really has happened here is that the company ever since its inception has been fortuitously put together by people who really enjoy our form of management. And therefore, through 10 to 11 years now they have insisted that it continue. When someone comes in who thinks he's above somebody, he's almost immediately exposed. He becomes the kind of a thing that is bad taste.

The differences between people are only relative—man-made differences. We at the top are merely people who, because of our position, are supposed to have a broad perspective: we are supposed to see everything that's going on in the company.

When I'm talking with company people, I sometimes draw the organization as a series of concentric circles instead of as the usual pyramid. That helps to eliminate the notion of levels and status. [See the *Exhibit* on page 84.]

That's a somewhat unconventional way of thinking about organizational relationships.

The trouble with the pyramid is that it accents up and down, and we attach values to up and down. Up is good, down is bad. If you're down, you're lower. Down is almost always lower in our value systems. It's like other opposites in values—black and white, light and dark. So the pyramid sets people's minds in a prejudicial fashion. They get conditioned to thinking that up is the only way to go.

What we want to say in our organization scheme is that an increase of responsibility is commensurate with a broadening of one's view. Now, the pyramid is legitimate in the sense that the higher you go on it, like a mountain, the more you can see. But in this circular design I look at things another way. It's a way of saying that a company doesn't just start from one point and go up or down. Rather, it starts from one point and radiates in all directions.

The circles are a symbol that all efforts lead to one thing, which is the company's survival.

If you're at the center of the circles, how do you relate to people in the outer circles?

You do it by being interesting. By not being too detailed, not becoming picayunish. Not meeting people only when disciplinary action is necessary. Talking over what is of mutual interest, not just writing memoranda or reports. Celebrating together when we do something right.

Do you publish this scheme for all employees? Is it part of the company literature?

No, we don't advertise it. It is something I have developed myself and use sometimes in talks about management. It is another way of saying we all have joined our fortunes together, and therefore we might as well cooperate. It's a way of looking at the company as a whole. If you look inside each department, you'll see a structure of authority that looks very much like a pyramid, so in that respect we're not radically different from many other companies.

Within this circular scheme there are still promotions and incentives and rewards?

Yes, and with them goes a certain amount of status that attends the person who is very good at his or her job. But no job is higher or lower in importance than another job—that is what we say with the circular design. How do you compare the importance of a salesman who overachieves his quota by 30% with a person who invents something new? You can't. You have to say that their values to the company have no levels or heights.

How do you communicate this idea to people in Versatec?

To begin with, we do it with the building itself. Take our offices. An office can be designed to bring together or to separate. My office here is the same size as the marketing vice president's across the way. Now my office could be bigger, and I could have a very good reason for that—for example, to have a conference room in here. That would be functional, that's okay. But suppose I have a rosewood desk when everybody else has only imitation rosewood. My rosewood desk wouldn't change the functions of my office. It would be designed only to separate me from other people.

Exhibit
The organization as a series of concentric circles

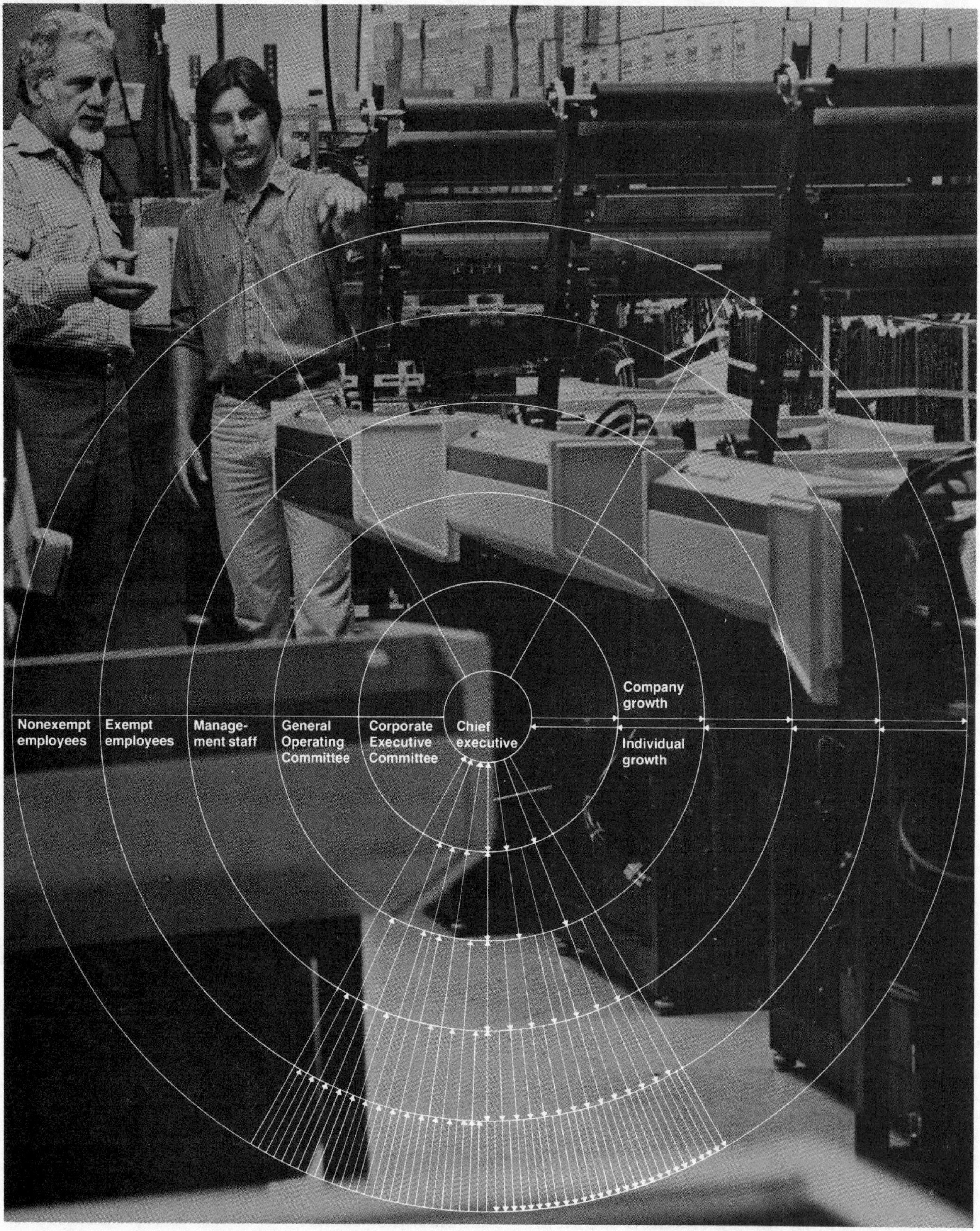

What you're saying is, the more psychological separation there is, the poorer the communication.

I want someone coming in here to feel at ease because I like the person. If I were the kind of person who didn't want to get close to people, I could make this place into a mausoleum so that when they walked in here they would really be afraid. Then I would always have the upper hand. But then I would lose the final game because the final game depends on the employee being enough at ease with me to reveal what he's doing so that I can understand his situation. In our organization circles, I'm not "on top" of others. I can only be on top on a pyramid.

What about the offices that don't have windows?

Oh, there are differences. But what I'm saying is, we try to minimize the differences and make sure that people do not use certain things for status symbols. Now there will be status symbols, no question about it. And there will be differences. But we try to make these things functional. We say the engineer has an office and a desk to put up his feet, while the operator has a lathe. The desk for the feet is very much a tool for the engineer who's thinking through a design, as the lathe is a tool for the operator.

Are there other ways in which you communicate your concept of the company?

Yes. We do as little standing on ceremony as possible. There are no private parking places, and there will never be any here because there's no need for that. Reserved parking, it seems to me, is based on the notion that the president's time is more valuable, which is fundamentally nonsense. What time I spend here is really my own business, and it will not be improved by somebody giving me a parking place in front. That is not a privilege that goes with rank. It's a privilege that separates me from the other people. So if I want to be friendly, I want to be able to talk to someone coming into the parking lot. If I have a white spot reserved where nobody else can park, that removes me from the rest of the people, and that attitude goes right down the line.

You emphasize the simple, everyday physical closeness of people in the company. Could you give other examples of how this promotes the spirit of openness and equal importance?

Many times I answer my own phone. People walk in and out of offices. Starting at four o'clock every

Wednesday we have meetings where we spend a lot of time with various groups of people. Some of these are meetings for the whole company—for everyone working here. Off and on we all have drinks together and some food, and we talk. Seeing the top manager in the company is therefore not an event. If it's not an event, people don't think it is extraordinary, and if they don't think it's extraordinary, they don't think of the structure so much as up and down, as being a pyramid.

Isn't it difficult for you, with all the other demands on your time, to make yourself so accessible?

You see, that's the myth. If I want people to talk with me, I have to have relationships with them. Executives who fly around so that nobody sees them don't develop relationships. My own feeling is that most executives, when they begin to make a lot of money, almost feel embarrassed and guilty. They feel they have to do something to make it appear that the money is in the proper place. So they develop the syndrome of appearing very busy and put themselves at the end of a corridor behind a door with a whole bunch of doormen. People say it's lonely upstairs, but that's only if you close the door and stay out of sight.

Your philosophy, then, is that busyness is not good business, or at least, not good management.

The late Alan Watts, the philosopher who popularized Eastern thought in the West, affected quite a bit of my thinking, especially with his concept of the path of least resistance. The essence of any kind of success is to be able to say that a person's talents, natural talents, fit the requirements of the job. This is what I would say is working in an effortless manner. That is, you naturally fit what you're asked to do.

If that is the situation, then the person gets out the most for the amount of input he or she puts in. What I'm trying to stress is that people who come in here should really look forward to enjoying themselves. My definition of hard work is to go against your grain. If you are in a position in which things go along with your talents, it is not hard work anymore.

Suppose you have an engineer who is a very good engineer and has the talents you want but perhaps is not good at communicating. Do you tell him, "No, you don't fit," or do you work with him or her to develop skill at communicating?

The requirements of the job may be such that the engineer works individually. In that case, the communication problem isn't a serious one. The question is: If there is much of a disparity between what the person can do and what the job objectives are, what do you do about it? It all depends on how critical this disparity is to getting the work done. There is no way of having people or things be exactly what you want them to be, and I don't care if we're talking about employees, wives, husbands, kids, parents, church members, lodges, or foreign countries. There will always be some sort of disparity between what you want and what occurs with another person. So as a manager or an employee, no one is going to fit the demands of the company completely.

So if what you want from the engineer is a technical contribution, and that is what he can do with the "least effort," it doesn't matter so much if he's not good at communicating?

Yes, let me put it another way. I can never do everything. There are certain things I will overlook or not get to. Ideally, those things won't matter a great deal. What I should do depends on what we call the "critical path," that is, the truly necessary aspects of my job. The critical path is carrying the water when you go across the desert, and you give that job to a very competent person. Now, other things that are not as essential you give to others. What I'm saying is, the fit you look for between people and jobs depends a lot on how critical the jobs are to the success of the company.

For you, then, being accessible and communicating is part of the "critical path."

Absolutely, and that goes for many other managers. There have been people whose employment we've needed to terminate because they would not communicate, and their jobs required them to do so. For example, a large part of what an engineering manager should do is discuss designs with people. If that doesn't happen, the people starve for contact and the whole department begins to falter. So in that kind of situation we have to step in and do something about it.

Is there a corollary here, that sometimes you try to change the job to fit the person?

Oh sure, we are full of eccentrics, from what I'm told, and we just bend to suit their needs. If there's some star inventor sitting in a laboratory creating something important, we bend over backward not to require much communication from him or her. We work around it. But it has to be possible to work around it; that is, it must be possible to sit alone in that lab and stay on one of the critical paths without spending a lot of time talking. If we have to compensate too much, if it gets too tiring to hold hands with the person, we stop doing it.

We have been talking about communication, but the result you want at Versatec is innovation and creativity. How do you relate communication to the innovative spirit?

One of the worst things you can do is put people in situations where nobody cares about what is going on. In a lot of research laboratories, people sit in rooms and nobody pays much attention to what they've developed. The way to keep people innovative—constructively innovative—is to react to what they are doing. Your reaction can be positive or negative. You can say they are failing or they are doing something great. Both statements say that you care. They answer the person's question: "Am I doing something useful that anyone cares about? How am I doing?"

I think it's important to define the problem or need in its least constrained form. Creativity is the process of inventing new combinations of old things. If I have a screwdriver and a hammer, and I put them together in some new way with the screwdriver at one end and the hammer at the other, that's an invention. The hammer isn't new, the screwdriver isn't new, but the combination is original. Now, if I define the problem in a very narrow form, people won't invent anything. If I say, "Look, try to design a bottle this way," I limit the solution too much. I'm not giving enough room for manipulation. I'm not leaving enough risk and uncertainty about how to do it.

How do you present the problem then?

What I need first of all to do is to present a challenge—"Invent a new toner bottle that doesn't leak so that a person can put it on the system without ruining his hands or getting them dirty. You see what I mean? See what you can do. We'll meet in two or three months, okay?" Then, they've got the ball and maybe they'll invent something. It's got to matter to us whether they succeed, and there has to be full confidence that they will succeed, but also there's got to be some risk. They must see that things won't necessarily work out.

You leave them with some anxiety, in other words, as well as freedom?

One has to instill an anxiety about success for people to become productive. But it must be what I call manageable anxiety. It must be a challenge that doesn't break them down but that gives them an interest in living and solving new problems. If there isn't any anxiety, life is too easy and they atrophy.

Do they understand that there are penalties for failure?

It is understood that it is permissible to fail. It is also understood that it is preferable not to. A lot depends on how desperate they are to succeed. If they are very desperate about succeeding, they won't create anything new because of worry about the result. So they have to know that the maximum help will be given to bring about success. Almost everything we do here is very difficult, very risky, new. It goes without saying that the game we play is dangerous. But then it also goes without saying that life isn't worth living without danger. The attitude has to be one of mutual support—"Maybe it will work, maybe it won't, we'll have to do it together."

There is a kind of group pride, then.

The pride of working for an organization that is awake, progressive, that insists on excellence. We talk a lot about competence. We talk a lot about doing the job right, and if the job is not done right, the failure surfaces fast. And when it does, we take action to change the budget, the resource, the engineers—whatever must be corrected. People can feel almost chauvinistic about being members of such a group.

Can you give an example of when people here have felt like that?

Yes, when we got our first order for our wide plotter—it's a big machine, about six feet wide—we had what seemed like an impossible deadline. The order came in in June 1979, and the machine had to be delivered by September twentieth to an industrial show in Philadelphia—the first order for a new piece of equipment, and only a few months to construct it in.

Before the last 30 or so days of the job, I made a handwritten calendar of tasks and due dates. We put it in the laboratory and checked off every day until time zero. In the space for certain days we drew lit-

tle pictures of milestones like "All the parts are here" and "Test begins at this point."

You'd be surprised how eager the people were to come in and scratch off the day each job was done. There was a very strong interest in the approaching deadline. "Time zero is approaching, guys. Have you got everything?" "Is it really going?" "How are we doing?" "Don't tell me tomorrow we didn't do it!" A kind of crescendo built up. It's amazing what incredible things can happen when people tune in. It's like the business of resonance in physics, when all the frequencies match so there can be a transfer of energy.

Is the 30-day chart a technique regularly used?

Oh no. If you do something like that too often, it becomes phony and it won't work, like always smiling at someone.

Were the people who made that prodigious effort on the wide plotter rewarded?

We rode it out in record time—9:30 on a Tuesday night. I invited everybody who was there to my house for a big party that very evening. We played pool, we sang—lots of things. But the reward was in the celebration, in our feelings, you see, not in anything valuable in a monetary way.

You may give a person a bottle of Grand Marnier, you know, if he or she gets a special order the company wants. But the reward is like the ancient Greek wreath for the victor. The wreath was made of laurel, and laurel was a weed which had no value. The idea of the laurel wreath was to remove physical value from the reward. It was the event that was valuable in people's minds. No gold in the award, like the Romans later made it—in Greece the award was pure.

Now, there is a big difference in philosophy between making the award an expensive, gaudy thing and making the idea or event precious. And I believe that most of the people at an organization like Versatec are more grateful if their image is enhanced rather than just their wealth. Therefore, if you improve their image, you meet one of their important needs.

Do you ever get negative reactions to your rewards?

Yes, and I'll give you an example. We have a practice of awarding pins to employees for each five years of service. A lot of companies give five-year pins. When an employee has served five years, I ask the person to lunch with me. The person's supervisor, the vice president for the area, and a personnel department representative usually join us.

But once a lady here said, "I don't want to go to lunch with you." I said, "That's perfectly okay. I would be interested to know why if you want to tell me." She answered, "I think it's sort of a phony thing. Here you don't pay any attention to me for five years, and now it's a five-year pin just because I've been here that long. Big deal!"

I said, "Well, I guess it appears that way, doesn't it? But if I don't pay attention to you at the end of the five years, I pay less than I'm trying to now. And really it would be impractical, you understand, for me to spend time regularly with every employee. At least we make an organized effort once every five years to see you and say, 'Hey, how do you feel about things?' "

Do you think the woman felt she was being typed?

Certain people have a need to be individualistic. They want to be different. So when someone says,

"Look, there's the president driving a five-year employee to lunch," their reaction is, "I am not going to be one of those."

My attitude is, "That's fine. I respect that. If you don't want to socialize with me, that's your business. But I am going to make the offer because I have to be true to myself." It gives me pleasure to invite someone to lunch whom I don't see normally and to take an hour or two to sit around and ask how things are going. I know that we could talk in my office, but I think with most people you want to get out of the framework of work and go to some place different and relax.

However, if this seems too mechanical to the other person, I will not argue. I have only made the offer, and in another five years I will make the same offer because that is what I want to do.

You've mentioned how your philosophy may affect a production effort or meeting a deadline. What about an example of innovation?

Well, we had a program called "gorilla." The gorilla project was the development of a very low-cost machine—a small, tabletop model of our standard electrostatic plotter. The project got that name after I wrote a sketchy memorandum to my boss at Xerox saying that we needed funds to produce a low-cost model in two and a half years. Of course we followed up the proposal with a budget, return-on-investment calculation, and so on. Presented with that proposal, the Xerox executive said, "Even a gorilla would think that that is a good plan." So we called it the gorilla project after that.

Gorilla went from me to Bill Lloyd, our vice president of research, development, and engineering and one of the most inventive people here. Then he brought a fellow we recruited in England into the project—Ian Turner. He's now director of development and engineering after two years at Versatec. The new machine was announced last spring.

What does it do?

What it does is reduce the cost of a printer-plotter by about one-third. Doing this required a great deal of inventiveness because our printers and plotters don't work in a mechanical way but on the basis of semiconductor technology. New semiconductors have become available that are cheaper, and we have taken advantage of that and other innovations to invent a machine that works at much lower cost. It is very successful. Its development is right on schedule.

Earlier today you were out on the plant floor. Was it the gorilla project you were looking at?

I was downstairs looking at how a line of production for another product was doing, and I saw some machines sitting there alone. I asked if there was a problem with people. I was told we have shortages on the line and we cannot work on those machines, that maybe next week we will have the proper people there. I asked how the month was going. Were we going to have a crunch at the end?

Then somebody comes in and brings some Philippine egg rolls, and he says, "Hey, you want to eat some?" So he gives me a napkin and we eat the egg rolls on the line. Bill Lloyd comes down, and he eats an egg roll. And we discuss fishing at the same time. Then somebody nearby has a technical problem, so we go and look at it—the machine's not writing correctly. I am at the production line and everywhere else in the company at least twice a day.

Does the company use any organizational techniques to keep people in touch with each other?

We have what we call the Management Advisory Group—"MAG"—eight people who represent employees from all parts of the company. There's a person from marketing, one from manufacturing, one from cost control, and so on. They meet once a month and talk about the problems of the company.

What power does MAG have?

Advisory, but they can come straight to me or straight to our executive committee members and have a séance with them. MAG doesn't have to go through supervisors or channels.

It is a way for people at the periphery to tell top management how the hell things are going, and when something is wrong, we decide what's to be done about it. For a group to have value doesn't mean it has to make major policy decisions. If what it says is taken very seriously, it has quite a bit of influence.

Where are the policy problems discussed?

The Corporate Executive Committee does that. This group is the half dozen or so people who report directly to me, and they are what we call the inner circle. If you're in the inner circle, we say, you're supposed to have a perspective on the whole company's goals. You're supposed to think about your department—marketing or manufacturing or whatever—but you're also supposed to see how your department ties in with the fortunes of the company, and vice versa. The executive committee worries about general things like what businesses we're in and morale, not so much about operating problems.

And whose concern is operating problems?

Those are for the General Operating Committee, the people who really make things happen, the directors of quality analysis, industrial relations, manufacturing, engineering, field sales, and so on. The rest of the company reports to them. They meet periodically during the month. There are 18 of them. In the circular chart they are shown as the second circle out. Their perspective is one specific field of responsibility rather than what the whole company's doing.

In the Exhibit [see page 84] you have some smaller fields of responsibility shown within a director's field.

The next smaller field is for members of the management staff—about 60 people on this circle. The narrowest fields, shown on the next circle, are 250 or so people who, though not managers, are still exempt. On the outer circle are the nonexempts—people like wire weavers, clerical workers, quality controllers.

But the circular scheme isn't really an organization chart.

No. It shows how closely all our functions are connected. It describes an attitude. It is not something we start with. It's something we end up with.

So management still has to resolve conflicts and make rules?

Of course. Business is, you might say, an activity that has rules. If it doesn't have rules, you don't know what the game is. As in tennis, you have to have lines to know what is a good shot and what is a bad shot. So we say we're going to have a structure and have certain people report to certain other people, and this goes clear to the center.

Now this is okay, except that employees have interests that often conflict with what the company wants to do. I can have a game outside of here that has other rules. Say my wife wants me to do something, wants me to be there at 5:30, but the company says we're having a meeting and it's not yet finished. Now the question is, how does one negotiate that? What do you do about conflicts between the games employees play outside the company and the games they play inside the company?

There's a universal game going on. Versatec is not the only game in town. It shouldn't be. What happens is that we must watch that the people who don't do a job right because of other conflicting games do not hurt the people adjacent to them or the people on the next circle. You can have a marvelous setup at the center that says this is the way the company should behave, but that center still must have feedback from the periphery.

What kind of feedback do you look for?

It depends whether you reward effort or results. Needless to say, we reward effort—for instance, an employee who has worked many years for us. But the thing we talk most about is results.

Life is very much responsibility for producing results, and effort does not compensate for lack of results. So if somebody says, "I'm busy," he's talking about effort—it's an activity-oriented statement. But when the person says, "This is what I've done," it's a different story. And it doesn't make any difference how long he took, because the ultimate thing is what he did, what really happened. Of course, the most marvelous thing is to do the least amount and get the most out of it. That's what I want people here to call efficiency.

Suppose you find that a person is not efficient, that he or she is not getting results. Do you feel a responsibility to keep him employed?

If I learn that my understanding of what a person could do is erroneous, that he or she doesn't meet the need, my responsibility is to tell him or her as fast as possible that I think I've made a mistake. It has to happen in a company like this that's growing at a rate of 40% per year.

Suppose we have a manufacturing manager who, let's say, is very good at producing 3 million printer-plotters for shipment per year. As the company grows, the job may totally outgrow him. He may be poor at getting 12 million printer-plotters out the door every year. The monitors and controls he used a few years ago may be useless now.

Or, take the star who does everything by himself, like the financial manager in a small organization. The organization grows, and pretty soon he needs a controller, then a receivables manager, a chief accountant, and so on. He's not right for the job anymore because he has to work through them. He can't be the star. I don't believe that a person is promoted to the level of his incompetence, as the Peter Principle says. What happens is more subtle. What happens is that the requirements of the job change.

Would you try to reassign the person instead of firing him?

Oh, of course, because the role of a manager is to arrange talent. It's the same as with a painting. Here is available talent sitting all around like paints. The question is, how do you put them together so that the composition is right? And then, if the composition isn't right, what do you do? You don't say that the red is wrong or the green is wrong. What you actually say is that the green should be red and that the red should be blue or a different shade of red. So you arrange, and if the arranging isn't right, you try to rearrange.

We have had people who were good engineers, but when they were made engineering managers they were not so good. So they became senior scientists, where they make just as much money but are better suited because of their talents and fears or wishes about communication.

Lots of executives think of being nice to people as quite time-consuming. But you see it as efficiency.

Yes, because if I can explain to people, by virtue of my relationship with them, the position we're in and the problems we have to solve, they'll go ahead and solve them. I don't have to hold their hands or crack the whip or direct their activities. Now, I cannot do that if I am apart from them, separate and distant. Because then, if I go to criticize someone, how am I going to make it possible for him or her to understand that what I'm saying is not hostile?

Is there any hindrance to continuing this management style that you have, this desire to have communication radiating from the center out and from the periphery toward the center?

It all depends on who runs the company in the future. It depends on who the people coming in are, and if top management changes, the company will change. There are many ways to manage people. We, as I say, are the kind of people who enjoy this. I think there are many people here today who believe in the present philosophy—they are very much disciples of it.

Let people do what they do well the way they want to do it

Bill Lloyd, vice president of research, development, and engineering: My reason for wanting to form a company had to do with the thought of developing something new and exciting that would at the same time offer us the opportunity to run an organization in a different way.

I had a strong interest in making a printer product out of the technology I'd been using, and the five of us who founded Versatec wanted more freedom to manage business in our own style.

HBR: Was it your invention that this company was formed around?

Well, yes. It developed out of a number of inventions I had in the field of electrography and the product development that followed.

It's been much easier to get new product developments started in our own company. If someone's got an idea he wants to work on, he doesn't have to interface with anyone else or any other group. It's all internal, and within budget constraints we each do our own thing.

In order to have that freedom, we normally budget approximately one-quarter of the research budget every year for what we call "blue sky activities." These are projects that are undefined at the beginning of the year and that are totally controlled by the people in this department.

What have some of those activities been?

About a year ago we decided that using our kind of equipment for color looked interesting. Marketing certainly wouldn't support nor did they want anything to do with color at that point, so we took some money out of our blue sky funds and made some color samples that satisfied our need to see what could be done with this technology. And then we let it lie.

When marketing finally comes around and says, "Hey, we want a color device," we'll be able to talk intelligently about it. This kind of thing is very important to us.

There are other things we've done with blue sky money that have improved our technology. We've looked into different techniques for doing things we've been doing in particular ways for a long time —as an example, the use of hybrid technology. It's an old technology, but we hadn't been using it in high voltage devices. Someone said, "I want to look into the use of hybrids," so he made use of some blue sky funds. As a result, today most of our products are made with hybrids, which save us money and use less board space, and you know, while this may not be a major advance, it is of importance to the company.

Can anybody initiate an idea?

Absolutely. Within the RD&E organization, anyone can come up with an idea and try to promote it within the department and then sell it to management.

What do you have to go through to turn an idea into a regular project, one that's not a blue sky project?

The engineers are the most likely to initiate and promote an idea, but anyone can. Generally that person brings it to one of the managers' attention—the head of research, the head of systems, or the head of engineering—and tries to get funding for it.

One thing this company is very good at, unlike many larger companies, is being so flexible that if we start a program and find that it's a bummer and there's a better one, we can change in midstream and say, "The heck with the other one. It's not the right one. Let's go with this one." We don't get too hung up on pet projects.

Just recently someone spent a lot of his own time at home building a wooden mock-up and demonstrating a new approach to one of our wide plotter projects. He did an excellent job; and we all admired his stamina and ability. When we finally decided which way to go with that product, we decided against his approach. Here was a case of a guy promoting something that lost.

That's not often the case. When people really get turned on to an idea, we usually go along with it, and more often than not, that idea will have something to do with improving our present product line or describing a new product concept.

Normally we try to sell marketing on new ideas. In the early stages of this company almost all new product ideas came from marketing. Today I would say that some new product ideas come from engineering, and some from marketing. Incidentally, I believe that RD&E has been just as successful as marketing in judging the value and even the marketability of products.

This kind of flexibility must've been something you wanted to bring to the company too.

Absolutely. We tend to let people do what they do well the way they want to do it rather than try to influence them to come around to someone else's method of doing things.

The three people that report to me vary tremendously in the way they manage each of their groups. One manages a systems activity, one manages a research activity, and one manages the development and engineering arm. And I don't try to change or influence their behavior. That's up to them.

We have total informality with each other. We have interesting conversations and interplay, and we don't have a structure that would cause anyone to be concerned about telling me, "That's wrong." They say it. We use a lot of very plain language. We don't attempt to be too gentle with one another in discussions about technology or management techniques.

The function of the top management of the company varies from time to time. There are times when we keep our noses out of certain areas that are working well. But if some area has serious trouble functioning, all of us become involved in its support or management.

We're not so structured that I sit up here and say to somebody, "You go down and solve that problem." I get the calls, and I decide whether I should send someone else down to solve the problems or whether I should go down myself. Normally I find that I do a lot of it—partly because I like to and partly because I'm probably best at it because I have the most experience with some of the older products.

What have you found to be most important in managing creative people?

I think a lot of freedom is probably the key element. I think it's very difficult to get creative people to accept someone else's ideas. I think creative people tend to want to do their own thing, and I find it difficult to force my ideas on people.

There are times, of course, when we get to a head-butting stage, where someone has to yield, and more often than not that's me. Occasionally I do win out and get my way. It's difficult to manage creative people. And there is no single formula. I think that everyone I've known who's creative has had a different personality and therefore that a different interface must occur.

Would you say that the company has brought about most of the changes that you were hoping to make in forming it?

I think so. I think that we are probably not as good today at keeping people happy as we were in the earlier days, though.

Oh, why is that?

I think it has to do with what happens as we grow—people don't get the personal attention they used to, and I think creative people demand a lot of attention, no matter what the field. People like to be talked to and feel that they're part of the same team. I think that as we grow people get a little farther apart. That's when you start to feel the need for rewards other than money.

One of the things we can do to supplement financial reward is to have a close relationship with the people who work here. I socialize with the people in my department and with many people in other departments.

I just took a group out fishing on my boat this past weekend. I believe that there is a real benefit to the company and to each of us in this type of socializing in that the next time a business interface with that person occurs it will prove to be more comfortable and very likely more productive.

We try to operate according to what people here want. We're a very people-oriented company.

A thousand hours of conversation —sketching things out

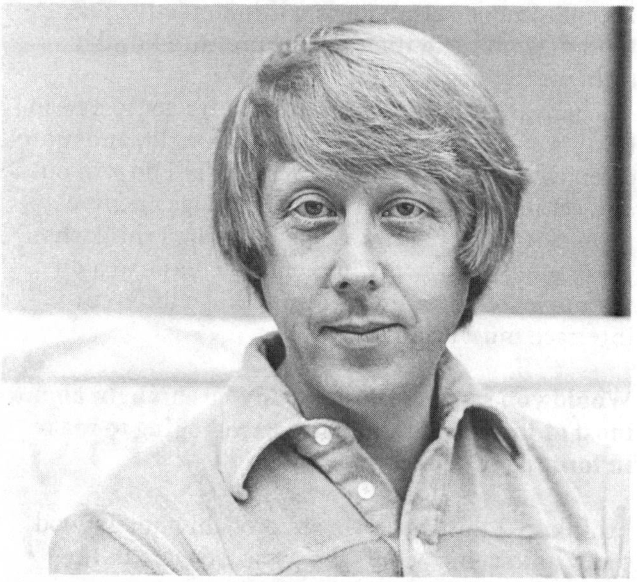

Ian Turner, director of development and engineering: A company needs to have the ability to innovate built right into its structure. Accountability and responsibility should be coincident. What happens in most companies is that the manager says, "I hold you responsible, but I'm going to approve everything you do." Worse than that, quite often there are large committees of people whose opinions about a new idea must be congruent before any progress can be made. And above that level there is usually nobody. So nobody is accountable. It's a committee with some guys responsible over here and other guys accountable somewhere else. That means that if one person dissents or misses a meeting, you get into a morass with nothing coming out of it.

Versatec understands that problem. What it says it that one person is champion; one person has the responsibility and is also held accountable and is given the tools to make it all come true.

HBR: What kind of tools are you given here?

Freedom. It's everything. It includes powers of signature, the chance to organize, the right to veto other people's ideas and sometimes to be terribly autocratic. You can build teams the way you want to and not have other people second-guessing you. It all comes back to the fact that the guy who does the innovation is seen to be in control of what happens. And you have a power over the system.

Now, as it turns out, I don't use all the power. My own style is very participative. I like to generate agreement as a group. But the point is that there is a way it can be controlled from a single point. We don't have some poor devil down here running this bit, and some other poor devil down there running that bit, and no consistency in the baseline.

How do you generate this agreement?

I think you have to get what's called goal congruence. You have to paint the dream in space so vividly and so realistically that everyone sitting at the baseline will say, "I like that dream too" and "We will all work toward it." The way you specify the dream has got to be sufficiently vague that they don't see conflict with their own activities. Somebody down in the quality assurance department, for example, has to be able to say, "I see what my job is with respect to getting it out the door." And therefore, he becomes a positive rather than a negative power.

The way I do that is that I don't sit in my office very much. I don't usually shut the door. I walk around a lot. I don't use the telephone unless it's absolutely necessary. I walk to people's offices to set up meetings, and I talk a lot.

I talk about the objectives. I talk about the dream. But I talk about it in a semi-nebulous way so that nobody can become a bureaucratic role player and say, "Hey, the plan said this." The concept is what we're hanging onto. It says we're going to try to achieve this goal, and the route toward it is arbitrary to some extent.

So you give the people under you a kind of freedom too?

Yes, it applies all the way down the chain, but they only get freedom if their dream coincides. My job is to watch them work without directly controlling them. Every so often we'll go into a three-hour discussion about the manner in which their procedures differ from what I think should happen. Rather than say "Do this, do that," it's a case of saying "Aren't we all trying to get to this point?" and "What you're doing doesn't seem to be contributing in the way I think it should." The only thing that I have is a kind of power of veto, but you rarely actually have to use it if you discuss every problem thoroughly.

The management team that works directly for me is very social. We're definitely friends as distinct from co-workers. We're very open about our failings and our strengths. They can attack me on my weaknesses, which I don't defend. I've got weaknesses. Other guys have got weaknesses.

We spend a lot of time making sure that we cover for each other. If I go out of the office for a month, any one of the guys can run the whole show. They may not do it quite the way I would, but they have all the same information at their disposal, so they know roughly where the whole thing is going.

What interested you about coming to Versatec?

I worked in research originally—I was a physicist by training—but I very rarely took a problem to solution and got the chance to make it into a product. I saw coming here two and a half years ago as a chance to innovate and to take the whole thing right through for the first time.

Are you working on inventions of your own now?

Yes and no. I don't make as much technical contribution as I used to. I don't sit down and draw diagrams and compute things. What I do do is sit in brainstorming meetings with other people who have their own points of view. I try to create an atmosphere which lets people be creative. I stop people from shooting each other down too early.

In this kind of team meeting, somebody may say, "But plastic bends" and someone else may say, "Ah, we could use the fact that it bends," and then someone else builds on that, and over a half an hour an idea starts to grow. It's the person who points it out who gets to be considered the inventor, but he doesn't actually invent the thing.

It's very rare that you can point to one person and say, "He did it." I don't believe there's ever been a patent like that that's any good. We deal patents out so that we all get our names on one or more of the patents that are issued as a result of group brainstorming.

In these meetings do you have not only the managers but also the engineers and the draftsmen?

Yes, anybody who's around. We're very informal about it. I don't call a meeting. What often will happen is that an engineer will be working on something and will come to a problem. And I'll go and sit on the end of his desk and say, "How're you going with this?" During the course of the conversation, somebody else will walk past and we'll say, "Hey, what do you think?" Then the meeting kind of grows impromptu. A set of ideas comes in. You watch them crystallize over the next week or so.

I can spend 20 minutes with one of the engineers and then go off to somebody else as a result of what he wants and say, "Why don't you two talk about that?"

Have you had the chance to be innovative that you wanted at Versatec?

Yes, on many levels of innovation. In the case of the V80—the gorilla project, which is the machine I'm most involved with right now—there were no examples to extrapolate from. We looked at things that had very loose connections. When you try to create a solution to a design problem, what you don't do is plan the route to it. Otherwise, you'll get exactly what you expect and there'll be no room for innovation.

For the V80, the specification was to make a graphics output printer that would make marks on paper at two inches a second for a price of about $3,000. Now, there is no easy way to do that. It turns out that the price for existing technologies is $10,000 to $12,000. It needed innovation at the very outset to be successful.

That innovation wasn't one single idea. It had to be a total package that somehow fitted together and that minimized the cost.

How did you get that package?

That's to ask how the design process normally goes.

What we started with was the notion that the product is a set of things that must happen. It's made up of sets of objects—what we call "subsystems." At the very limit there are parts. Some of these parts relate together to do something, and their functions may be overlapped.

The first thing you have to do is get agreement on what the subsystems are and what they must do. The perception of a set of things varies according to the designers working on them. People think their perceptions of the world are right. If you get two guys looking at something differently and they haven't communicated that fact, the communication breaks down, and they don't even know why. So what I do is say, "Let's move to some common ground that says we can at least communicate about what we're doing."

It takes about a month to get agreement on which subsystems to talk about. If you don't do this first step, you'll have all kinds of design problems downstream.

What's the next step as you see it?

Then you sit down with the designers and discuss specific solutions for each subsystem problem. From there on, you come to conclusions about what is critical to the design. You discuss whether A is more fundamental than B and whether B is more fundamental than C. After a while it becomes pretty obvious to all of them which things are going to kill them and which ones aren't, until eventually the team commits. Not only are they committed to the idea of what the subsystems are, to what is special and personal to the team that they're going to deal with, but they've also roughly agreed on the order in which things should go and how important they are from a cost and a design point of view.

Then what you do is look at the numbers of solutions you've got for each subsystem design problem, and there aren't many—probably two or three. Whichever solution you choose is very cost sensitive. It also probably interacts with the rest of the system a lot.

Next you say, "If I pick this one, what's its effect on this other subsystem?" Now, you just beat down these lines of reasoning as far as you've got time, money, effort, and intellect to do. You rapidly see an end to some of these lines. You often find that one's impossible or that another doesn't meet the product specs. Or people will say, "That's terrible. I bet they'll run out of plastic in two years' time" or "That process is unreliable" and so on.

How long does this design process take?

Oh, you spend three, four, or five months sketching things out, doing research on the cost of components, brainstorming for solutions—because now you're actually into the creative phase. That's when you say, "If I'm clever, I can reduce the criticality of this factor or that. I could actually find ten more total solutions by thinking of one idea that may have never been thought up before."

When you've done that, you've really got the whole thing cracked. At that point, you haven't drawn a single design parameter. You've got a few grubby sketches, a few notes, and probably a thousand hours of conversation. But the team is committed to the approach. You don't get people later saying, "Did we decide that? Maybe it was wrong."

For this gorilla project, you went all through this kind of process?

Absolutely, and we found some interesting things as a result. We found that the electrical interconnection between our writing head and the electronics which drive it is critical to the design. That means the wires. Who would have thought the wires so important? But there are 128 of them, each with difficult technical problems, and how to put them together had always been designed last.

It turns out that that component was not only costing a lot, it was dominating a lot of other subsystems in the machine. There had been lots of Band-Aid solutions used to correct the mistakes that had been made.

Gorilla was made possible by finding the criticality of that one component and designing the whole machine around it.

Renn Zaphiropoulos says he likes to think of this company as a series of concentric circles. Have you heard him talk about this?

Yes, and I think that that picture is very accurate. The caliber of a manager is how far out toward the periphery he can retain contact. Companies get quite good but dried up managers who've got six people working for them, and those six people they know well and work well with. But the next level down, nothing—no contact, no communication, no leadership. That guy is a caretaker manager really. He doesn't influence the spirit or the morale of the team. He's the guy who's in his office with a real battle-ax secretary whose orders are to prevent anyone from talking to him unless he chooses.

If you find a manager who is recognized four or five levels down—they speak to him and smile—he really has a talent that's superior to that other person from a human point of view. It doesn't mean attention to detail. It means contact. His leadership influences many people.

Renn, for example, goes right down. He goes very far out to the periphery of this organization. Face-to-face communication with lower-level people is critical.

I get people stomping in here red in the face and saying, "Let me tell you what's going wrong." Probably only 3% of all the grumbles come to me that way, but I respond completely to that 3%. At least that way people feel that the leadership is sensitive.

How do you prevent the company's self-assurance from getting in the way of further innovation?

You don't, unfortunately. There's a dilution that probably occurs anywhere. Take the executive group: it's a unique bunch of people, a rare group to put together in one place—outrageous personalities and talents. They recruit other people who are slightly less outrageous and perhaps slightly less talented for positions below them. And so on down. By the time you get to the lower levels in the organization, it's just a cross-section of society.

That's fine because the leadership is still outrageous. But as the company grows, the lower levels start to rise in power without being reselected for the growing jobs that they have. So after a time, you end up with less of the original type of talent at the top levels than you would like. You start to get analysts and the kind of person who shuts his office door. You begin to see a dilution of the company's theme.

What if you have an engineer who feels he has to shut the door because he's trying to work out a design problem? Do you mind if he says, "I really have to concentrate by myself for the day"? Do people feel free to work that way too if they need to?

Yes, in fact the door is a very useful tool. The door shut is a symbol that says "Right now I don't want to be disturbed" without having to direct a secretary to say "Go away" and thus create a barrier between oneself and someone else. If you open the door again, people will put their heads around the door and start talking.

What kind of reward do you find that creative people working under you are most interested in getting?

In my environment, I think 50% peer accolade and 50% approval from me and the other managers. Once they get a competitive salary, money is no longer a driving force for most creative people.

So when somebody here succeeds in presenting an innovative idea, an upgrade in salary is not necessarily used as the reward?

Money is used, but it's expected anyway, so it's not a reward. If you do well, you expect to get more money. That's built into the philosophy of the society; therefore, it goes away as an incentive. It would be negative if you didn't give it, but it's not positive when you do give it.

The day after people get their raises, they feel the same as they did the day before. At the time, they enjoyed the experience of being told; it has no motivational aspects after that. On one project recently some people worked late at night very often, so we wrote up a citation—The "You Want It When?" Award for Insane Behavior. We had them printed up and put into little scrolls. There were about 12 of them.

We took the people out to lunch, gave them a slap-up Chinese meal and then a humorous but full presentation of the scrolls that said in effect, "We appreciate this and you didn't go unnoticed." These are the kinds of rewards that mean the most.

[Continued on page 98]

Management here has always been visible and approachable

Bobbette Johnson, manager of employee relations and training: I'm a sort of vocal, "can-do," opinionated person and also a woman, and I have worked in personnel departments where I got silent messages which said, "Sit down, shut up, and don't rock the boat." At Versatec I get verbal messages which say, "It's quite all right to stand up, sound off, and rock the boat." I need that in a work environment for myself. I have had the opportunity to do that, which is why I have stayed with the company for six years.

We at Versatec encourage people to be bold, which suggests that you don't simply sit still for things, or take orders, or do something just because someone in a revered position tells you to do it. You do it because you believe that person to be right or to be just.

We have several recourses here—the Management Advisory Group is one of them—which allow any kind of rules or practices to be challenged and explored. If we were a company that took an authoritarian point of view, we wouldn't bother to create such organizations.

HBR: Has the Management Advisory Group been created since you've been here?

Yes, MAG was created about five years ago to formalize something we were already doing informally. Employees have always challenged things here. Management here has always been visible and approachable. The problem-solving path, though, as we get larger is longer, and MAG shortens that path so that comments that come from the outer levels of our organization can go on a direct express to this inner level. MAG is just a formal expression of what we've always done naturally.

Where did the idea for it come from?

It came from Renn.

If you think back over the MAG meetings you've been to, what do you remember MAG challenging and influencing?

Small changes in the company have come as a result of creating an awareness in management that there are problems. For example, the group was instrumental in creating smoking and nonsmoking sections in the cafeteria recently and in establishing a mileage reimbursement increase because of the escalating gas prices.

People wanted a way to voice reactions to the cafeteria that weren't positive, so we created an anonymous hotline. Employees can put reactions into a box. They're gathered and responded to weekly by the cafeteria staff and posted in a public place in the cafeteria. It's this kind of thing that MAG influences.

Another thing that comes to mind is the fact that the Management Advisory Group got together with the Safety Committee and took some photographs of areas that showed aisles that were not kept clear, debris not promptly removed, and so on. People in both of those groups created an awareness on the executive level of how bad and unsafe, from their point of view, housekeeping was.

What did top management do about it?

As a result of that, we instituted tally sheets and formalized reporting procedures by our Safety Committee to make sure that these areas would be kept tidy. And management implemented things that were possible to do, such as having our facilities technician establish gathering points for waste material.

Our product uses a lot of paper, and in testing it we create a mountain of paper. We decided to contract with an outside service to pick it up.

Can anyone at the company serve as a MAG member?

No, only nonsupervisory, nonmanagement people serve on MAG. Our management staff meetings, general operating committee meetings, executive staff meetings, and operations group meetings—which are for everybody who is exempt at the company—are established vehicles for bringing supervisors' and managers' problems to the surface. People who deal in nonmanagement, nonsupervisory areas—people who don't have this communication vehicle—need one, and MAG is it. People in the professional ranks are usually more concerned about issues other than the sort of thing we talk about at MAG.

Everybody in the company has a way of upward communication, of problem identification and reaching a solution. It's the equality thing, I guess. MAG is just offering the same opportunity that one segment has to the other segment, that's all.

One MAG member today introduced himself as a research chemist. Is his membership inconsistent with the others'?

Not really, because he was a guest. He may have been filling in for someone who was away, or he may have asked to attend a meeting. At the end of the MAG meeting minutes, we publish an invitation to people to sit in on meetings and to serve as future members. MAG members whose terms in office are over often choose their replacements from among the guests.

Who gets the minutes?

Everybody in the company.

Why is membership arranged this way instead of through election by employees?

They are elected by the MAG members themselves, not by co-workers. The MAG members say, "Yes, I want Joe to become part of this group."

MAG has this arrangement so that the group won't lose credibility. They can say, "Look, the eight of us who are members know that John Doe, in our collective opinion, is a raving maniac and we don't want him to represent what happens at this group. We don't think that John could correctly repeat one-two-three to somebody without having it come out four-five-six." So rather than the group having to deal with a person it gets stuck with, it has the option of saying, "Yes, we respect John Doe. We think he's going to do a good job. We wish him to join us."

Another reason we don't have election by co-workers is that it seems to suggest unions, and it almost implies that people here need representation, which isn't really the case.

Also, I think it would be administratively burdensome. The MAG members have short terms of office—three months extendable to six. You can see that with eight members and several guests and the many Versatec departments that would be having elections, it would soon become very cumbersome.

What happens is that the member who is about to exit lets everybody in his department know via a memo that says something like: "My term of membership in MAG is about up. I seek the names or the contact of those of you who are interested in exploring the group. Come with me as a guest to see if you want to throw your hat into the ring for three months."

Many members serve three months and then say, "I'm involved in the activities here and I want to see this action item through, so I will opt for another three months."

And can the people in the department say, "No, we don't want you"?

It's possible, but it never has happened.

Why are the terms of office so short?

We used to have six months and a year as terms. The reason that we feel the shorter term is beneficial is that the more people we get to participate, the more points of view the group gets to deal with. It just makes the group more relevant to the needs of everybody instead of just relevant to the needs of a few who have long tenure.

Where are the MAG meetings usually held?

In our main meeting rooms. One has a fancy table custom-built for this building by Renn and others on the management staff. When I started with the company, all the tables in our conference rooms were homemade. They were built at Renn's house.

Wasn't one of your marketing vice presidents—Milt Reed—at today's MAG meeting?

Yes, executives and directors attend as management representatives because they can be a source of information to the group. They can say things like "Here's what I know about the flex-time decision" and give the straight scoop.

The executive or director also gets information from the group. He learns what people have on their minds and can relay that to his peers when he goes to their meetings, just as Milt did, for example, when he took up the issue of employees feeling so strongly about late performance reviews. The day after the MAG meeting in which this issue came up, there was a management staff meeting in which for 30 minutes Milt discussed the concern that had been brought to his attention through the MAG people.

So now personnel lets Renn know when there is a review that's late. He will then contact the supervisor and say, "If you wish me to make this employee's pay retroactive, then you must tell me why he's getting his performance review late."

Do supervisors ever attend MAG meetings?

No, because supervisors are several management tiers down and are not necessarily in an appropriate place to be able to give information. Our top management is in a place to be helpful to the group. In addition, the supervisors may be part of the problem being brought up.

Is there antagonism generated then among the supervisors when they hear there's a MAG meeting coming up?

Sometimes, yes, because MAG brings up issues that they may not want to deal with.

Do the supervisors have any vehicle for voicing their opinions and complaints?

Yes, the management staff meeting. There they sometimes identify the Management Advisory Group as a problem.

But there are lots of ways to solve the problems that come up here. MAG is just one of many employee options.

Out of all the issues that came up today, which one were you especially glad to hear?

I was glad to hear all of them articulated, especially the action steps we have taken toward issuing reviews on time and reducing the danger of driving into the busy traffic outside our building. The purpose of this group is to deal with problems that affect everyone in the company, not department problems or personal things.

We are all concerned about the traffic, for instance. In the last year and a half, this has become an issue. It was brought up again and again at MAG meetings. Renn said, "It seems ridiculous to me that we can't make any headway. Make sure that a MAG person, myself, and anyone else able to influence the outcome are clued in on when the next City of Santa Clara meeting is held to discuss traffic."

So one of the MAG members took on the role of expediter. He talked with Renn and the personnel director, and they all went down to the meeting together to make a plea to have a traffic light put in at our intersection. The result is that the city has agreed to put a light in a year from now—quick for them, they say.

Do you remember anything coming up in one of the meetings that Renn Zaphiropoulos has called for the whole company which made you feel that the people in this company were working together more than they might have without his leadership?

I guess the last total company announcement that Renn made was last fall. He called us together in the parking lot for what we called a "bold finish" party. It was to create an awareness of where we all were in relation to meeting our goal for the end of the year, where we wanted to be, and the fact that we wanted to work together as a team and with the understanding that all our jobs were different but important to meeting the goal.

How did you find people reacting to what Renn said about this?

The comments I have heard to Renn's addresses, including this one, have been generally favorable. People who are new to our company and who come from companies of comparable size or larger ones tell us that before they came here they rarely saw a company president and that if they did it was by "Hey, that fella crossing the floor way over there is our president." Rarely was there a time when he got out into a parking lot with a band and beer and dancing and tomfoolery as our president does.

I think that Renn's philosophy of quick response to MAG establishes its credibility. Renn sets the tone for it, and I believe that the people who visit this group as management representatives follow that philosophy through. I certainly try to, and I think that that's part of the reason MAG works.

Do you think it could function without Renn being here?

I think that it would function on its own as long as whoever was managing the company at the uppermost levels of it continued Renn's practice of being a living expression of the belief that employees have worth and should be responded to.

I believe that MAG is going strong because it actually solves problems. It really does involve the participation of the workers who have the problems themselves and who represent others like them. I think MAG's a strongly working kind of thing that contributes to the betterment of the company.

You know, I think Versatec is a place of many options that express an individual's preference, an individual's feeling about what's appropriate for tackling issues.

If it's important to us, someone will back us up

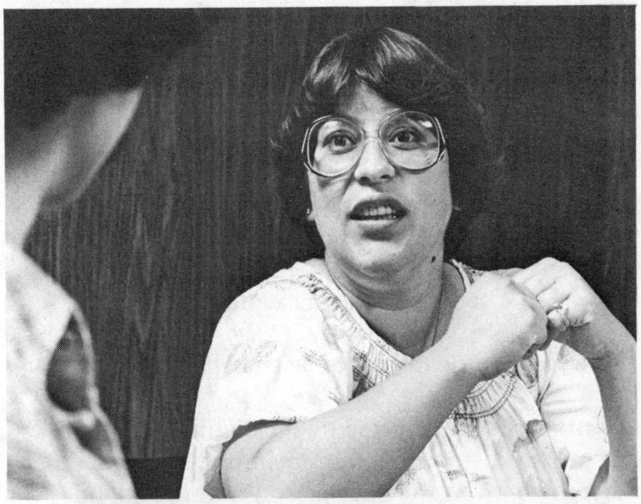

Cynthia Trainer, chairman of the Management Advisory Group: I weave wires onto boards on what we call "the head" in a Versatec machine. That's where the wires that make the marks on the paper connect with the power supply. I've been here six months, and I'm now a head weaver II. The wires have to be woven, soldered, and cleaned. You make mistakes, you fix them, which isn't easy when you have thousands of wires.

Vitória (Vickie) Cardoza, member of the Management Advisory Group: I'm a quality assurance inspector, and I've been here a year.

HBR: How does someone get to be on MAG?

Vickie: You're chosen by MAG. I really wanted to get into MAG, so when one of the MAG members left the company, she asked me if I'd like to take her place, and I said, "Yes, I really would."

Had you been a guest at the meeting?

Vickie: No, but I had wanted to go. Being a guest is usually how MAG chooses its new members. Each member serves a term of three to six months, and then someone new is chosen from the department he or she represents.

Cynthia: At the end of the MAG minutes, which every employee gets in printed form, there's a form you can fill out with your name and department to say, "I'm interested in being a guest at MAG."

How does someone get to be chairperson of MAG?

Cynthia: You're elected by the eight MAG members. You're nominated from among the eight members. I was the only person nominated, but I think a lot of people don't want the responsibility. It's a lot of extra work. I put in a lot of my own time that I don't put on my time card. You've got to really want to help, to get things going and be concerned about company problems—not just your own job's, but everyone's.

How do you find out what is of concern to the people you represent?

Cynthia: Sometimes people will say, "I want to talk to you," so you meet with them. As soon as the people in the headroom found out I was in MAG, they brought me so many things. "I want this brought up, I want that brought up." You know, they had all these questions and problems.

Also, there's a suggestion box. People can put their concerns in there. Others write their problems on slips of paper and leave them in my tool box.

Vickie: Most of the time, with me anyway, they approach me and say, "Gee, I've got a big problem. How about helping me out? Can you bring this up at MAG?" I listen to them and take notes and then investigate. Some things I have to do a little research on before I bring them up.

Usually, my way of handling it is to look into the problem myself. If I can't find help or answers to their questions, then I'll bring it up at MAG.

Cynthia: A lot of times problems are covered by policies in the personnel manual, which we all have. I also have a log of minutes from day one when the committee was started, too, so I have all these minutes I can go back through and see what the decision was at another time to answer a question, and then it's not necessary to bring it up again.

And sometimes it's just common sense. Somebody once said, "I got a nail in my tire the other day. Take my complaint to MAG." That was really a matter for the facilities crew to clean up.

As you think over yesterday's MAG meeting, what do you remember as being important?

Vickie: I felt it was a little argumental at times, but that's because we—the MAG members—are pressured by the people. They feel strong about certain subjects, and we try to bring them out the best we can, even if it's just the privilege of playing a radio or requiring that performance reviews be issued on time, as it was in yesterday's meeting. And we ourselves want to be heard too.

If it takes a little bit of argument, you've got to give it to MAG. Otherwise, nothing will be solved.

The things that I was mentioning yesterday—performance reviews being late and radios at work—are little things to some people. I realize that. But they are very important to the rest of the people who are out here working every day, so I try to fight for them.

Cynthia: Reviews aren't considered little.

Vickie: Well, maybe insignificant to other people. But to these people here, it means a lot. And when they come in on Saturdays, they like to have a few more privileges like playing a radio. They are getting extra pay, but then it's the weekend. It's their day off. The company's asked, "Will you help us out?" It's not mandatory, coming in on Saturdays—Versatec is great that way. But we want to make money for the company, we want to make everyone happy, so we say, "Yeah, we're coming in."

So the radios are not unimportant either?

Vickie: Right, and I don't really think they're a hazard. Not everybody brings a radio. There's usually just one in each department if any at all.

Cynthia: The thing is, there's the other side—it depends on your work, and people don't all like the same kind of music.

When I'm working on a wide plotter, if I miss one little tiny wire, I have to go back and find that mistake, and if I've already soldered one side, the whole head is ruined. Any noise where I work is really distracting.

I felt I should cut the discussion short yesterday because it was out of our hands anyway. There's a company policy against radios.

Vickie: But you should allow people to express themselves in whatever way they can.

Cynthia: Right, but when you have so much business to conduct in two hours, you've got to stick to essential business.

Would you say that there was some more essential issue that came up yesterday?

Vickie: I thought performance review was really the most important issue.

How often are you supposed to get reviews?

Vickie: Three months after you're hired, and then after that it's every six months. The paperwork gets to the supervisors in plenty of time, so reviews should be given to the employees on time too.

Why don't you like getting them late?

Cynthia: Because of the pay. If a review is late, then your raise, if you get one, starts late.

Vickie: It's not only the pay that's important. It's the supervisor's evaluation of your performance. We like to know how we stand here in the company. How can we improve ourselves? If we're not told this, we'll just continue in our old patterns.

Of course we all like to get a raise at review time. Who doesn't? This is the world, and you've got to make money to survive. Things are getting tighter every day, so it's nice to get an evaluation. Any time your supervisors want to give you their own opinions of your performance, I think it's a great thing.

And if you feel like you need improvement, then, you know, you'll say, "I'm going to get with it because I really like it here and I want to learn and progress."

Renn Zaphiropoulos says he likes to think of the company as a series of circles because he feels that all of you are working side by side, that you're all more or less on the same level. Does it seem that way to you?

Vickie: We're on a first-name basis—everyone, even Renn. It's like a friendly family here. You see Renn around and you say "Hi," and he always acknowledges you.

Cynthia: You see him a lot in the headroom, too. The headroom, I guess, is kind of a central point as far as manufacturing goes. He takes people through, and he comes around to see what's going on. It's kind of neat, you know. He'll say, "Hello. Good morning. How are you?"

Vickie: That's something you don't see in very many companies. Usually a president or a vice president or people in high offices will stay in their own areas, but he always comes around and makes us feel very comfortable and happy.

What about the person from management who was at the MAG meeting yesterday?

Cynthia: He's one of the ones who's very open. He's there to represent top management, but he also brings his own viewpoint in. In the discussion yesterday, he would explain things and make you understand why something's got to be done a certain way instead of just telling you, "This is it."

Vickie: He makes sure that if the topic needs working on, he'll get right down to the bottom of it. He won't let things slide, no matter how little they are. If it's important to us, he'll be right there to back us up.

Cynthia: That's the way it is here for most things. If I really need something done or have a question, I can demand to be answered and I'll get an answer from somewhere. I know if my managers don't know, I can go to their manager or I can go to MAG. We have so many different places to take problems to.

Vickie: That's what's good about this company. We have an open door policy, and everyone who works for Versatec can speak through it to their benefit.

Cynthia: And if you do speak, you don't have to worry about losing your job. ▽

Harvard
Business Review

Thomas H. Fitzgerald

Why motivation theory doesn't work

We should discard the dismal vocabulary of motives, motivators, and motivation and think about becoming a society of persons

Foreword

Is it possible that people cannot be "motivated"? This is certainly not a pleasant question to ponder, especially for those managers confronted with mounting problems of high employee turnover, low productivity, and poor morale. The author of this article suggests, however, that the roots of such problems go deeper than is generally recognized, and the major tenets of motivation theory offer solutions that are not quite relevant to what is going on in the workplace. Instead of thinking of employees as objects, to be manipulated by this or that theoretical approach, management must strive to effect fundamental, value-oriented changes in the structure of rationalized work systems.

Mr. Fitzgerald, who was himself a first-line supervisor, is Director of Employee Research and Training Activities at the Chevrolet Motor Division of General Motors Corporation. *Reprint number 71407*

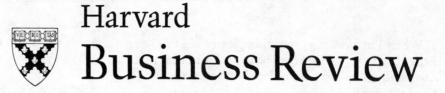

Rising costs and recessionary pressures have prompted the business community, as well as administrators of public agencies, to seek economies. One potential source of savings is in labor costs, but these have resisted reduction because of the downward rigidity of wage rates and the difficulties of increasing aggregate labor productivity. The growing pressures for economy and productivity also stress other labor problems that increase costs: absenteeism and turnover, idleness and featherbedding, product defects and errors. All this is reflected in one of the more familiar questions one hears at management seminars, "How can I motivate my employees?"

Equally familiar to most of us are the recurring themes concerning the motivation problem developed by perhaps a score of business theorists and commentators. Their speeches and publications, together with a number of widely distributed educational films summarizing their views, have arrived at a common core of mid-range theory. What this theory says about employee motivation, both in diagnosis and prescription, is a significant advance from naive conceptions of "morale" during the World War II era, the discredited industrial engineering approach prior to that, and the casual omniscience of the popular press. But what, really, does it tell us?

Briefly, we are told that the concept of motivation is complex, but can and should be understood. Humans have basic physiological needs that must be satisfied, but these are supplemented by numerous other biosocial and culturally derived needs. The individual's actual movement to satisfy his needs depends not only on their state of readiness within himself but also on the objective situation in which he moves (i.e., the field containing other actors), together with his perception of the situation, which is in turn influenced by his own past experiences—i.e., successes or failures in finding satisfaction.

Seeds of doubt

In the business environment, exchanging time for money may take care of a few of the worker's important needs, but it does nothing for those other "higher" needs such as sense of competence, recognition, and so on, that emerge after he has achieved a minimum amount of security. But the work must be performed in any case, and its failure to fill these higher needs results in frustration, antagonism, indolence, and malingering.

When motivation is found thus failing, management's response may not be to throw out the carrot-and-stick theory but to conclude either: (a) that work is inherently irksome and new and more interesting carrots are required, or (b) that workers are a shiftless and lazy lot and stronger sticks are required. The first conclusion, of course, has not solved the problem, while the second is self-validating and defeatist, and leads to more controls, more resentment, more "shiftless" behavior.

What can be done? The advice of the motivator fraternity shows a remarkable unanimity and, with some minor injustice to the subtlety of individual perception and diagnosis, can be summarized in the following three counsels:

1. Enlarge or enrich [1] jobs to make the work more interesting by restoring challenge and the potential for achievement satisfactions. Employees will be motivated to perform well those tasks that are in themselves worth doing.

2. Institute training to modify supervisory style. Supervisors are encouraged to be employee-centered and to assist workers in defining and reaching their job goals. They should act as friendly helpers rather than as policemen.

3. Foster employee "participation" by encouraging workers to take part in the decision process. Participation ranges from such elementary forms as giving employees advance notice of changes or explanations of these changes to more involved forms like stating a problem and requesting employee solutions. The final phase, still largely conceptual, is for the employees themselves to identify the problems, discuss possible solutions, and then arrive at joint decisions. Under these conditions, relationships would no longer be superior/subordinate or master/menial, hence characterized by antagonism and anxiety; instead, they would reflect a refreshing mutuality, trust, honesty, and concern in a climate where organizational goals coalesce with individual goals.

My purpose in this paper is to express doubts about these counsels and to suggest that their general adoption will be more difficult than anyone has recognized publicly. This is not meant to imply that the counselors claim general solutions; they admit difficulties and limitations and the fact that positive motivation in some situations, such as conventional assembly lines, is remote. But their writings, films, and public addresses have an unmistakable hortatory character and require a reasoned demurrer.

My thesis is that the proposed remedies are not adequate because the seriousness of the motivation problem has been underestimated. In what follows, I shall examine some early developments in the organization of rational-

1. Some theorists distinguish between job enlargement and job enrichment; see, for example, Frederick Herzberg, "One more time: How do you motivate employees?" HBR January-February 1968, p. 53. I find, however, that little distinction is made between them in actual practice and use enlargement here as a blanket term.

ized work systems which, from the perspective of contemporary society, reflect assumptions that have become increasingly less valid and at the same time generate extensive tensions and strains. After discussing the advice commonly prescribed to mitigate this distress (the three counsels mentioned earlier), I shall offer some prescriptions of my own.

Roots of rationality

The problem of employee motivation has its origins in certain fundamental conditions of industrial society, and is magnified by the cumulative effect of historical and cultural trends. The roots of the problem are implicit in three early assumptions in the organization of rationalized work systems and will require more extensive changes in our interdependent, multidimensional systems than most businessmen, motivational theorists, and consultants would like to think.

1. Stopwatch measurement

An early assumption of the factory system involved the choice of a time frame in which certain utilitarian calculations were made. Since workers were paid a daily or hourly wage, the value of their output was computed on the same basis, while the use of the stopwatch made it possible to calculate output-value minute by minute, thereby firmly establishing utility in the short run. Production operations were rationalized to maximize output in this short run through detailed process planning and narrow division of tasks. This system simplified the tabulation of worker outputs and allowed effective control of large quantities of unskilled labor, but let us consider some of its other effects:

◇ The imperatives of short-run efficiency disrupted work group solidarities, and, simultaneously, the mass employment system and the extensive size of the plants hindered their formation; thus an important source of day-to-day, small group control of individual deviance was weakened, and the transmission and continuity of those values that make up the workmanship ethic were obstructed.

◇ Decisions on the quality of workmanship made by individual workers in the handicraft era were largely replaced by machine process control, which was made necessary in any case by the utilities of standardization and of interchangeability of parts.

◇ The vast elaboration of structure, together with the separation and, later, remoteness of ownership from management made it more difficult to identify with, or even see, the patrons of one's efforts.

It is scarcely now disputed that these dysfunctional consequences and the miscalculation of their real costs in a longer time frame are expressed in workplace problems such as employee hostility or indifference and unthinking dependency. What is important here, however, is that a narrow division of labor, churning of labor markets, and large-scale units are intrinsic parts of rationalized production systems where costs are computed in the short run (i.e., "false maximization"). Any attempt to resolve worker and workplace problems must recognize these structural sources.

2. Objective decision making

Another assumption of rationalized production has to do with what might be called the "spatial" frame; that is, the failure to foresee a widening of rational attitudes to the work force. As rationality became characteristic not only of production operations, but of engineering, investment, marketing, and management generally, calculation of objective inputs and outputs became the habitual basis for decisions. The broader effects of these decisions, however, as well as the cognitive style of the decision makers, could not long go unnoticed within the company. Difficulties arose when the same rational habits of mind infected the work force, displacing existing class and ethnic styles or causing doubts about the continuance of an earlier patrimonial solicitude.

However, the problem becomes more complicated when everyone decides to base the application of his efforts on pleasure-pain, input-output calculations as do utilitarian managers. This is especially true if, as is now the case, schedules of rewards are truncated by single rate pay systems and uniform work standards, while schedules of punishments are partly neutralized by a full employment-welfare system and the protection possible for individuals through combination (unions). Workers are transformed into job itinerants who do not identify with any one employer; the "rational" worker can blandly ask, "What's in it for me?"

But there is a further infection: that is to say, the spread of "competitive" attitudes to the managers and supervisors of the work force. The ethos of competition—of one against all, of individual maximization—belongs, properly speaking, to entrepreneurs and among entrepreneurs. When it spills over into the work force (or is even cultivated there by management that naively asserts it as a general good), it leads to a self-perpetuating cycle of suspiciousness, blaming and reprisals, withholding of information—either bad news or necessary facts—errors, defensiveness, and more distrust (although admittedly, one hears less of that competitive bravado with the growth of a systems approach to management).

3. *Rigid value system*

Perhaps the most important assumption concerns the availability of certain *nonrational* elements necessary to the work force, and implicit in the operation of rational organization as we know it. That is to say, the personality traits and values (orderliness, accuracy, neatness, punctuality, specialization of knowledge in a career path, success striving, deference to rank and authority, predictability, impersonality, reliance on rules and procedures, etc.) that "fitted into" the needs of rational bureaucracy so well, were not seen as possible *variables* but as a natural, continuing "given"—as was the society that bred these traits, the culture which was saturated with them.

Clear evidence to the contrary, of course, existed in anthropological reports of other societies in remote places, but now such evidence is widely available here in our own society. The lack of a temperament impelled toward assiduous effort or habitual striving for ever higher goals and the incomplete internalization of certain aescetic values and normative controls appear not only as an "exception" among ghetto blacks (who explicitly reject them) or the alienated white youth in the street culture, but increasingly in other sectors of society as well.

That there is now a widespread indifference to, or even contempt for, authority, both as "idea" and reality (ascribed status, deference, the legitimacy of externally imposed sanctions, tradition) has been widely reported. A persistent populism and egalitarianism, reinforced by the spread of empirical or "scientific" attitudes and demystification of "divine right," "natural law," and so on, seems to be responsible for the change. Professionalization of knowledge also increasingly strains against the authority of rank.

A further difficulty with this third assumption has been noted by Charles Reich in his book, *The Greening of America*.[2] He points out that the rising volume of industrial production, which is the inevitable result of successful, rationally organized enterprises, must be disposed of by means of a pervading and utopian advertising, which in turn is gradually disrupting industry's own foundation, the work force.

Workers, regularly instructed as consumers in a ceaseless acquisition of goods and services, lose their willingness to bear with the common drudgery. The offers of independence, the encouragement to self-aggrandisement, and the persistent flattery they experience as audience all contrast unfavorably with the discipline and the subordination which they experience as employees. Work loses its "religious" character, its centrality as the locus for the self. It is replaced by a sort of populist hedonism, ranging from compulsive accumulation to the new connoisseurship.

Even if consumption were not thus stimulated, human beings are not satisfied with constant rewards—unlike Professor Skinner's pigeons, one grain at $T_1 \neq$ one grain at T_n. The escalation of human wants, once satisfaction is achieved, produces a continuing problem. As workers "use up" their material shelter-survival needs, they seek such intangibles and unbuyables as freedom and autonomy (one might add, following Baudelaire: beauty, clarity, luxury, and calm). These, obviously, are incompatible with the life of organized production.

A realistic reappraisal

Questions seem to leap from a recognition of the increasing vulnerability of the foregoing assumptions, especially the third assumption. Will it be possible to continue to operate "efficient," closely synchronized, and interdependent organizations if change in the personality-culture system continues in the same direction? Put in another and more value-oriented way: How much personal freedom is *possible* in a hierarchical, bureaucratic authority system? At what point does individual style become incompatible with order?

2. New York, Random House, 1970.

To push it further, what is the potential for becoming an authentic self in a system characterized by well-defined role behaviors and role expectations that inherently demand reification and internalization?

Other questions, however, are at issue here: Are job enlargement, training, and employee participation realistic approaches to solving the new—as well as the old—motivation problem in industry? Are they practical? Will they work? It is to these counsels that we now turn.

The enlargement counsel

Job enlargement is more modest than participation, less ambitious in its objectives, and apparently easier and less disruptive "to do." This prescription also has more substance than the talk therapies of the training-climate approach to motivation. While there is some empirical validation of the value of job enlargement, I am skeptical over its applicability in a wider variety of work situations and, more importantly, over a longer period of time.

There is probably little disagreement anymore about the desirability of eliminating as much as possible of egregiously repetitious operations, much as we correct poor lighting or dirty lavatories. In fact, in both shops and offices, a really repetitious job is an obvious candidate for automation or computerization. But after the more monotonous jobs are eliminated, we arrive at a wide range of operations where perception, rather than objective reality, is crucial.

Individuals differ vastly in their need for variety, responsibility, and competence, just as they vary in their need for independence or security. The job Jones finds moronic and insufferable is okay with Smith, yet too much for Brown. Restructuring and/or enlarging jobs are brave attempts to fit the job to the man, but *which* man? Do we have different sets and sequences of the same operations for people of varying competence, interest, and drive? Does turnover, then, imply continued rearrangement?

The school solution would reply: it's a matter for employment and placement to select similar people. But, of course, things don't work out that neatly in practice. Additional investments must also be made to broaden employee skills to meet increased responsibilities, although it is not yet clear whether employees will (a) expect greater compensation for this, or (b) be satisfied with increased psychic income.

It is obvious, however, that management's present flexibility in reallocating unskilled labor without loss of training investment would be reduced.

Finally, as time passes, one cannot but wonder how much of the added challenge remains, whether the broadened responsibility persists in its motivational propensity, or the worker merely paraphrases the well-known question, "What have you enlarged for me lately?" (How else to explain the faded motivation of those with amply challenging jobs—say, bored executives, doctors, or college professors?)

The training counsel

A second prescription for improved motivation—to enhance supervisory style and the climate of communication through in-house education and training—shares limitations similar to those cited for job enlargement: it does not get at enough of the basic incongruence between individual needs and organizational goals.

The fact that there is *some* congruence can be readily admitted, but this does not change the tension that exists anymore than does the recognition of the inconsistency of certain needs within the individual himself. The difficulty is that attention to improving attitudes and undesirable behaviors is usually directed at surface symptoms, without significant attempts to correct the underlying source. If a group of supervisors behave in a bossy, condescending, and insensitive manner, it is rarely because anyone *told* them to act that way, but because of other influences in the organization that are just as real as talk. For example:

◇ The system of selecting supervisors from the work group may make it clear that one type of personality will succeed, but others will not.

◇ Supervisory styles are perpetuated by modeling, and by the success of those who learn from the successful models. Attitudes about what is really important are conveyed not only by the official mottoes on posters, but in every conversation, in every inquiry and direction.

◇ An invidious system of monetary and status rewards must of necessity produce relative deprivation for some workers. The resulting competition to achieve rewards (or avoid deprivation) tends to encourage withholding of information and a lack of trust. Blaming, scapegoating, and defensiveness follow.

◇ Punishments and reprisals for deviance or poor performance in themselves provide satisfactions to those who have made the sacrifices necessary to self-discipline.

◇ Dependency is often cultivated at the lower levels because it is thought to ensure predictability of actions.

And so it goes. If we want to change all that, we have to ask (here, in behavioral terminology), "What are those forces in the situation that reinforce specific behaviors while acting to extinguish others?" Even where the supervisory attitudes themselves are found to be a cause of the motivation problem, change may be difficult because these attitudes are linked in with larger value systems—the belief that a supervisor should be dominant, assertive, even truculent, is supported by a more general mythology of masculine authority and prowess, and by a leadership imagery borrowed from athletics or the military.

Structural considerations: The failures of other attempts to change attitudes, as, for example, in efforts to eliminate racism in this country, have led to a reorientation of tactics of change toward more substantive methods; that is, to get inside "the black box" of institutional and organizational process. The lesson of that experience, however, is not necessarily that talk cannot change attitudes for the better, as well as encourage those who are ready to change. Some things are good in themselves, and a management that promotes a decent concern for employees' integrity, growth, and well-being should not have to look to an economic payoff as justification. The point here, however, is that education in itself has limited potential for producing and sustaining improvement unless changes, consistent with officially sponsored values, are also made in process and structure.

The participation counsel

While participatory management is often urged by corporate liberals these days as the most desirable avenue of change, analysis of its dimensions and their implications for contemporary organizations suggests that it is questionable whether participation can correct pervasive apathy and indifference, let alone provide an unqualified good.

Of course, much of the advice is noble, urging the development of an improved climate of communication, trust, acceptance, mutuality, and so forth; but it is often unclear how, objectively, these attitudes are to be brought about and maintained. Also an open question is whether any significant percentage of the work force even wants to participate, other than perhaps for the novelty of doing so.[3] Although the advocates of this prescription for motivational health have failed to supply many important details of actual implementation, it is not hard to surmise what new difficulties might evolve.

Pressure for more involvement: Participation is not a simple or linear gradation of acts. It means more, for example, than giving accurate information, listening to responses, answering questions, seeking advice or ratification. It may mean interactions with groups of employees, as well as one-over-one relationships. The subjects of participation, moreover, are not necessarily restricted to those few matters that management considers to be of direct, personal interest to employees, or to those plans and decisions which will benefit from employee advice. Neither of these positions can be maintained for long without (a) being recognized by employees as manipulative or (b) leading to expectations for wider and more significant involvement—"Why do they only ask us about plans for painting the office and not about replacing this old equipment and rearranging the layout?"

Once competence is shown (or believed to have been shown) in, say, rearranging the work area, and after participation has become a conscious, officially sponsored activity, participators may very well want to go on to topics of job assignment, the allocation of rewards, or even the selection of leadership. In other words, management's present monopoly—on initiating participation, on the nomination of conferees, and on the limitation of legitimate areas for review—can in itself easily become a source of contention.

Potential for disruption: Another difficulty with participation has to do with organizational effectiveness. The dysfunctions of bureaucratic systems are now well known, while the motivational potential of employee involvement is, if yet unrealized, at least widely anticipated. But the dysfunctional, disruptive effects of participation on rationally organized systems should not be ignored either. Before embarking on participatory management, advocates should consider the following points:

3. See, Robert Dahl, "The Case for Worker Control," New York Review of Books, November 19, 1970.

☐ It is not at all clear how the highly variable competence of employee participants can contribute to the solutions of corporate problems that have specific technical constraints, even though these employees are affected by the results. As the store of knowledge expands (and becomes more opaque) along with the need for its accurate application, organizations rely increasingly on experts and professionals, and it may in fact be true that the girls on the carton-folding operation really have nothing to contribute to almost anything important about running a container company. Once again, meritocracy confronts democracy.

☐ The scale of contemporary industry makes the implications of decisions, and the interaction of their effects, hard to foresee, although the need for precision is now greater. At some point the "critical mass" of large organizations is reached where their manageability even by the few—much less the many—becomes questionable. The closely linked, synchronized, interdependent nature of the numerous subsystems that now comprise large organizations would appear to make serious participation questionable not only in its technical aspects but in its goal-directed behavior. Inevitably, participation to any significant degree will cause indeterminacy and delay, loss of consistency and coherence, diluted and compromised objectives.

☐ Although it hasn't been discussed much yet, when blacks and women finally integrate supervisory and mid-management ranks, they may coalesce into identity groupings to seek representation. We already have examples of teachers, college students, welfare recipients, and others who have been demanding the right to participate as groups to help determine not only conditions within the system but its operation and outputs as well. Aside from the real costs in reduced effectiveness (partly balanced, of course, by better motivation, higher output, less waste, and so on) the impact of this new participation on the process and structure of management, though hard to estimate, must be anticipated, because what is really involved is politics, the conscious sharing of control and power. History does not offer many examples of oligarchies that have abdicated with grace and goodwill.

Once again, all this is not to imply that because gross efficiency and productivity may be reduced, we should not proceed toward alternatives. Given the goal of maximizing utility, however, there does seem to be a necessary trade-off between precision, on the one hand, and motivation through participation, on the other hand, and we shouldn't assume that we can have it both ways, just as we now admit that we can't have both full employment and price stability. The amount of each we want (or can tolerate), the location of the best trade-off point, is a matter of experimentation and calculation. Viewed from a wider perspective, it is also entirely possible for organizations to pursue new, multiple, even divergent goals, although the trade-off problem then becomes much tougher, involving basic values, or as they say these days, "priorities."

Conclusion

It may be that the question, "How do I motivate my employees?" is not quite relevant to what is going on. Truth is sometimes damaged in the process of analysis and reconstruction, and concepts can easily become more "real" than the reality from which they were cut. When transplanted from the laboratory, the language of motivation may become subtly elitist by suggesting that the employee resembles a captive rodent in a training box equipped with levers, trick doors, food pellets, and electric grids. Talking about a majority (perhaps, in fact, a minority?) of people and how they live as being "motivated" may provide only a pretentious terminology which deflects understanding.

When a man gets up in the morning, we can say this act is a conditioned response to the stimulus of an alarm, but that doesn't *tell* us anything important. To say he is motivated by hunger may be true, but perhaps he is not hungry and thinks instead, "Seven o'clock; *time to get up.*" What he does the rest of the day may have much the same toneless character of going from one thing to another and getting by. This may very well be the way it is for a great many people, at least during the time they spend in the shop or the office, because most of what they really care for is in other places and at other times. A few of them may not even care strongly for much of anything, almost anywhere. Is it just possible that some whom we employ *can't* be motivated?

Some alternatives

I am aware, following a critique such as this, of expectations for suggesting alternatives. They can be offered so as not to deny my wider meliorism; yet their statement should not distract from the main thrust of the argument presented here: the problem of employee motivation is rooted in certain fundamental conditions of industrial society, and its solution will require costly and extensive changes in our interdependent, closely linked systems. Just as most of the signs point to a pervasive consumerism, environmentalism, and governmental surveillance in the market economy, so we should anticipate a persistent alienation of industrial and business manpower in relation to its employers.

What can be done; what is being tried? At very little cost we can avoid giving offense or being intrusive. Merely talking with people also does a lot of good, although it does not seem to be easy for many managers. Here is a brief overview of other possibilities:

◇ Inexpensive means such as emblems, slogans, contests, and sets of monogrammed glasses function as attention getters, but their transference value is always speculative.

◇ Praise and approval can produce temporary improvement of individual effort.

◇ Company-sponsored recreation and house organs are also comparatively cheap and seem to have a positive effect on some of the people part of the time.

◇ Money is recurrently popular as an incentive for more and better work, but the general decline of piecework and profit-sharing plans testifies to the experience that these monetary incentives are not really effective in practice, due in part to intervening variables such as employee perception of an ambiguous means-ends relationship.

◇ Reducing the size of a productive or service unit seems to increase identification and improve motivation, but may introduce inefficiencies (especially as viewed by traditional costing methods) with no assurance of net gain.

◇ Stripping away the baroque elaborations of office may result in loss of the mystique of authority, but it could help create the conditions for unity.

Increasingly more expensive than the foregoing —in original investment as well as in maintenance—are mixes of "training" to improve skills and climate, of job enlargement, and of organizational development and participation. All imply substantial alterations in the way organizations are wired together and in communication and controls. They will eventually involve examination of reward and succession systems, priorities, and ends. Participation especially, as pointed out earlier, not only may start out as an unpleasant ride for those who are accustomed to being fully in charge, but also may become one from which it is increasingly hard to dismount.

What is needed is not merely the "willingness to confront change" (already a safe thought-cliché) but a commitment to go beyond changes in structure and procedures. What may even be required is relinquishing certain behaviors and beliefs, such as an ideology of certitude and constraint, a habit of objectifying people because of ranking or role ascription, or a style of address characterized by cant and bravado—difficult to give up, but not impossible.

We have seen progress in other areas where we once would not have expected it. We look back now at personality testing, slightly incredulous at its colonialist mentality and its banality of concepts, wondering how we could have been taken in by its promises of penetration and mastery. Similarly, perhaps yet in our time, we will be willing to discard the dismal vocabulary of motives, motivators, and motivation and start to think seriously about how to go about becoming a society of persons.

> One man that has a mind and knows it can always beat ten men who haven't and don't.
>
> George Bernard Shaw
> *The Apple Cart* (1929), *Act I*

3

Can we learn anything from international competitors?

Peter F. Drucker

What we can learn from Japanese management

Decision by 'consensus,' lifetime employment, continuous training, and the godfather system suggest ways to solve U.S. problems

Foreword

Businessmen in the United States and Europe know Japanese industry as an important supplier, customer, and competitor. But they should also know it as a teacher. Three important sets of ideas we can learn from Japan are described in this article. They could have a far-reaching impact on the quality of our executive decision making, corporate planning, worker productivity, and management training.

Mr. Drucker is well known to HBR subscribers for a series of memorable articles dating back to 1950. He is also well known in Japan, which he has visited often and studied for many years. Professor of Management at New York University's Graduate School of Business since 1950, he is the author of *The Effective Executive, The Practice of Management*, and other books published by Harper & Row.

Reprint number 71202

What are the most important concerns of top management? Almost any group of top executives in the United States (or in many other Western nations) would rank the following very high on the list:

○ Making effective decisions.

○ Harmonizing employment security with other needs such as productivity, flexibility in labor costs, and acceptance of change in the company.

○ Developing young professional managers.

In approaching these problem areas, Japanese managers–especially those in business–behave in a strikingly different fashion from U.S. and European managers. The Japanese apply different principles and have developed different approaches and policies to tackle each of these problems. These policies, while not *the* key to the Japanese "economic miracle," are certainly major factors in the astonishing rise of Japan in the last 100 years, and especially in Japan's economic growth and performance in the last 20 years.

It would be folly for managers in the West to imitate these policies. In fact, it would be impossible. Each policy is deeply rooted in Japanese traditions and culture. Each applies to the problems of an industrial society and economy the values and the habits developed far earlier by the retainers of the Japanese clan, by the Zen priests in their monasteries, and by the calligraphers and painters of the great "schools" of Japanese art.

Yet the principles underlying these Japanese practices deserve, I believe, close attention and study by managers in the West. They may point the way to a solution to some of our most pressing problems.

Decisions by 'consensus'

If there is one point on which all authorities on Japan are in agreement, it is that Japanese institutions, whether businesses or government agencies, make decisions by "consensus." The Japanese, we are told, debate a proposed decision throughout the organization until there is agreement on it. And only then do they make the decision.[1]

This, every experienced U.S. manager will say with a shudder, is not for us, however well it might work for the Japanese. This approach can lead only to indecision or politicking, or at best to an innocuous compromise which offends no one but also solves nothing. And if proof of this were needed, the American might add, the history of President Lyndon B. Johnson's attempt to obtain a "consensus" would supply it.

Let us consider the experience of Japan. What stands out in Japanese history, as well as in today's Japanese management behavior, is the capacity for making 180-degree turns—that is, for reaching radical and highly controversial decisions. Let me illustrate:

☐ No country was more receptive to Christianity than sixteenth-century Japan. Indeed, the hope of the Portuguese missionaries that Japan would become the first Christian country outside of Europe was by no means just wishful thinking. Yet the same Japan made a 180-degree turn in the early seventeenth century. Within a few years it completely suppressed Christianity and shut itself off from all foreign influences—indeed, from all contact with the outside world—and stayed that way for 250 years. Then, in the Meiji Restoration of 1867, Japan executed another 180-degree turn and opened itself to the West—something no other non-European country managed to do.

☐ Toyo Rayon, the largest Japanese manufacturer of man-made fibers, made nothing but rayon as late as the mid-1950's. Then it decided to switch to synthetic fibers. But it did not "phase out" rayon making, as every Western company in a similar situation has done. Instead, it closed its rayon mills overnight, even though, under the Japanese system of employment, it could not lay off a single man.

☐ As late as 1966, when I discussed this matter with officials, the Ministry of International Trade and Industry was adamantly opposed to any Japanese companies going "multinational" and making investments in manufacturing affiliates abroad. But three years later, the same Ministry officials, working for the same conservative government, had turned around completely and were pushing Japanese manufacturing investments abroad!

Focusing on the problem

The key to this apparent contradiction is that the Westerner and the Japanese mean something different when they talk of "making a decision." With us in the West, all the emphasis is on the *answer* to the question. Indeed, our books on decision making try to develop systematic approaches to giving an answer. To the Japanese, however, the important element in decision making is *defining the question.* The important and crucial steps are to decide whether there is a need for a decision and what the decision is about. And it is in this step that the Japanese aim at attaining "consensus." Indeed, it is this step that, to the Japanese, is the essence of the decision. The answer to the question (what the West considers *the* decision) follows its definition.

During this process that precedes the decision, no mention is made of what the answer might be. This is done so that people will not be forced to take sides; once they have taken sides, a decision would be a victory for one side and a defeat for the other. Thus the whole process is focused on finding out what the decision is really about, not what the decision should be. Its result is a meeting of the minds that there is (or is not) a need for a change in behavior.

All of this takes a long time, of course. The Westerner dealing with the Japanese is thoroughly frustrated during the process. He does not understand what is going on. He has the feeling that he is being given the runaround. To take a specific example:

It is very hard for a U.S. executive to understand why the Japanese with whom he is negotiating on, say, a license agreement, keep on sending new groups of people every few months who start what the Westerner thinks are "negotiations" as if they had never heard of the subject. One delegation takes copious notes and goes back home, only to be succeeded six weeks later

1. See Howard F. Van Zandt, "How to Negotiate in Japan," HBR November-December 1970, p. 45.

by another team of people from different areas of the company who again act as if they had never heard of the matter under discussion, take copious notes, and go home.

Actually—though few of my Western friends believe it—this is a sign that the Japanese take the matter most seriously. They are trying to involve the people who will have to carry out an eventual agreement in the process of obtaining consensus that a license is indeed needed. Only when all of the people who will have to carry out the agreement have come together on the need to make a decision will the decision be made to go ahead. Only then do "negotiations" really start—and then the Japanese usually move with great speed.

There is a complete account of this process at work—though it does not concern a business decision. The account deals with the decision to go to war against the United States in 1941.[2]

Undertaking action

When the Japanese reach the point we call a decision, they say they are in the *action stage*. Now top management refers the decision to what the Japanese call the "appropriate people." Determination of who these people are is a top management decision. On that decision depends the specific answer to the problem that is to be worked out. For, during the course of the discussions leading up to the consensus, it has become very clear what basic approaches certain people or certain groups would take to the problem. Top management, by referring the question to one group or the other, in effect picks the answer—but an answer which by now will surprise no one.

This referral to the "appropriate people" is as crucial as the parallel decision in the U.S. political process which baffles any foreign observer of American government—the decision as to which committee or subcommittee of the Congress a certain bill is to be assigned. This decision is not to be found in any of the books on U.S. government and politics. Yet, as every American politician knows, it is the crucial step which decides whether the bill is to become law and what form it will take.

Increased effectiveness

What are the advantages of this process? And what can we learn from it?

In the first place, it makes for very effective decisions. While it takes much longer in Japan to reach a decision than it takes in the West, from that point on they do better than we do. After making a decision, we in the West must spend much time "selling" it and getting people to act on it. Only too often, as all of us know, either the decision is sabotaged by the organization or, what may be worse, it takes so long to make the decision truly effective that it becomes obsolete, if not outright wrong, by the time the people in the organization actually make it operational.

The Japanese, by contrast, need to spend absolutely no time on "selling" a decision. Everybody has been presold. Also, their process makes it clear where in the organization a certain answer to a question will be welcomed and where it will be resisted. Therefore, there is plenty of time to work on persuading the dissenters, or on making small concessions to them which will win them over without destroying the integrity of the decision.

Every Westerner who has done business with the Japanese has learned that the apparent inertia of the negotiating stage, with its endless delays and endless discussion of the same points, is followed by a speed of action that leaves him hanging on the ropes. Thus:

It may take three years before a licensing agreement can be reached, during which time there is no discussion of terms, no discussion of what products the Japanese plan to use, no discussion of what knowledge and help they might need. And then, within four weeks, the Japanese are ready to go into production and make demands on their Western partner for information and people which he is totally unprepared to meet.

Now it is the Japanese who complain, and bitterly, about the "endless delay and procrastination" of the Westerner! For they understand our way of making a decision and acting on it no better than we understand their way of considering a decision and acting on it.

The Japanese process is focused on understanding the problem. The desired end result is certain action and behavior on the part of people. This almost guarantees that all the alternatives will be considered. It rivets management attention to essentials. It does not permit commit-

2. See *Japan's Decision for War, Records of the 1941 Policy Conferences*, translated and edited by Nobutuka Ike (Stanford, California, Stanford University Press, 1967).

ment until management has decided what the decision is all about. Japanese managers may come up with the wrong answer to the problem (as was the decision to go to war against the United States in 1941), but they rarely come up with the right answer to the wrong problem. And that, as all decision makers learn, is the really dangerous course, the irretrievably wrong decision.

Improved focus

Above all, the system forces the Japanese to make big decisions. It is much too cumbersome to be put to work on minor matters. It takes far too many people far too long to be wasted on anything but truly important matters leading to real changes in policies and behavior. Small decisions, even when obviously needed, are very often not being made at all in Japan for that reason.

With us it is the small decisions which are easy to make—decisions about things that do not greatly matter. Anyone who knows Western business, government agencies, or educational institutions knows that their managers make far too many small decisions as a rule. And nothing, I have learned, causes as much trouble in an organization as a lot of small decisions. Whether the decision concerns moving the water cooler from one end of the hall to the other or phasing out of one's oldest business makes little emotional difference. One decision takes as much time and generates as much heat as the other!

To contrast the Japanese approach and the Western approach, let me illustrate:

I once watched a Japanese company work through a proposal for a joint venture received from a well-known American company, one with which the Japanese had done business for many years. The Orientals did not even discuss the joint venture at the outset. They started out with the question: "Do we have to change the basic directions of our business?" As a result, a consensus emerged that change was desirable, and management decided to go out of a number of old businesses and start in a number of new technologies and markets; the joint venture was to be one element of a major new strategy. Until the Japanese understood that the decision was really about the *direction* of the business, and that there was need for a decision on that, they did not once, among themselves, discuss the desirability of the joint venture, or the terms on which it might be set up. It has, by the way, been doing very well since its formation.

In the West we are moving in the Japanese direction. At least, this is what so many "task forces," "long-range plans," "strategies," and other approaches are trying to accomplish. But we do not build into the development of these projects the "selling" which the Japanese process achieves before the decision. This explains in large measure why so many brilliant reports of the task leaders and planners never get beyond the planning stage.

U.S. executives expect task forces and long-range planning groups to come up with recommendations—that is, to commit themselves to one alternative. The groups decide on an answer and then document it. To the Japanese, however, the most important step is understanding the alternatives available. They are as opinionated as we are, but they discipline themselves not to commit themselves to a recommendation until they have fully defined the question and used the process of obtaining consensus to bring out the full range of alternatives. As a result, they are far less likely to become prisoners of their preconceived answers than we are.

Security & productivity

Just as many Americans have heard about consensus as the basis for Japanese decisions, so many of us know about Japanese "lifetime employment" policies. But the common understanding of "lifetime employment" is as far off the mark as is the common interpretation of consensus.

Myths & realities

To be sure, most employees in "modern" Japanese business and industry have a guaranteed job once they are on the payroll. While they are on the job, they have practically complete job security which is endangered only in the event of a severe economic crisis or of bankruptcy of the employer. They also are paid on the basis of seniority, as a rule, with pay doubling about every 15 years, regardless of the type of job. To be accurate, the picture must be qualified with such facts as the following:

◇ Women are almost always considered "temporary" rather than "permanent" employees; so they are exempted from the benefits.

◇ In most "traditional" Japanese businesses, such as workshop industries producing lacquer, pottery, and silk, workers are hired and paid by the hour.

◇ Even in the "modern" industries there is a slowly shrinking, but substantial (perhaps 20%), body of employees who, by unilateral management decision, are considered "temporary" and remain in that category for many years.

But, while job security and compensation are quite favorable for Japanese workers as a whole, the picture does not have the implications a Western businessman might expect. Instead of a rigid labor cost structure, *Japan actually has remarkable flexibility in her labor costs and labor force.* What no one ever mentions—and what, I am convinced, most Japanese do not even see themselves—is that the retirement system itself (or perhaps it should be called the nonretirement system) makes labor costs more flexible than they are in most countries and industries of the West. Also, it harmonizes in a highly ingenious fashion the workers' need for job and income guarantees with the economy's need for flexible labor costs.

Actually, most Japanese companies, especially the large ones, can and do lay off a larger proportion of their work force, when business falls off, than most Western companies are likely or able to do. Yet they can do so in such a fashion that the employees who need incomes the most are fully protected. The burden of adjustment is taken by those who can afford it and who have alternate incomes to fall back on.

Official retirement in Japan is at age 55—for everyone except a few who, at age 45, become members of top management and are not expected to retire at any fixed age. At age 55, it is said, the employee, whether he is a floor sweeper or a department head, "retires." Traditionally, he then gets a severance bonus equal to about two years of full pay. (Many companies, strongly backed by the government, are now installing supplementary pension payments, but by Western standards these payments are still exceedingly low.)

Considering that life expectancy in Japan is now fully up to Western standards, so that most employees can expect to live to age 70 or more, this bonus seems wholly inadequate. Yet no one complains about the dire fate of the pensioners. More amazing still, one encounters in every Japanese factory, office, and bank, people who cheerfully admit to being quite a bit older than 55 and who quite obviously are still working. What is the explanation?

The rank-and-file blue-collar or white-collar employee ceases to be a permanent employee at age 55 and becomes a "temporary" worker. This means that he can be laid off if there is not enough work. But if there is enough work—and, of course, there has been during the past 20 years—he stays on, very often doing the same work as before, side by side with the "permanent" employee with whom he has been working for many years. But for this work he now gets at least one third less than he got when he was a "permanent" employee.

The rationale of this situation is fairly simple. As the Japanese see it, the man has something to fall back on when he retires—the two-year pension. This, they freely admit, is not enough to keep a man alive for 15 years or so. But it is usually enough to tide him over a bad spell. And since he no longer has, as a rule, dependent children or parents whom he has to support, his needs should be considerably lower than they were when he was, say, 40 and probably had both children and parents to look after.

If my intent were to describe the Japanese employment system, I would now have to go into a great many rather complicated details, such as the role of the semiannual bonus. But I am concerned only with what we in the West might learn from the Japanese. For us, the main interest of the Japanese system, I submit, is the way in which it satisfies two apparently mutually contradictory needs: (a) job and income security; and (b) flexible, adaptable labor forces and labor costs. Let us look at the way this is done and draw comparisons with the U.S. system.

Meeting workers' needs

In the West, during the last 25 years, more and more employees have achieved income maintenance that may often exceed what the Japanese worker gets under "lifetime employment."

There is, for instance, the Supplementary Employment Compensation of the U.S. mass-production industries which, in effect, guarantees the unionized worker most of his income even during fairly lengthy layoffs. Indeed, it may well be argued that labor costs in U.S. mass-production industries are more rigid than they are in Japan, even though our managements can rapidly adjust the number of men at work to the order flow, in contrast to the Japanese practice of maintaining employment for "permanent" employees almost regardless of business conditions. Increasingly, also, we find in the heavily unionized mass-production industries provisions for early retirement, such as were written in the fall of 1970 into the contract of the U.S. automobile industry.

Still, unionized employees are laid off according to seniority, with the ones with the least seniority going first. As a result, we still offer the least security of jobs and incomes to the men who need predictable incomes the most—the fathers of young families (who also may have older parents to support). And where there is "early retirement," it means, as a rule, that the worker has to make a decision to retire permanently. Once he has opted for early retirement, he is out of the work force and unlikely to be hired back by any employer. In short, the U.S. labor force (and its counterparts in Europe) lacks the feeling of economic and job security which is so pronounced a feature of Japanese society.

We pay for a high degree of "income maintenance" and have imposed on ourselves a very high degree of rigidity in respect to labor costs. But we get very few tangible benefits from these practices. Also, we do not get the psychological security which is so prominent in Japanese society—i.e., the deep conviction of a man of working age that he need not worry about his job and his income. Instead we have fear. The younger men fear that they will be laid off first, just when the economic needs of their families are at their peak; the older men fear that they will lose their jobs in their fifties, when they are too old to be hired elsewhere.

In the Japanese system there is confidence in both age groups. The younger men feel they can look forward to a secure job and steadily rising income while their children are growing up; the older men feel they are still wanted, still useful, and not a burden on society.

In practice, of course, the Japanese system is no more perfect than any other system. There are plenty of inequities in it; the treatment of the older people in particular leaves much to be desired—especially in the small workshop industries of "preindustrial" Japan and in the multitude of small service businesses. But the basic principle which the Japanese have evolved—not by planning rationally, but by applying traditional Japanese concepts of mutual obligation to employment and labor economics—seems to make more sense and works better than the expensive patchwork solutions we have developed that do not come to grips with the problem itself. Economically, it might be said, we have greater "security" in our system—we certainly pay more for it. Yet we have not obtained what the Japanese system produces, the psychological conviction of job and income security.

More meaningful benefits

Today there is talk—and even a little action—in U.S. industry concerning "reverse seniority" to protect newly hired blacks with little or no seniority in the event of a layoff. But we might better consider applying "reverse seniority" to older men past the age of greatest family obligations, since so many labor contracts now provide for early retirement after age 55. Under current conditions, these men may be expected to be laid off when they qualify for early retirement. Why not give them the right to come back out of early retirement and be rehired first when employment expands again? Some such move that strengthens the job security of the younger, married employee, with his heavy family burdens, might well be the only defense against pressures for absolute job guarantees with their implications for rigid labor costs.

Even more important as a lesson to be learned from the Japanese is the need to shape benefits to the wants of specific major employee groups. Otherwise they will be only "costs" rather than "benefits." In the West—and especially in the United States—we have, in the last 30 years, heaped benefit upon benefit to the point where the fringes run up to a third of the total labor cost in some industries. Yet practically all these benefits have been slapped on across the board whether needed by a particular group or not.

Underlying our entire approach to benefits—with management and union in complete agreement, for once—is the asinine notion that the work force is homogeneous in its needs and wants. As a result, we spend fabulous amounts of money on benefits which have little meaning for large groups of employees and leave unsatisfied the genuine needs of other, equally substantial groups. This is a major reason why our benefit plans have produced so little employee satisfaction and psychological security.

Willingness to change

It is the psychological conviction of job and income security that underlies what might be the most important "secret" of the Japanese economy: cheerful willingness on the part of employees to accept continuing changes in technology and processes, and to regard increasing productivity as good for everybody.

There is a great deal written today about the "spirit" of the Japanese factory, as reflected in the company songs workers in big factories sing at the beginning of the working day. But far more important is the fact that Japanese workers show little of the famous "resistance to change" which is so widespread in the West. The usual explanation for this is "national character"—always a suspect explanation. That it may be the wrong one here is indicated by the fact that acceptance of change is by no means general throughout Japan. For example:

□ The Japanese National Railways suffer from resistance to change fully as much as any other railway system, including the U.S. railroads. But the numerous private railways that crisscross the densely populated areas of Japan seem to be free from such resistance. That the Japanese National Railways are as grossly overstaffed as any nationalized industry in the world may be part of the explanation; the workers know that any change is likely to create redundancy.

□ The other industries in Japan that suffer from resistance to change are also the ones that are organized according to Western concepts of craft and skill. The industries that apply Japanese concepts, as do the private railways (on the whole), do not suffer from resistance to change, even though their employees may know that the company is overstaffed.

The secret may lie in what the Japanese call "continuous training." This means, first, that every employee, very often up to and including top managers, keeps on training as a regular part of his job until he retires. This is in sharp contrast to our usual Western practice of training a man only when he has to acquire a new skill or move to a new position. Our training is promotion-focused; the Japanese training is performance-focused.

Second, the Japanese employee is, for the most part, trained not only in his job but in all the jobs at his job level, however, low or high that level is. To illustrate:

□ The man working as an electrician will automatically attend training sessions in every single area in the plant. And so will the man who pushes a broom. Both of them may stay in their respective jobs until they die or retire. Their pay is independent, in large measure, of the job they are doing, and is geared primarily to the length of service, so that the highly skilled electrician may well get far less money than the floor sweeper. But both are expected to be reasonably proficient in every job in the plant that is, generally speaking, at the same level as their own job.

□ An accountant is expected to be trained—or to train himself through a multitude of correspondence courses, seminars, or continuation schools available in every big city—in every single one of the professional jobs needed in his company, such as personnel, training, and purchasing.

□ The president of a fairly large company once told me casually that he could not see me on a certain afternoon because he was attending his company's training session in welding—and as a student, rather than as an observer or teacher. This is an exceptional example. But the company president who takes a correspondence course in computer programming is fairly common. And the young personnel man does so as a matter of course.

It would take a fat book on Japanese economic and industrial history to explain the origins of this system—though in its present stage it is just about 50 years old and dates back to the labor shortages during and right after the First World War. It would take an even fatter book to discuss the advantages, disadvantages, and limitations of the Japanese system. The limitations are very great indeed. For example, the young, technically trained people—scientists and engineers—resent it bitterly and resist it rather well. They want to work as scientists and engineers and are by no means delighted when asked to learn accounting or when shifted from an engineering job into the personnel department.

Moreover, there are exceptions to the rule. Such highly skilled and highly specialized men as papermakers and department store buyers usually are not expected to know other jobs or to be willing to fit into them. But even these types of workers continue, as a matter of routine, to perfect themselves in their own specialty long after any training in the West would have ended.

Built-in advantages

One result of the practices described is that improvement of work quality and procedures is built into the system. In a typical Japanese training session, there is a "trainer." But the real burden of training is on the participants themselves. And the question is always: "What have we learned so we can do the job better?" A new tool, process, or organization scheme becomes a means of self-improvement.

A Japanese employer who wants to introduce a new product or machine does so in and through the training session. As a result, there is usually no resistance at all to the change, but acceptance of it. Americans in the management of joint ventures in Japan report that the "bugs" in a new process are usually worked out, or at least identified, before it goes into operation on the plant floor.

A second benefit is a built-in tendency to increase productivity. In the West we train until a "learner" reaches a certain standard of performance. Then we conclude that he has mastered the job and will need new training only when he moves on or when the job itself is changed. When a learning curve reaches the standard, it stays on a plateau.

Not so in Japan. The Japanese also have a standard for a job and a learning curve leading up to it. Their standard as a rule is a good deal lower than the corresponding standard in the West; indeed, the productivity norms which have satisfied most Japanese industries in the past are, by and large, quite low by Western measurements. But the Japanese keep on training. And sooner or later, their "learning curve" starts breaking above the plateau which we in the West consider permanent. It starts to climb again, not because a man works harder, but because he starts to work "smarter." In my view, the Japanese pattern is more realistic and more in tune with all that we know about learning.

In the West we are satisfied if the older worker does not slacken in his productivity. Declining performance is a problem, too, in some Japanese industries; young women assembling precision electronics, for instance, reach the peak of their finger dexterity and their visual acuity around the age of 20 and, after age 23 or so, rapidly slow down. (This is one reason that the Japanese electronics industry works hard to find husbands for the girls and to get them out of the factory by the time they are 21 or 22.)

But on the whole the Japanese believe that the older employee is more productive; and their figures would bear this out. With pay based on seniority, the output per yen of wages may be much higher in a plant in which the work force is largely new and young. But output per man-hour is almost invariably a good deal higher in the plant that has the older work population—almost the exact opposite of what we in the West take for granted.

Lifetime training concept

In effect, the Japanese apply to work in business and industry their own traditions. The two great skills of the Samurai, members of the warrior caste that ruled Japan for 300 years until 1867, were swordsmanship and calligraphy. Both demand lifetime training. In both one keeps on training after one has achieved mastery. And if one does not keep in training, one rapidly loses one's skill. Similarly, the Japanese schools of painting—the Kano school, for instance, which dominated Japanese official art for 300 years until 1867—taught that even the greatest master spends several hours a day copying. Thus, he too keeps in "continuous training." Otherwise, his skill, and above all his creativity, would soon start to go down. And the greatest judo master still goes through the elementary exercises every day, just as the greatest pianist in the West does his scales every day.

When employees and efficiency experts take this attitude toward work, the result is a subtle but important change in emphasis. A leading industrial engineer of Japan told me one day:

"One difference I find hard to explain to my Western colleagues is that we do exactly the same things that the industrial engineer does in Detroit or Pittsburgh; but it means something different. The American industrial engineer lays out the work for the worker. Our industrial engineers are teachers rather than masters. We try to teach how one improves one's own productivity and the process. What we set up is the foundation; the edifice the worker builds.

"Scientific management, time and motion studies, materials flow—we do all that, and no differently from the way you do it in the States. But you in the States think that this is the end of the job; we here in Japan believe it is the beginning. The worker's job begins when we have finished engineering the job itself."

'Generalist' vision

The concept of "continuous training" in Japan goes a long way toward preventing the extreme specialization and departmentalization plaguing U.S. business. Generally speaking, there are no craft unions or craft skills in Japanese industry. (The most significant exception is the Japanese National Railways, which imported craft specialization from Great Britain and from Germany, together with steel rails and locomotives, and which is perhaps even more fragmented by craft and jurisdictional lines than American or British railroads are.) Part of the explanation is historical. In the early days of Japanese industrialization, craftsmen flatly refused to work in the new factories. The plants therefore had to be staffed by youngsters, fresh from the farm, who had no skills and who had to be taught whatever they needed to know to do the job.

Still, it is not really true, as Japanese official doctrine asserts, that "men are freely moved from job to job within a plant." A man in a welding shop is likely to stay in a welding shop, and so is the fellow in the next aisle who runs the paint sprays. There is much more individual mobility in office work, and especially for managerial and professional people. A Japanese company will not hesitate to move a young manager from production control into market research or the accounting department.

The individual departments in an office tend to be rigidly specialized and highly parochial in the defense of their "prerogatives." Yet the tunnel vision afflicting so many people in Western business is conspicuously absent in Japan. For instance:

The industrial engineer I quoted earlier insists meticulously on the boundaries between the industrial engineering and personnel functions. He himself never worked in any other function, from the day he graduated from engineering school to the day when, at age 55, he was made president of an affiliate company in the corporate group. Nevertheless, he knew the work of every other function. He understood their problems. He knew what they could do for his industrial engineering department and what, in turn, his people had to do for them. He is the purest of specialists in his own work, and yet he is a true "generalist" in his knowledge, in his vision, and in the way that he holds himself responsible for the performance and results of the entire organization.

This approach he attributes to the fact that throughout his career he was subjected to "continuous training" in all the work going on at his job level. When he was a junior industrial engineer, he took part in the training sessions of all juniors, whether engineers, accountants, or salesmen, and since becoming a member of top management, he has belonged voluntarily to a group which meets two evenings a week, usually with a discussion leader from the outside, to train itself in the work of top management.

Adapting the concept

We in the West emphasize today "continuing education." This is a concept that is still alien to Japan. As a rule, the man or woman who graduates from a university there never sets foot on campus again, never attends a class, never goes back for "retreading." Normal education in Japan is still seen as "preparation" for life rather than as life itself.

Indeed, Japanese employers, even the large companies and the government, do not really want young people who have gone to graduate school. Such people are "too old" to start at the bottom. And there is no other place to start in Japan. Graduate students expect to work as "specialists" and to be "experts" rather than submit to training by their employers. Resistance to the highly trained specialist is considered by many thoughtful management people in Japan to be the greatest weakness of Japanese business—and of government. There is little doubt that, in the years to come, "continuing education" will become far more important in Japan than it now is, and that the specialist will become more important, too.

But, at the same time, Japan's continuous training has something to teach us in the West. We react to worker resistance to change and increased productivity largely along the lines of Mark Twain's old dictum about the weather. We all complain, but no one does anything. The Japanese at least do something—and with conspicuous success.

Continuous training is not unknown in the West. A century ago it was developed by the fledgling Zeiss Works in Germany and applied there to *all* employees in the plant even though most of them were highly skilled glassblowers and opticians with many years of craft training behind them. The world leadership of the German optical industry until World War I rested in large measure on this policy, which saw in advanced craft skill a foundation for, rather than the end of, learning.

With craft jurisdictions in the United States (and Great Britain) frozen into the most rigid and restrictive union contracts, continuous training is probably out of the question for many blue-collar workers on the plant floor. But it could be instituted—and should be instituted—

for nonunionized employees. To be sure, many companies not only have massive training programs, but encourage their younger technical, professional, and managerial people to keep on going to school and to continue their education. But in all too many cases the emphasis in these programs is on a man's becoming more specialized and on *not* learning the other areas of knowledge, skills, and functions.

In most of the U.S. company training programs I know, the emphasis is entirely on the one function in which a young man already works; at most he is being told that "other areas are, of course, important." As a result, he soon comes to consider the other areas as so much excess baggage. And when it comes to education outside—in evening courses at the local university, for instance—a young man's supervisor will push his subordinate into taking more work in his specialty and away from anything else.

The approach should be the opposite: once a young man has acquired the foundations of a specialty, he should be systematically exposed to all the other major areas in the business—whether in company training courses or in "continuing education" programs outside. Only in this way can we hope to prevent tomorrow's professional and managerial people from becoming too departmentalized.

Care & feeding of the young

The House of Mitsui is the oldest of the world's big businesses; it dates back to 1637, half a century before the Bank of England was founded. It also was the largest of the world's big businesses until the American Occupation split it into individual companies. (As these companies come back together into a fairly close confederation, it may well become again the world's biggest business.)

In the more than 300 years of its business life, Mitsui has never had a chief executive (the Japanese term is "chief *banto*"—literally, "chief clerk") who was not an outstanding man and a powerful leader. This accomplishment no other institution can match, to my knowledge; the Catholic Church cannot, nor can any government, army, navy, university, or corporation.

What explains this amazing achievement? In Japan one always gets the same answer: until recently, the chief *banto*—himself never a member of the Mitsui family but a "hired hand"—had only one job: manager development, manager selection, and manager placement. He spent most of his time with the young people who came in as junior managers or professionals. He knew them. He listened to them. And, as a result, he knew, by the time the men reached 30 or so, which ones were likely to reach top management, what experiences and development they needed, and in what job they should be tried and tested.

Appraisal & assignment

At first sight, nothing would seem less likely to develop strong executives than the Japanese system. It would seem, rather, to be the ideal prescription for developing timid men selected for proved mediocrity and trained "not to rock the boat." The young men who enter a company's employ directly from the university—and by and large, this is the only way to get into a company's management, since hiring from the outside and into upper-level positions is practically unknown—know that they will have a job until they retire, no matter how poorly they perform. Until they reach age 45, they will be promoted and paid by seniority and by seniority alone.

There seems to be no performance appraisal, nor would there be much point to it when a man can be neither rewarded for performance nor penalized for nonperformance. Superiors do not choose their subordinates: the personnel people make personnel decisions, as a rule, often without consulting the manager to whom a subordinate is being assigned. And it seems to be unthinkable for a young manager or professional to ask for a transfer, and equally unthinkable for him to quit and go elsewhere.

This practice is being questioned by highly trained technical personnel, but it is changing very slowly. It is still almost unheard of for a young man to take a job in another company except with the express permission of his previous employer. Indeed, every young managerial and professional employee in Japanese organizations, whether business or government, knows that he is expected to help his colleagues look good rather than stand out himself by brilliance or aggressiveness.

This process goes on for 20 to 25 years, during which all the emphasis seems to be on conforming, on doing what one is being asked to do, and on showing proper respect and deference. Then suddenly, when a man reaches 45, the Day of Reckoning arrives, when the goats are separated from the sheep. A very small group of candidates is picked to become "company directors"—that is, top management. They can stay in management well past any retirement age known in the West, with active top management people in their eighties by no means a rarity. The rest of the group, from "department director" on down, generally stay in management until they are 55, usually with at best one more promotion. Then they are retired—and, unlike the rank-and-file employees, their retirement is compulsory.

Limited but important exceptions to this rule are made in the case of outstanding men who, while too specialized to move into the top management of the parent company, are assigned to the top management of subsidiaries or affiliates. In such positions they can stay in office for an indefinite period of time.

Informal evaluators

To an outsider who believes what the Japanese tell him—namely, that this is really the way the system works—it is hard to understand on what basis the crucial decision at age 45 is made. It is even harder to believe that this system produces independent and aggressive top managers who have marketed Japanese exports successfully all over the world and who have, in the space of 20 years, made into the third-ranking economic power in the world a nation that, at the eve of World War II, was not even among the first dozen or so in industrial production or capital.

It is precisely *because* Japanese managers have "lifetime employment" and can, as a rule, be neither fired nor moved, and *because* advancement for the first 25 years of a man's working life is through seniority alone, that the Japanese have made the care and feeding of their young people the first responsibility of top management. The practice goes back at least 300 years, to the time when the Samurai, as retainers of a military clan, were organized in tight hereditary castes with advancement from one to the other officially not permitted. At the same time, the government of the clan had to find able people who could run the clan's affairs at a very early age and take their opportunities without offending higher ranking but less gifted clansmembers.

Today, of course, it is no longer possible for the chief *banto* of Mitsui to know personally the young managerial people as his predecessor did a few generations ago. Even much smaller companies are too large and have far too many young managerial and professional employees in their ranks for that to be done. Yet top management is still vitally concerned with the young. It discharges this concern through an informal network of senior middle-management people who act as "godfathers" to the young men during the first ten years of their careers in the company.

Managerial godfathers

The Japanese take this system for granted. Indeed, few of them are even conscious of it. As far as I can figure out, it has no name—the term "godfather" is mine rather than theirs. But every young managerial employee knows who his godfather is, and so do his boss and the boss's boss.

The godfather is never a young man's direct superior, and, as a rule, he is not anyone in a direct line of authority over the young man or his department. He is rarely a member of top management and rarely a man who will get into top management. Rather, he is picked from among those members of upper-middle management who will, when they reach 55, be transferred to the top management of a subsidiary or affiliate. In other words, godfathers are people who know, having been passed over at age 45 for the top management spots, that they are not going to "make it" in their own organizations. Therefore, they are not likely to build factions of their own or to play internal politics. At the same time, they are the most highly respected members of the upper-middle management group.

How is a godfather chosen for a young man? Is there a formal assignment or an informal understanding? No one seems to know. The one qualification that is usually mentioned is that the godfather should be a graduate of the same university from which the young man graduated—the "old school tie" binds even more tightly in Japan than it did in England. Yet everybody inside the company knows who the godfather of a given young man is and respects the relationship.

During the first ten years or so of a young man's career, the godfather is expected to be in close touch with his "godchild," even though in a large company he may have 100 such godchildren" at any one time. He is expected to know the young man, see him fairly regularly, be available to him for advice and counsel, and, in general, look after him. He has some functions that reflect Japanese culture; for instance, he introduces the young men under his wings to the better bars on the Ginza and to the right bawdy houses. (Learning how to drink in public is one of the important accomplishments the young Japanese executive has to learn.)

If a young man gets stuck under an incompetent manager and wants to be transferred, the godfather knows where to go and how to do what officially cannot be done and, according to the Japanese, "is never done." Yet nobody will ever know about it. And if the young man is errant and needs to be disciplined, the godfather will deal with him in private. By the time a young man is 30 the godfather knows a great deal about him.

It is the godfather who sits down with top management and discusses the young people. The meeting may be completely "informal." Over the sake cup, the godfather may say quietly, "Nakamura is a good boy and is ready for a challenging assignment," or "Nakamura is a good chemist, but I don't think he'll ever know how to manage people," or "Nakamura means well and is reliable, but he is no genius and better not be put on anything but routine work." And when the time comes to make a personnel decision, whom to give what assignment, and where to move a man, the personnel people will quietly consult the godfather before they make a move.

An outsider's glimpse

A few years ago I found myself, by sheer accident, a "temporary godfather." My experience may illustrate how the system works:

One of my ablest students in 20 years at New York University's Graduate Business School was a young Japanese. Let me call him Okura. The son of a diplomat, he went to Oxford for his undergraduate work and then took the Japanese Foreign Service Examination, which he passed with honors. But then he decided to go into business instead, came to our school in New York, and went to work for one of Japan's big international companies.

A few years ago, while I was in Japan, he came to see me. I said, "Okura, how are things going?" He said, "Fine, but I think I may need some help. This is why I have come to see you."

I shall mention just the highlights of the story he told me. "Not having gone to school in Japan, I do not really have anyone in my company who feels responsible for me," he said. "All our management people have gone to school in Japan. As a result, there is no one in upper management who can tell the personnel people that I am ready for a managerial job in one of our branches abroad. I know they considered me when they filled the last two vacancies in South America, but no one knew whether I wanted to go there, whether I was ready, and what my plans were. I know that you are going to have lunch with our executive vice president in a day or two, and, having been my professor, you can speak for me."

I asked, "Okura, won't your executive vice president be offended if an outsider interferes?" He said, "Oh, no. On the contrary; he'll be grateful, I assure you."

He was right. When I mentioned Okura's name to the executive vice president, his face lit up and he said, "You know, I was going to ask you to do us a favor and talk to Okura-san about his plans. We think he is ready for a big management assignment abroad, but we have no way of talking to him; none of us went to the same university he went to."

Three months later Okura was posted to head the company's branch office in a fairly important country in Latin America!

Implications for the West?

In the West, though relationships are far less formal, we still need, just as much as the Japanese do, the senior manager who serves as a human contact, a listener, a guide for the young people during their first ten years or so in business. Perhaps the greatest single complaint of young people in the large organization today is that there is nobody who listens to them, nobody who tries to find out who they are and what they are doing, nobody who acts as a senior counselor.

Our management books say that the first-line supervisor can fill this role. That is simply nonsense. The first-line supervisor has to get the work out; all the sermons that "his first job is human relations" will not make it otherwise. A supervisor tries to hang on to a good man and not let him go. He will not say, "You have learned all there is to learn in this place." He will not say, "You are doing all right, but you really don't belong here." He will not ask a young man, "Where do you want to go? What kind of work do you want to do? How can I help you to get there?" In fact, the supervisor is almost bound to consider any hint of a desire to change or to transfer on the part of a young and able subordinate a direct criticism of himself.

As a result, young managerial and professional people in American business and industry—and in Europe too—"vote with their feet." They quit and go elsewhere. The absence of a genuine contact is an important reason for the heavy turnover among these people. Often, when I talk with them, I hear them make statements like these:

○ "The company is all right, but I have nobody to talk to."

○ "The company is all right, but I am in the wrong spot and can't get out of it."

○ "I need someone to tell me what I am doing right and what I am doing wrong, and where I really belong, but there isn't anybody in my company to whom I can go."

They do not need a psychologist. They need a human relationship that is job-focused and work-focused, a contact they have access to, a mentor who is concerned with them. This is what the Japanese have had to supply for a long time because of the impersonal formality of their rigid system. Because they cannot admit officially that the godfather practice exists, they have set it up in the right way. For it is clearly a strength of their system that the godfather function is not a separate job, is not a part of personnel work, and is not entrusted to specialists, but is discharged by experienced, respected, and successful management people.

But it is not only the young people in American and European companies who need a communication system. Senior executives could also make good use of it. Let me illustrate:

In a number of companies with which I have been working, an attempt has been made to have senior executives meet fairly regularly with younger men—outside of office hours and without respecting lines of function or authority. In these sessions the senior man does not make a speech, but asks, "What do you have to tell me—about your work, about your plans for yourself and this company, about our opportunities and our problems?" The meetings have not always been easy going. But the young people, though at first highly suspicious of being patronized, after a while have come to look forward to the sessions. The real beneficiaries, however, have been the senior executives. They have learned what the young managers are thinking.

The godfather concept of the Japanese may be too paternalistic for us in the West; it may even be too paternalistic for the young Japanese. But the need for some system enabling young managerial and professional people to become the special concern of senior men is especially acute in this age of the "generation gap."

Conclusion

Any Japanese executive who has read this article will protest that I grossly oversimplify and that I have omitted many salient features of Japanese management. Any Western student of Japan who has read this will accuse me of being uncritical. But my purpose has not been to give a scholarly analysis of Japanese management or even to attempt an explanation of Japan's managerial performance. I am fully aware of the many frustrations of the young manager in Japan. I am aware of the tremendous tensions in the Japanese economy and society created by the nation's economic achievement—tensions which are so great as to make me highly skeptical about all those current predictions that the "twenty-first century will be Japan's century." Indeed, if I were a Japanese, this prediction would scare me out of my wits.

Whether anyone can learn from other people's mistakes is doubtful. But surely one can learn from other people's successes. While the Japanese policies discussed in this article are not the "keys" to Japan's achievement, they are major factors in it. And while they are not the answers to the problems of the West, they contain answers to some of our most pressing problems, suggest help for some of our most urgent needs, and point to directions we might well explore. It would be folly to attempt to imitate the Japanese; but we might well try to emulate them.

Japanese poetry has as its subject the human heart.

Kamo Mabuchi, 1697-1769
Writings

Why Japanese factories work

They succeed not by using futuristic techniques but by paying attention to manufacturing basics

Robert H. Hayes

Japan's rapid evolution into a major industrial power has aroused in U.S. managers both awe and the wish to discover the "secret" of Japanese manufacturing success. Contrary to popular opinion, this evolution has not come about through the use of techniques like quality circles and advanced technologies like robots. What Japan has created is the factory of the present, operating as it should. Japanese managers have never stopped emphasizing the basics. To them, every stage of the manufacturing process—from product design to distribution—is equally important. They constantly work to improve equipment design, inventory control systems, and worker skills through cooperation at all levels. The ultimate goal? Perfect products and error-free operations.

U.S. industry can also redress the decline in its manufacturing competitiveness, says the author, by using its enormous resources and talents to do the basics better. As always, this—and not some magical solution—is the route to manufacturing success.

Robert Hayes is professor of business administration at the Harvard Business School. He is currently doing research on how different U.S. manufacturing companies are attempting to improve their productivity. His most recent HBR article, coauthored with William J. Abernathy ("Managing Our Way to Economic Decline," July-August 1980), won the 1980 McKinsey Award.

Illustrations by Karen Watson.

Reprint number 81408

Twenty years ago, most Americans pictured the Japanese factory as a sweatshop, teeming with legions of low-paid, low-skilled workers trying to imitate by hand, with great effort and infrequent success, what skilled American and European workers were doing with sophisticated equipment and procedures. Today, shocked and awed by the worldwide success of Japanese products, Americans tend to rationalize Japan's industrial prowess by imagining gleaming factories peopled by skillful robots—both human and otherwise—all under the benevolent sponsorship of "Japan, Inc."

My research (see my note on this page for a detailed description) suggests that this new stereotype is probably as incorrect as the old one. The modern Japanese factory is not, as many Americans believe, a prototype of the factory of the future. If it were, it might be, curiously, far less of a threat. We in the United States, with our technical ability and resources, ought then to be able to duplicate it. Instead, it is something much more difficult for us to copy; it is the factory of *today* running as it should.

The Japanese have achieved their current level of manufacturing excellence mostly by doing simple things but doing them very well and slowly improving them all the time. "The nail that sticks up is hammered down," says the Japanese proverb. In the factories I visited, all the nails appeared to have been hammered down.

In describing some of the ways in which this "hammering" has been done, I shall not discuss the effect of Japanese cultural or social norms on management behavior, the distinctive aspects of Japanese management systems, or the virtues of Japanese industrial policy. They are all im-

Author's note: In the course of my work, I visited the manufacturing facilities of six Japanese companies (all located in or near Tokyo): Toshiba, Sanyo, Yokogawa Electric, TRW Tokai (a subsidiary of TRW Inc., where I toured three separate plants), Mitsubishi Melcom Computer Works, and Molex Japan (a U.S. subsidiary). These variously sized companies represent a broad range of industries and ownership histories. I made the first three plant visits with a group of about 25 manufacturing managers from General Electric; the last three tours I made on my own.

portant topics, but all have been the subject of innumerable books and articles. (See the ruled insert at the end of this article for a list of related reading.) Instead, I will focus simply on how the Japanese manage their manufacturing functions.

What I did *not* see

For the most part, Japanese factories are *not* the modern structures filled with highly sophisticated equipment that I (and others in the group) expected them to be. The few "intelligent" robots I encountered were largely still experimental; the general level of technological sophistication that I observed was not superior to (and was usually lower than) that found in comparable U.S. plants.

Automation consisted mainly of simple materials-handling equipment used in conjunction with standard processing equipment—just as it is here. Nor do the Japanese run this equipment at higher rates or for longer hours than U.S. factories do. Because of government regulations against women working after 10 P.M., very few Japanese facilities operate more than two shifts a day.

Similarly, the famed "quality circles" did not appear as influential as I expected. They were not widely adopted until several years after the Japanese Union of Scientists and Engineers had given them its official support in the mid-1960s. Most of the plants I visited had in fact experienced problems with QCs for three to four years after their introduction. Moreover, most of the companies I talked to already had enviable reputations for high-quality products by the time they adopted QCs.

One company treated quality circles as secondary, peripheral activities; another had eliminated them altogether ("temporarily," it said). But the quality levels at these plants were just as high as at others where QCs were active.

Finally, I did not observe the use of uniform compensation systems. I had been led to expect wage systems based strictly on seniority, bonuses based on corporate profitability, no incentives based on individual performance, and no time clocks. Yet at one plant I found wages based on level of skill and commuting distance as well as on seniority. At another, by agreement with the union, bonuses equaled a certain number of months of regular salary independent of recent corporate profitability. At a third, the general manager wanted to tie compensation more directly to individual performance measurement—almost on a piecework basis. And I did see a few time clocks in operation. In short, there appeared to be few general rules covering employee compensation.

What I *did* see

Although I found no exotic, strikingly different Japanese way of doing things, I did notice several areas to which the Japanese had directed special attention.

Creating a clean, orderly workplace

The factories I visited were exceptionally quiet and orderly, regardless of the type of industry, the age of a company, its location, or whether it was a U.S. subsidiary. Clearly, this orderliness was not accidental. The meticulousness of the Japanese worker was not, in my opinion, the major reason for the pervasive sense of order that I observed but seemed instead to result from the attitudes, practices, and systems that plant managers had carefully put into place over a long period.

The workers' uniforms (provided, of course, by the company) were clean, their machines were clean, and so were the floors around their machines. Sources of litter and grime were carefully controlled: boxes placed to catch metal shavings, plastic tubs and pipes positioned to catch and direct oil away from the workplace, spare parts and raw materials carefully stored in specified areas. The rest areas were centrally located, tastefully decorated (often with plants and flowers), and immaculate. As one American manager observed, "If you clean up the factory floor, you tend to clean up the thought processes of the people on it too."

Keeping their workplaces and machines in good order was a responsibility assigned to the workers themselves, along with maintaining output and quality and helping fellow workers. Moreover, each worker was trained to correct the minor problems that often arose in the course of the day, to conduct regular preventive maintenance, to monitor and adjust equipment, and to search continually for ways to eliminate potential disruptions and improve efficiency. The object was simple: to avoid any breakdown of equipment during working hours.

Eliminating 'the root of all evil'

In the factories I saw, the sense of order also resulted from an almost total absence of inventory on the plant floor. Raw materials were doled out in small batches only as needed. In many cases, vendors maintained stores of materials and purchased parts that the company "called off" periodically. Suppliers often made three or four deliveries a day to avoid excess stock in the plant. Finished goods were removed immediately from the floor and either transferred to a separate warehouse or shipped directly to customers or distributors. The little inventory I did observe was carefully piled in boxes in specified places around the plant—marked, as were the aisles, with painted stripes.

Even work-in-process inventory was minimal. Material moved along steadily, assisted by materials handlers, by automated equipment, and by the workers themselves. Buffer inventories of partially completed work at various stations were unnecessary, for stoppages caused by breakdowns at earlier process stages almost never occurred. Because the incidence of rejects was very low, rejects did not pile up in baskets or on the floor (I discuss this at length in the next section). In short, most of the plants I saw appeared to have instituted materials movement systems similar to Toyota's famous "just in time" system: inventory is minimized if every part arrives precisely when needed or when a machine is available.

Why do U.S. companies have such large work-in-process inventories? One major reason is their emphasis on producing "economic batches," which seek to balance inventory costs against the setup costs created by changing from one item to another. In contrast, the Japanese believe that inventory is by definition bad, and they therefore seek to avoid the rationale for large-batch production by directing their attention and ingenuity to reducing setup costs. Toyota, for example, estimated that one U.S. auto company took six hours to change the presses in its hood- and fender-stamping department. Volvo and a German competitor took four hours. Toyota's changeover time was 12 minutes.

As one senior manager phrased it, "We feel that inventory is the root of all evil. You would be surprised how much you simplify problems and reduce costs when there are no inventories. For example, you don't need any inventory managers or sophisticated inventory control systems. Nor do you need expediters, because you can't expedite. And, finally, when something goes wrong, the system stops. Immediately the whole organization becomes aware of the problem and works quickly to resolve it. If you have buffer inventories, these potential problems stay hidden and may never get corrected."

Keeping Murphy out of the plant

The inventory control system I describe requires iron discipline, not just on the plant floor but, more important, throughout the plant's managerial infrastructure: vendor relations, production planning, industrial engineering, manufacturing/process engineering, and quality assurance. Everywhere I saw evidence of Japanese managers' determination to prevent Murphy's law ("If something can go wrong, it will go wrong") from taking effect and to make sure that problems which do arise are resolved before they get to the plant floor.

"Before you can increase productivity or improve quality, you must have stability and continuity in your manufacturing process," argued one manager. "How can you have stability when crises are occurring? Our job is to keep crises from developing on the production floor so that our production workers can focus their attention on quality and productivity."

Preventing machine overload

Tools, dies, and production equipment were not overloaded. In fact, machines often operated at slower rates than they were designed for—and at less than the usual rate in U.S. factories. This practice reduced the possibility of jams and breakdowns as well as the wear on machine parts and dies.

Along with regular preventive maintenance and constant cleaning and adjustment, machines last longer with reduced rates of use. I expected to be impressed by the newness of Japanese machine tools compared with those used in the same industries in the United States. (The average age of machine tools in U.S. industry is about 20 years; in Japan, 10 to 12.) But the machines were not really that much newer; they just *looked* newer. And they *ran* newer.

One American manager who has studied closely the Japanese companies in his industry estimated that, even though they used equipment similar to that found in the United States, it lasted two to three times longer. Another summarized the difference as follows: "They use their machines; we abuse ours."

Monitoring systems

Most factories I saw used comprehensive equipment monitoring and early warning systems. These devices checked the process flow, signaled when jams occurred, measured dimensions and other characteristics of finished parts, indicated when these characteristics approached tolerance limits, and kept track of rates of use (number of strokes, shots, or impressions) of tools and dies and indicated when to adjust or regrind them.

These monitoring systems, together with the widespread use of simple materials-handling equipment, allowed Japanese workers to oversee the operation of more machines than their U.S. counterparts. American managers, when walking around the floor of a Japanese factory, are often struck by the sense of being in a virtually untended forest of machines. Sometimes they *are* untended. The Japanese have such trust in the error-free functioning of their equipment that they often load up a machine with work at the end of the last shift and let it run through the night.

No-crisis atmosphere

Production schedules were based on capacity measures derived from actual performance data (not, as one often sees in the United States, from theoretical or obsolete standards). They were established at least a day in advance—generally several days. And unlike U.S. companies, where manufacturing is expected—with good grace and a can-do attitude—to react to last-minute changes imposed by marketing personnel, these schedules were ironclad. (How can you change a production schedule when the inventory required to produce something different is not available?)

No expediting and no overloading were allowed. Work was meted out to the plant in careful doses instead of being, as one U.S. manager put it, "dumped on the floor so the foreman can figure out what to do with it." In short, I never detected an atmosphere of crisis in any of the plants I visited or anything like the "end-of-the-month push" and the "Friday afternoon crisis" so familiar to many American factories.

One plant I visited, which produced electronic instruments in low volume, had a different approach. Production schedules were made up two weeks in advance, and at the beginning of each two-week period all the materials required to meet that schedule were distributed along the production line. At the end of the period, the inventory was used up and a new batch brought in. Workers therefore had the satisfaction of cleaning up the plant floor every two weeks and were exposed to continual, controlled pressure to meet production quotas.

Another company with a very broad product line imposed a simple constraint on production schedulers to reduce the frequency of equipment changeovers: it allowed no more than eight product changes a day. Salespeople might complain and schedulers might be pushed to the limits of their ingenuity, but the rule was firm. If it became impossible to operate within the constraints of this rule, the company reduced its product line or increased the minimum size of customer orders—but the factory did not become burdened with confusion over additional product changes.

The crisis prevention programs like those I have just described generally extended to a company's suppliers as well. A company often informed a supplier several months in advance of its schedule of deliveries to a plant. Any change in the plant's production schedule was translated automatically into a revised delivery schedule for its supplier. The fact that Japanese companies tend to favor nearby suppliers reinforced this tight linkage.

As one American manager put it, "Doesn't Murphy's law work here?" Perhaps one reason Murphy lives in America is that American managers actually *enjoy* crises; they often get their greatest personal satisfaction, the most recognition, and their biggest rewards from solving crises. Crises are part of what makes work fun. To Japanese managers, however, a crisis is evidence of failure. Their objective is disruption-free, error-free operation—operation that doesn't require dramatic fixes.

Management & manufacturing

It became clear to me that what sets Japanese factories apart is not so much what managers do but, rather, how well they do the things they have decided to do—that is, how they view their roles and responsibilities.

'Pursuing the last grain of rice'

Japanese products have a worldwide reputation for precision, reliability, and durability. Many Americans still find this reputation somewhat incongruous because "Made in Japan" used to mean cheap and shoddy products. The important point, however, is *not* that the Japanese have made a remarkable transition but that it took 25 years of hard work to do it.

"Pursuing the last grain of rice in the corner of the lunchbox" is a Japanese saying that describes, somewhat disparagingly, a person's tendency to be overscrupulous. But it conveys volumes about the Japanese character. As managers and as workers, the Japanese are smart and industrious—and never satisfied. They regard *all* problems as important.

Their concept of "zero defects" is a good case in point. As one Japanese scholar phrased it, "If you do an economic analysis, you will usually find that it is advantageous to reduce your defect rate from 10% to 5%. If you repeat that analysis, it may or may not make sense to reduce it further to 1%. The Japanese, however, will reduce it. Having accomplished this, they will attempt to reduce it to 0.1%. And then 0.01%. You might claim that this obsession is costly, that it makes no economic sense. They are heedless. They will not be satisfied with less than perfection."

Indeed, in most of the Japanese factories I visited, the quality charts on the walls measured the defect rate not in percentages but in parts per million: 1,000 ppm represents a 0.1% defect rate. These companies' current defect rate was 300 to 500 ppm, and their "near-term goal" was 100 to 200 ppm. And the long term? "Zero, of course."

"It's not just that we are idealistic," one Japanese manager stated, "but we realize that your willingness to stop at 95%, coupled with our unwillingness to accept 95%, is what makes us able competitors." Another, with perfect sincerity, informed me that "a defect is a treasure." So few of them turned up in his company that each could be studied individually and mined for the information it contained about the remaining bugs in his production process.

It is important to add that a Japanese manager who talks about a quality problem in an operation is as likely to be talking about a design problem or a productivity problem or an inventory problem or a delivery problem or an absenteeism problem as about defective products. Quality, to the Japanese, means error-free operation. Any defect in any part of the manufacturing operation, therefore, becomes a quality problem in management's view—another "grain of rice" to be pursued and eliminated.

High quality, after all, is not achieved by a few random management decisions but by a complex, all-encompassing, interactive management system that has the uncompromising long-term support of top management. The basis of this system is not simply an appropriate arrangement of people and machines. It is a way of thinking.

'Thinking quality in'

Japanese managers have taken the familiar American slogan, "You don't inspect quality into a product, you have to build it in," one step further: "Before you build it in, you must *think* it in."

Planning: Managers think it in, first, by careful planning in the product design stage. Interminable discussions among engineering, production, quality assurance, and sales personnel take place before the design is made final. Right from the start, manufacturing and industrial engineers help in developing machine specifications, methods, and standards. Product design is viewed as part of a total product-process system.

Training: Once production begins, managers concentrate on holding to these standards. Therefore, they think quality in by training workers to deliver consistently high-quality products while developing in them expectations of producing high quality.

Japanese production workers automatically check the parts they receive to make sure that they are defect-free. They work meticulously, knowing that any defects arising from their operation will be spotted and ultimately—and embarrassingly—tracked to them. When the system works well, making high-quality products becomes a source of pride, and management attitudes and actions constantly reinforce this feeling.

Feedback: Managers encourage production workers and quality inspectors to identify and correct any quality problems that arise (even when they are so minor that the product still passes final inspection). Everybody works together to ascertain the causes of problems and to eliminate them.

By contrast, in many U.S. companies a "we against them" attitude prevails between production workers and quality inspectors. As a result, workers keep potential problems hidden and shunt off defects to be reworked, and the pressure to meet delivery deadlines makes quality inspectors reluctant to delay delivery because of minor quality problems.

In Japanese companies "we" is everybody, and "them" are defects. Feedback from production workers, quality inspectors, salesmen, vendors, and customers is encouraged. Field service organizations often report directly to the manufacturing manager rather than, as in most U.S. companies, to the sales manager.

Materials: Managers also think quality in by recognizing that even the most carefully designed and stable production process cannot maintain high quality if the materials that enter the process are defective. Japanese companies therefore devote intensive effort to screening incoming parts and materials and to feeding the results back to suppliers. One hundred percent inspection is often the rule until a supplier proves its reliability.

The pressure put on suppliers to improve the quality of their own materials is incredible to an American, but Japanese manufacturers do not think that simple pressure is sufficient. Instead, they work with suppliers to ascertain why problems arise and to help solve them. They even conduct seminars for employees of supplier companies. The message: "If you follow these steps, you will learn to meet our requirements." Given the long-term relationships between suppliers and customers in Japan, suppliers cannot refuse or take lightly such assistance and advice.

Benefits of the system

Driving this quality consciousness—long before Japan's determined assault on export markets—are the realities of the Japanese domestic market. As one senior government official put it, "A 1% defect rate means that if you sell 100,000 units of a product, 1,000 of them will be defective. In a country as small geographically and as crowded as ours is, it is simply unacceptable to have that many dissatisfied customers 'unselling' your product to their friends." Moreover, the practice in some U.S. companies of shipping off-spec products to remote or less favored customers is unthinkable.

The Japanese have learned how to exploit the inevitable. They have come to realize that the same conditions which promote defect-free manufacturing operations also increase productivity. The apparent relationship between productivity and quality is supported by one American expert—Robert Lynas, group vice president at TRW—who notes that "a 2% reduction in defects is usually accompanied by a 10% increase in productivity."

This finding may simply be due to the fact that fewer defects mean more output without a corresponding increase in costs. As one Japanese manager pointed out, "If you eliminate the production of defective items, things become much simpler and less costly to manage. You don't need as many inspectors as before. You don't need to have production workers doing rework, or systems that manage the detection and flow of rework through the process. Waste goes down. Inventory goes down. But morale goes up. Everybody feels very proud when you produce only perfect products."

Time consciousness

In my tour, I was confronted time and again with concrete evidence of Japanese managers' emphasis on long-term commitments. The managers of U.S. companies jealously guard their "flexibility" and "reaction time" and therefore think in terms of "sales," "hourly workers," "vendors," and "stockholders." Japanese managers, on the other hand, are likely to think in terms of "everlasting customers," "lifetime employees," "supplier-partners," and "owners." This difference has enormous implications for both action and attitude.

Partnership

One simply does not develop a relationship with an everlasting customer in the same way that one makes a one-time sale—the two require completely different expectations and approaches. Nor does one disappoint an everlasting customer by delivering defective products or by failing to meet delivery schedules. One does not disappoint a supplier-partner by not buying from him if his prices are somewhat out of line, although one certainly works with him to help him get prices back in line with those of competitors. The objective, as in all partnerships, is a mutually beneficial long-term relationship—what many Japanese companies refer to as "codestiny."

American managers usually operate quite differently. One marketing vice president, for example, observed, "When I visit a U.S. customer, I am allowed to present my product and then out I go. When recently I visited [a Japanese customer], on the other hand, I was told we would meet with a group of 4 people—which turned into a group of 12. I was told we would probably be there for an hour, but we were there for four hours as they questioned and probed me for information on what was happening in other areas and with other manufacturers.

"All the time I was speaking they were making notes frantically; after I finished, they had a discussion in Japanese to ensure that they had all the necessary information. I was then asked to tour their factory and make suggestions and recommendations to improve their product. I think," he concluded, "that the Japanese approach is more fruitful."

When asked to comment on this difference in U.S. and Japanese companies' treatment of vendors, American managers usually justified their short, directed meetings on the grounds that they were too busy to spend time in meetings like the one just described. But where do Japanese managers find time to be so thorough? Perhaps they do such a good job of creating error-free operations that their plants can run without their active supervision and intervention. Or perhaps they have a different notion of how important their suppliers are to the ultimate success of their businesses and therefore allocate time differently.

Lifetime employment

The Japanese custom of lifetime employment, which has attracted much attention in the West, dates in its current form only from the end of World War II and is still not the rule in all Japanese companies. Even today, less than a third of all Japanese workers are lifetime employees. Only the elite companies (that is, the biggest and most successful, whose products typically appear in international markets) usually practice it—and even they dilute it by using both subcontractors and large numbers of temporary workers hired on a monthly or yearly basis.

The impact of lifetime employment on these companies is enormous, for it both expresses and forces a certain kind of management thinking about workers. "I get the impression," remarked one Japanese visitor to the United States, "that American managers spend more time worrying about the well-being and loyalty of their stockholders, whom they don't know, than they do about their workers, whom they do know. This is very puzzling. The Japanese manager is always asking himself how he can share the company's success with his workers."

Lifetime employees are, in the Japanese view of things, "human capital"—and expensive capital at that. A Japanese worker will earn about 100 million yen ($500,000 in 1980 dollars) in salary and bonuses during his life employment and another 30 to 50 million yen ($200,000) in fringe benefits—not too much less than U.S. workers.

As a U.S. manufacturing manager pointed out, "U.S. managers analyze, rationalize, and agonize until their office walls are covered with paper before committing to a piece of equipment requiring an investment of $500,000—and therefore an annual depreciation charge of $50,000. Yet the process of evaluating and making recommendations regarding the training, compensation, and career path of a $50,000 a year (including benefits) engineer typically requires one-half of a piece of paper, reluctantly prepared in one-half hour once a year!" This difference in priorities is puzzling, particularly when one recognizes that a machine is simply the embodiment of an engineer's skill.

As with all expensive capital investments, choosing lifetime employees requires considerable management planning and screening. Because a company limits the number of its lifetime employees, it must increase their value through training programs, skill-enriching job assignments, and the like. Then, whenever a problem arises, managers have an additional source of expert advice on which to rely: the workers. After all, insisted the managers we met, "They are the experts." This is neither lip service nor false modesty, for management has seen to it that they are.

Such emphasis on continually developing the skills and, thus, the productivity of workers made an enormous impression on the American managers who confronted it. As one commented, "Our whole philosophy has been to 'deskill' our work force through automation, so we end up having relatively unskilled people overseeing highly sophisticated machines. The Japanese put highly skilled people together with highly sophisticated machines and end up with something better than either."

Another observed, "U.S. industry has divided up the total work that has to be done and assigned various parts of it to specialists. This has resulted in production jobs that are repetitive and uninteresting, while the skilled jobs are centralized and moved away from the production floor where they are needed and where corrective action must be taken."

It is important to remember that a company's commitment to its lifetime employees also leads to a reciprocal commitment from employees to the company. Recognizing that a no-layoff policy requires a work force level that lags behind sales demand, Japanese workers in the companies I visited willingly worked up to 60 hours of overtime per month (3 hours per day) when demand was high.

Their willingness to do so was encouraged by their knowledge that management understood intimately the difficulties and pressures under which they operated and was working just as hard as they were. Workers know that potential managers typically begin their careers with a year or so in relatively low-level occupations—the shop floor or the trading desk—to learn about the day-to-day concerns of operating people. Over time they work their way up the ladder, but a sense of identification with the workers remains. In the plants I visited, everybody—from the most junior production worker to the plant manager—wore the same company uniform.

Equipment independence

Another aspect of management thinking in Japan that surprised and, at first, perplexed me was the insistence on designing and fabricating production equipment in-house. Most of the companies I visited claimed that at least 50% of their production equipment was built by their own engineers and machinists and that most of the remainder was designed in-house as well. One Japanese magazine has estimated that roughly 40% of Japanese R&D goes for process or equipment improvement.

By contrast, the conventional management wisdom in the United States, where a much smaller percentage of process equipment is developed in-house, says that equipment manufacture is best left to experts. Equipment producers, so the reasoning goes, can afford the high fixed costs of using specialized engineers and can amortize these and other developmental expenses over long production runs, thus reducing the cost of their product.

The Japanese will have none of this. "Every machine represents a compromise among various users and, therefore, various uses," one manager told us. "We prefer to design equipment that is directed toward our own needs. Not only do we get better equipment, but our costs are lower and our delivery times less."

Why is this so? One reason is that machines designed in-house cost less because they do not need the safety margins and "design cushions" that equipment manufacturers build into their general-purpose machines. More to the point, the same manager informed us, "We always need machines when business conditions are good—which is when everybody else wants machines. The equipment manufacturing industry is notorious for its cyclical behavior. During these periods of high demand, they stretch out their lead times and they raise prices. If you are dependent on them, you soon regret it."

But what about the slack times, when companies must carry underused manufacturing engineers and skilled machinists? Then Japanese managers use these skilled resources to upgrade the company's existing equipment and perfect the new drive mechanisms, computerized controls, materials-handling equipment, and the equipment monitoring and warning devices mentioned earlier. Observed one manager, "The advantage of having highly skilled people (like manufacturing engineers) around is that they can always find something useful to do!"

Re-solving 'the problem of production'

During the past 15 to 20 years, a number of important U.S. manufacturing industries have acted as if they had entered into a tacit agreement to compete on grounds other than manufacturing ability. They appeared to think they had, as John Kenneth Galbraith phrased it, "solved the problem of production" and therefore directed attention and resources to mass distribution, packaging, advertising, and developing incremental new products (to round out product lines or attack specific market segments)—but neglected to upgrade continually their manufacturing capabilities.

As a result, U.S. plant and equipment have been allowed to age. Our technological advantage has eroded because of reduced expenditures on new-product R&D and on new process technologies. Our best managerial talent has been directed toward fast tracks that often do not include direct manufacturing experience. At the same time, promotions to top corporate positions have increasingly favored specialists in finance, marketing, accounting, and law.

This complacent attitude toward the problem of production did not impair the competitiveness of U.S. manufacturers for a number of years—until, that is, they began to encounter companies (like those in Japan) that *did* compete on such mundane grounds as reliable, low-cost, defect-free products and dependable delivery. Then U.S. businesses found themselves increasingly displaced in international markets and, more recently, in their home markets as well. This sudden weakness has come as a shock to many American managers who, in searching belatedly for causes and explanations, have often looked for dramatic, easily imitated or purchased solutions: quality circles, government assistance, and the use of intelligent robots.

The Japanese have never considered the production problem solved, never underestimated the challenge of building and improving the "factory of the present." There are no magic formulas—just steady progress in small steps and focusing attention on manufacturing fundamentals. This is why their example will be so hard for American companies—and American managers—to emulate.

Yet it is not beyond our capabilities. Many of the attributes that characterize Japanese manufacturing management are valued in America too. Although we emphasize our "rugged individualism" (and criticize, in the same breath, the fact that "everybody is out for himself"), Americans love to work in smoothly functioning teams.

Nor is the Japanese concept of self-reliance—by which they refer to the importance of developing their own production equipment in-house and of modifying purchased equipment to meet their own specific needs—foreign to us. Americans are inveterate tinkerers with a tradition of self-reliance that springs from frontier roots. Our dependence on "off-the-shelf" solutions developed by outside experts—whether these individuals be equipment producers, company-hopping executives, or consultants—is a recent phenomenon.

Nor is the concept of lifetime employment so strange. In most large U.S. companies, 30% to 40% of the work force has lifetime employment, in the sense that any production worker who has worked for more than 10 years is almost never laid off. Rather than making that fact explicit, however, and using it to increase workers' sense of self-worth and their commitment to the company, we continue to refer to them as "hourly workers." We thereby imply they are expendable—which they aren't.

And we blind ourselves to the opportunities for increasing their skills (and thus their value to the company) that we routinely employ to upgrade the capabilities of expensive capital goods—which in a sense employees are. We complain about workers who have no commitment to their company and conveniently ignore the fact that most companies make no commitment to their workers.

The "we're all in this together" attitude of Japanese companies is also reminiscent of the American management tradition of "let's roll up our sleeves and get it done." The lack of managerial elitism in the United States used to be a source of wonder to Europeans, whose managerial traditions reflected the deep divisions between social classes. With some shock, we recognize the emergence of elitism and lack of trust in the United States—managers who isolate themselves from workers, both physically and emotionally; who have no direct experience in the businesses they manage; who see their role as managing resource allocation and other organizational processes rather than as leadership by example.

Improving our manufacturing competitiveness does not lie with the "last-quarter touchdowns," the "technological fixes," or the "strategic coups" that we love so much. Instead, we must compete with the Japanese as they do with us: by always putting our best resources and talent to work doing the basic things a little better, every day, over a long period of time. It is that simple—and that difficult.

Related reading

Articles

Peter F. Drucker,
"What We Can Learn From Japanese Management,"
HBR March-April 1971,
p. 110.

Peter F. Drucker,
"Japan Gets Ready for Tougher Times,"
Fortune, November 3, 1980,
p. 108.

Peter F. Drucker,
"The Price of Success: Japan Revisited,"
Foreign Affairs, August 1978,
p. 28.

Byron K. Marshall,
"Japanese Business Ideology and Labor Policy,"
Columbia Journal of World Business, Spring 1977,
p. 22.

Richard Tanner Pascale,
"Zen and the Art of Management,"
HBR March-April 1978,
p. 153.

Howard F. Van Zandt,
"How to Negotiate in Japan,"
HBR November-December 1970,
p. 45.

Ezra F. Vogel,
"Guided Free Enterprise In Japan,"
HBR May-June 1978,
p. 161.

Books

Robert Cole,
Japanese Blue Collar: The Changing Tradition
(Berkeley, Calif.: University of California Press, 1971).

Chie Nakane,
Japanese Society
(Berkeley, Calif.: University of California Press, 1970).

Ezra F. Vogel,
Japan as Number One: Lessons for America
(New York: Harper & Row, 1979).

Innovation, not imitation

. . . A U.S. company attempting to introduce an alien management style in an adverse cultural environment may be inviting rigid bureaucratization without realizing the benefits of higher productivity. It may be better off leaving the fundamentals of the organization and company culture alone and instead attempt to change the characteristics of the industry. A successful change will bring the industry in harmony with the strengths of the U.S. environment, and will force the Japanese to defend their weaknesses.

For example, the U.S. company can invest in an industry, not in process improvements or in going down the learning curve, but to fundamentally change the nature of the product. This is what aircraft manufacturers have done. Such investments, if made boldly, can create enough uncertainty about the future of the industry that the community of Japanese decision makers is unable to tolerate the level of risk.

Another option is to shift technological innovation away from the factory floor where Japanese work culture provides advantages and into the design room or laboratory. This may involve willingness to scrap reliable existing technologies, hire seemingly unproductive PhDs, acquire the tangible and intangible assets of entrepreneurial companies and sell the soundness of the strategy to the financial community.

A third option is to set up global organizations that use local manufacturing and local marketing. The United States is a melting pot and its multinational corporations contain diverse nationalities and talents. . . . With few exceptions Japanese strengths have come from manufacturing operations located in Japan. A truly multinationally staffed and operated global business will give non-Japanese competitors significant advantages of market access and responsiveness in numerous international markets.

None of these options is without risks, but the ability to innovate and explore the uncharted is precisely what separates the leader from the industry follower. The Japanese system has shown great strengths in coming up from behind. But the kind of organizational skills that were needed for catching up are probably not appropriate for being at the cutting edge. In time, Japanese society and industrial organizations may transform themselves in order to fulfill these new tasks. Until then, non-Japanese competitors have real opportunities to hold their own by exploiting Japanese institutional rigidities.

From
Tino Puri and Amar Bhide, McKinsey & Company, "The Crucial Weaknesses of Japan Inc.," the *Wall Street Journal*, June 8, 1981. Reprinted with permission of the *Wall Street Journal* © 1981, Dow Jones & Co., Inc.

The new industrial competition

Thrown into a competitive turmoil, a mature industry can go through a rejuvenation— as U.S. auto manufacturing appears ready to do

William J. Abernathy, Kim B. Clark, and Alan M. Kantrow

The results of Japanese competition in U.S. markets are evident to all Americans. Repercussions from competitive pressures exerted by European and Japanese manufacturers have been or are being felt by U.S. producers of cars, machine tools, minicomputers, commercial aircraft, textile machinery, and color TV sets, to name a few traditional businesses. Taking auto manufacture as their case example, the authors of this article attribute the Japanese carmakers' success to superiority in the manufacturing plant, especially in their process systems and work force management.

The authors describe the current dilemma of U.S. car manufacturers, who find themselves at a crossroads because this struggle has changed the rules of the game. Now these producers face a situation in which advancing technology and the momentous changes it wreaks–instead of the incremental changes through styling, marketing, and service to which U.S. manufacturers are accustomed–will determine the winners and losers. As often happens in a mature industry when a new phase of competition appears, the auto industry may well undergo a renewal that transforms it. The challenge for U.S. companies in endangered industries is to recognize the altered situation, adjust to it, and learn to manage change.

William Abernathy is professor of business administration at the Harvard Business School. A noted expert on the automobile industry, he wrote The Productivity Dilemma: Roadblock to Innovation in the Automobile Industry *(Johns Hopkins University Press, 1978). Kim Clark, assistant professor of business administration at the Harvard Business School, is author of the National Academy of Sciences' forthcoming report on* The Competitive Status of the U.S. Automobile Industry. *Alan Kantrow, an associate editor at HBR, has written two previous HBR articles, the more recent being "The Strategy-Technology Connection" (July-August 1980.)*

Reprint number 81501

It is barely possible that in some remote corner of the United States a latter-day Rip Van Winkle awoke this morning fresh with shining images of American industry in the 1950s still fixed in his head. But it is not very likely. Who, after all, during the past few years could have slept undisturbed through the general chorus of lament about the economy? Who could have remained unaware that much of U.S. industry—especially the mature manufacturing sector—has fallen on hard times?

And who did not have a surefire remedy? Born-again supply-siders argued for the massive formation of capital; "new class" advocates of a more systematic industrial policy, for better allocation of existing capital; industrial economists, for enhanced productivity; organized labor, for a coherent effort at reindustrialization; subdued (if unrepentant) Keynesians, for more artful demand management; boisterous Lafferites, for a massive tax cut; congressional experts, for carefully targeted tax breaks on depreciation and investment; Friedmanites, for tight money; and Naderites, for an anticorporate economic democracy.

This loudly divided counsel on the best strategy for managing economic change reflects inadequacy in both perception and understanding: our current industrial malaise defies the usual interpretations and resists the usual prescriptions. Managing change successfully has proved difficult because policymakers in business and government, trained in an old economic calculus, have found it hard to see the new competitive realities for what they are—or to identify the best terms in which to analyze them.

Policymakers fail to understand that the old rules of thumb and worn assumptions no longer hold. Similarly, the traditional structural arrangements in many industries—the familiar relationship between, say, labor and management or producer and supplier—no longer square with the facts of competitive life. As a result, decision makers who continue to act as if nothing has happened are, at best, ineffective and, at worst, inadvertent agents of economic disaster.

Levers of change

What has happened? The two principal changes have been greater exposure to international competition and technical advances that alter competition. For a start, let's look at two basic major manufacturing industries that have experienced these forces.

One is color television:

☐ This industry was confronted with new competitors who emphasized high productivity, reliability, quality, and competent design (but not innovative design, except for Sony).

☐ Many competitors—Warwick, Motorola, and Admiral among them—did not survive the foreign thrust and were either taken over or went out of business.

☐ Foreign competitors' emphasis on manufacturing, a critical element, was transferred to their U.S. operations—witness Sanyo's management of the previously unsuccessful old Warwick plant, with many of the same employees and U.S. middle managers.

☐ Now technological changes have created a situation of potential renewal of the product life cycle—developments in videocassette recorders; videodiscs; flat, high-resolution screens; telecommunications; and computers may combine to revolutionize the television business.

... And another is textile machinery:

☐ Before the 1960s a few U.S. manufacturers (for example, Draper) dominated this business. Conglomerates acquired them (e.g., Rockwell International took over Draper).

☐ The U.S. manufacturers began to lose business primarily because of deterioration in product performance relative to European and Japanese models and failure to remain at the cutting edge of new technology.

☐ Because of insufficient investment (conglomerates treated them as cash cows), the once-dominant U.S. manufacturers have lost technical and market leadership to the Swiss, Germans, and Japanese.

Now consider two other industries that are facing the new forces of international competition.

One of them is computers:

☐ Fujitsu has introduced a mainframe computer that attacks IBM where its strength is—service. Fujitsu is doing this by building a high-quality, reliable machine that can *guarantee* 99% uptime. In a test run of strategy, Fujitsu has taken on IBM in Australia with this approach and bested the U.S. giant in obtaining some mainframe contracts. The experience there to date: 99.8% uptime.

☐ In minicomputers and home computers the Japanese are entering the U.S. market. Producers like Mitsubishi, Nippon Electric, and Hitachi will soon offer high-quality products that are cost competitive.

... And another is machine tools:

☐ Japanese producers have entered this market with a strategy built around a very reliable, high-quality product. Recently, for instance, a U.S. auto producer ordered transfer lines from an established U.S. machine tool manufacturer and from Toyota. The lines arrived at the U.S. plant at the same time. Toyota sent two engineers who had the equipment running and fully debugged in two weeks, while the competitor's team of eight engineers spent several months getting its line operational.

☐ Developments in new technology—electronics, optical and tactile sensors, lasers, and robotics—are creating opportunities for improved metalworking operations and are opening up new applications in areas like assembly and inspection, where mechanization and automation have hardly played a role. Integration of these advances with computerized design and manufacturing could change the very concepts on which traditional machine tools are founded.

A number of other long-stable U.S. manufacturing industries no doubt will be shaken in the not-distant future by these pressures. One is the air compressor field, which a few companies have dominated. A Japanese producer, Hokuetsu, entered its domestic market five years ago and now rules it. Among the companies left in its wake is Ingersoll-Rand, whose market share in Japan plunged from well over 50% to zero. Hokuetsu offers a dependable, good-quality product at half the cost of the comparable U.S. compressor.

Still another field is major household appliances, which the Japanese have slated for heavy export activity in this decade. Sanyo, Toshiba, and other companies are setting up U.S. plants and distribution systems. General Electric, for one, is worried; GE has begun a program designed to improve greatly the quality and productivity of its Louisville appliance complex.

The list of endangered industries goes on: jet engines, commercial aircraft, small forklift trucks, steel, electric motors, lawnmowers, and chainsaws, to name just a few.

Character of the new competition

Let us focus on a single industry to show in detail the character of the conditions that the imperiled U.S. industries face. An inkling of these conditions has entered the consciousness of all Americans as they witnessed Japan's extraordinary success in capturing a large share of the automobile market from the entrenched Big Three domestic producers. In this article we go beyond the previously known facts and show exactly how the Japanese implemented their strategy on the plant floor, on the engineers' design boards, and in the executive offices.

Until recently, developments in the U.S. auto industry were determined mostly by government policies and economic forces peculiar to North America. The sheer extent of the U.S. market and its productive base had long guaranteed the industry a largely self-contained posture. Over the past 15 years, however, the competitive boundaries have expanded drastically until now they are virtually worldwide in scope.

Accompanying this expansion has been a rapid increase in the number of healthy competitors. These new international players, moreover, have quite a different approach from that of the U.S. Big Three; their plan consists of radically new strategies, modes of operation, and production experience.

More to the point, the novel competitive challenge they present cannot be overcome by the familiar responses U.S. companies have long used against each other. Strategically, the Big Three are well prepared to fight not this new war, but the last one.

Many observers believe that the perceived low quality of Detroit's vehicles is a simple function of lethargy and past practice. This view ignores the close connection between poor quality and a disadvantage in costs. The productive capacity of some new entrants, notably the Japanese, enjoys a significant cost advantage over that of the Americans. The Japanese have been especially skillful in exploiting this advantage by adding performance and quality to their cars. This combination of competitive price and high quality has proved tremendously successful in reaching consumers in the American market.

What makes this advantage particularly troublesome is that it does not represent primarily an investment problem; if it did, it would be far easier to remedy. Instead, it arises to some extent from differences in wage rates and, more significant, from differences in productivity and management of operations.

In 1973, when Lee A. Iacocca was asked about the competitive advantage of innovation as perceived by Ford, he responded simply, "Give them [American consumers] leather. They can smell it." In Ford's reading of the U.S. market, innovation did not pay; styling did. Things are quite different today: technology matters.

In the 1950s and 1960s, product technology was competitively neutral. No auto company sought a competitive advantage through significant innovation. In the 1980s, however, the necessity for advantage through innovation is steadily growing. In fact, consumer preference for small, fuel-efficient automobiles has developed faster in the United States than it did earlier in Europe or Japan. Beset by unfortunate decisions in the past, the continued absence of a workable long-term energy policy, conflicting regulatory requirements, and the massive financial demands posed by a retooling of production capacity, U.S. producers find themselves at a serious technological disadvantage.

But this is not all. The edge that U.S. companies have long enjoyed in mass production technology and in the resulting economies of scale —an edge long believed essential to competitive success—no longer obtains. Most of the standard U.S. technology is either already widely diffused or easily transferable. Moreover, the process technology for the new, smaller autos is subtly but significantly different from that now in place. In other words, changing market preferences and changing rates of technology diffusion have diluted, perhaps destroyed, the established scale economies of U.S. producers.

Premium on management

Two main distinctions have largely provided the structure for discussions of manufacturing competitiveness. The first is the division between analysis and prescription of a "macro" sort (that is, having to do with such overarching questions of economic management as fiscal and monetary policy and tax incentives) and those of a "micro" sort (that is, having to do with issues relating to the management of particular companies). The second is the division between analysis and prescription based on "hardware" (equipment, buildings, and machinery) and those based on "software" (people management, organizational systems, and corporate strategies).

Considered together, these distinctions form the simple matrix shown in *Exhibit I.* Although the distinctions among these quadrants are rough, they are nonetheless useful. In practice, however, they are often neglected, which has left the unfortunate impression in some minds that the current industrial difficulties are composed equally —and indistinguishably—of problems in all the quadrants.

Exhibit I **Key elements in manufacturing competitiveness**

	Macro	Micro
	1. Government fiscal and monetary policies	**2. Production capability**
Hardware	Taxation	Plant
	Capital markets	Equipment
	Savings	
	3. Socioeconomic environment	**4. Corporate management**
Software	Work ethic	Organization
	Regulation	Administration
	Education	Production systems

This impression has been mischievous, for these difficulties and their remedies are distributed unevenly about the matrix. In the auto industry the key measures for meeting the new competition fall primarily into Quadrant 4.

Japanese micromanagement

The Japanese advantage in production costs and product quality in the auto industry, as well as many other established U.S. industries, is not only a fact defining the new competitive reality but also the result of a carefully honed approach to management—the stuff of Quadrant 4. Americans' talk of overregulation, underdepreciation, pervasive national culture, and markedly absent government support is misplaced.

Costs of production

Several estimates have placed the landed cost advantage in U.S. markets of Japanese-produced subcompact cars in the $400 to $600 range per vehicle. For example, Abraham Katz, then assistant secretary of commerce for international economic policy, testified last year that "the apparent cost advantage to Japanese producers may have been $560 per car in 1979."[1]

These estimates, in our view, seriously understate the advantage. In the first place, they fail to reflect both current rates of labor compensation and, perhaps more important, the great differences in productivity between Japanese and American manufacturers. Furthermore, they are often based on a narrow definition of the productive units to be compared, for they assume that the relevant comparison is between two original equipment manufacturers—say, Ford and Toyota—even though the really meaningful comparison lies between two productive systems, or "confederations"—that is, an OEM and its constellation of suppliers.

To get a truer picture of the Japanese cost advantage, we must therefore produce estimates that account for productivity differentials, labor costs, and industry structure.

The first step in developing these improved estimates is to update assessments of differential labor productivity. We know that in 1974 output per labor hour in the Japanese auto industry—OEMs and suppliers—was 88% of the level in the United States (that is, the ratio of Japanese to U.S. productivity was 0.88). Published data suggest that growth in labor productivity in the Japanese auto industry (motor vehicles and parts) averaged 8% to 9% in the 1970s; the comparable figure for the United States was 3% to 4%. Using a midrange estimate of the difference (5%), we arrive at a 1980 productivity ratio of 1.18. This means that in 1980 Japanese producers operated at a productivity level almost 20% above that of their American competitors.

This rapid growth was offset in part by higher rates of wage increase: in 1974 Japanese hourly compensation rates were about 37% of those in the United States, while in 1980 they were roughly 50%. Dividing the compensation ratio (0.5) by the productivity ratio (1.18) yields a unit labor cost ratio of 0.424—a figure that has remained more or less constant during the entire 1974-1980 period.

Table A in the *Appendix* translates this steady labor cost ratio into a Japanese advantage of $1,673. Subtracting $400 for freight and tariff costs yields a landed cost advantage of $1,273 on a 1980 subcompact that sells in the American market for about $5,500—a cost advantage of 23%.

Although the calculations in *Table A* are based on a number of undocumented assumptions about cost structure and labor content, reasonable adjustment of these assumptions would not affect the order of magnitude of the Japanese cost advantage. Indeed, we were biased conservatively throughout in estimating that cost advantage. Moreover, inclusion of general administrative and selling expenses, as well as the costs of capital and salaried personnel, would leave the Japanese cost advantage intact. So we figure that Japanese producers enjoy a $1,200 landed cost advantage on every small vehicle sold in the United States.

We can to some extent check these numbers against information in the annual reports of major U.S. and Japanese producers. These reports yield data on the costs of nonlabor inputs and salaried personnel but none on the labor embodied in components or materials.

Getting at these data, however, presents several analytic problems. Perhaps the most serious is the great difference between U.S. and Japanese OEMs in their degree of vertical integration and in the nature of their relationships with suppliers. At Toyota, for example, purchases account for almost 80% of the value of sales; but because Toyota holds an equity interest in many of its suppliers, this figure is somewhat misleading. Comparable data for U.S. companies show much less reliance on suppliers; GM, for instance, has a purchase-to-sale ratio of less than 50%.

A second problem is the quite different product mix of U.S. and Japanese OEMs. The data we use come from 1979, when medium-size cars dominated the U.S. Big Three's product lines. The Japanese were producing a much narrower range of vehicles and, of course, were emphasizing the subcompact segment.

Table B in the *Appendix* shows estimates of total employee costs per vehicle in 1979 at Ford and Toyo Kogyo (Mazda). Our calculations suggest that assembly of the average Ford vehicle required 112.5 employee hours; a Toyo Kogyo vehicle, only 47. Employee costs in building the Ford vehicle were $2,464; for Toyo Kogyo, $491.

As already noted, this sizable cost gap reflects differences in product mix and vertical integration as well as in labor costs and productivity. Information on value added in the annual reports and discussions with industry sources suggest that the Toyo Kogyo results should be increased by 15% to 20% to adjust for vertical integration. Using these higher estimates yields a per-vehicle total of 56 hours instead of 47. (To correct for product mix, we have estimated the cost to Ford of producing the Toyo Kogyo product mix. These calculations are presented in *Table C* in the *Appendix*.)

Our analysis of annual report data suggests that in 1979 the difference between Ford and Toyo Kogyo employee costs per small vehicle was about $1,300. Updating this figure to 1980 might increase the absolute dollar amount somewhat, but the evidence we cited on relative growth rates in productivity and compensation implies that the percentage gap would not change much.

Adjustment for changes in exchange rates would also have a negligible effect. Using a rate of 200 yen to the dollar (the approximate rate at the end of 1980) instead of 218 would reduce the gap by only $50. And when we adjust this $1,300 to reflect the U.S. advantage in administrative and selling expenses, the 2.9% tariff with the relevant freight costs for Japanese imports, and the Japanese productivity edge at the supplier level, we emerge with a landed cost advantage for Japanese OEMs of about $1,400.

Contrasts in product quality

It is, of course, true that the competitively important dimensions of auto quality are established not by experts but by the market. And many American consumers, who place a high value on quality of assembly workmanship (what the industry calls "fits and finishes"), on reliability, and on durability, seem to believe that Japanese cars are superior in each of these dimensions.

Exhibit II, which presents industry data on assembly quality, suggests that consumer perceptions are consistent with experience. Buyers rated the imports as a group superior in quality to the domestically produced cars, while the top Japanese models were ranked first and third among the nine rated. Japanese makes also had fewer defects after one month of service.

Similarly, subscribers to *Consumer Reports* gave high ratings to Japanese autos for reliability as measured by the incidence of repairs (see *Exhibit III*). Nevertheless, what little evidence exists indicates that U.S.-built vehicles have superior corrosion protection and longer-lived components and systems.

At any rate, American automobiles enjoy much less customer loyalty than do Japanese imports. *Exhibit IV*, which summarizes the data on loyalty, gives perhaps the clearest evidence of the differential customer perception of product value for each dollar spent.

Lessons of Quadrant 4

Most explanations of this Japanese advantage in production costs and product quality emphasize the impact of automation, the strong

1. Statement before the Subcommittee on Trade of the House Ways and Means Committee, March 18, 1980.

Exhibit II **Evidence on assembly quality of U.S. autos vs. certain imports**

	Vehicle category	**Condition at delivery** scale of 1-10; 10 is excellent		**Condition after one month of service** number of defects per vehicle shipped
	Aggregates	**Domestic**	**Imports**	
	Subcompact	6.4	7.9	
	Compact	6.2	7.7	
	Midsize	6.6	8.1	
	Standard	6.8	–	
Models	**Domestic**			
	Omni	7.4		4.10
	Chevette	7.2		3.00
	Pinto	6.5		3.70
	Rabbit (U.S.)*	7.8		2.13
	Horizon	7.5		NA
	Imports			
	Civic	8.0		1.23†
	Fiesta	7.9		NA
	Colt	7.8		NA
	Corolla	7.8		0.71‡

*European Rabbit averages 1.42 defects per vehicle shipped.

†Honda average.

‡Toyota average.

Source:
Aggregates – Rogers National Research, *Buyer Profiles*, 1979; models – industry sources.

support of the central government, and the pervasive influence of national culture. No doubt these factors have played an important role, but the primary sources of this advantage are found instead in the Japanese producers' mastery of Quadrant 4—that is, in their execution of a well-designed strategy based on the shrewd use of manufacturing excellence.

It may seem odd to think of manufacturing as anything other than a competitive weapon, yet the history of the U.S. auto market shows that by the late 1950s manufacturing had become a competitively neutral factor. It was not, of course, unimportant, but none of the major American producers sought great advantage through superior manufacturing performance. Except perhaps for their reliance on economies of scale, they tended to compete by means of styling, marketing, and dealership networks.

The Japanese cost and quality advantage, however, originates in painstaking strategic management of people, materials, and equipment—that is, in superior manufacturing performance. This approach, in our view, arose from the Japanese pattern of domestic competition and the need for an effective strategy to enter the U.S. market.

At that time the Japanese realized it would be foolish to compete head-on with the established domestic producers' competence in making elaborately (and annually) styled large cars with a "boulevard ride." They lacked the experience, the manufacturing base, and the resources. Instead, taking a lesson from Volkswagen's success, the Japanese concentrated on producing a reliable, high-quality, solid-performance small automobile and on backing it up with a responsible network of dealers.

Exhibit V outlines the seven factors most responsible for successful productivity performance and compares the Japanese practice in each with the American. On the basis of extensive discussions with U.S. industry executives, engineers, and consultants, we have ranked these factors in the order of their importance in determining the current state of the industry and have given them approximate relative weights.

Surprisingly, the hardware associated with technology—new automation and product design—proves relatively insignificant in assessing the competitive difficulties of the U.S. manufacturers, although its importance for the future of the industry grows ever larger. Despite the publicity given Japan's experimentation with industrial robots and advanced assembly plants like Nissan's Zama facility, the evidence suggests that U.S. producers have so far maintained roughly comparable levels of process equipment. However appealing they may be, Quadrant 2 explanations cannot themselves account for U.S.-Japanese differentials in manufacturing productivity.

Focus on 'process yield'

To the contrary, a valid explanation must start with the factor of "process yield," an amalgam of management practices and systems connected with production planning and control. This yield category reflects Japanese superiority in operating processes at high levels of efficiency and output over long periods of time. Although certain engineering considerations (machine cycles, plant layouts, and the like) are significant here, the Japanese advantage has far more to do with the interaction of materials control systems, maintenance practices, and employee involvement. *Exhibit VI* attempts to make this interaction clear.

At the heart of the Japanese manufacturing system is the concept of "just in time" production. Often called *Kanban* (after the cards or tickets used to trigger production), the system is designed so that materials, parts, and components are produced or delivered just before they are needed. Tight coupling of the manufacturing stages reduces the need for work-in-process inventory. This reduction helps expose any waste of time or materials, use of defective parts, or improper operation of equipment.[2]

Furthermore, because the system will not work if frequent or lengthy breakdowns occur, it creates inescapable pressure for maximizing uptime and minimizing defects. This pressure, in turn, supports a vigorous maintenance program. Most Japanese plants operate with only two shifts, which allows for thorough servicing of equipment during nonproductive time and results in a much lower rate of machine breakdown and failure than in the United States.

Pressure for elimination of defects makes itself felt not in maintenance schedules but in the relationships of producers with suppliers and in work practices on the line. Just-in-time production does not permit extensive inspection of incoming parts. Suppliers must, therefore, maintain consistently high levels of quality, and workers must have the authority to stop operations if they spot defects or other production problems.

Worker-initiated line stoppages are central to the concept of *Jidoka* (making a just-surfaced problem visible to everyone by bringing operations to a halt), which–along with Kanban–helps direct energy and attention to elimination of waste, discovery of problems, and conservation of resources.

It is difficult, of course, to separate the effects of Kanban-Jidoka on process yield from the effects of, say, job structure and quality systems –factors given a somewhat lower ranking by the experts we consulted (see *Exhibit V*). It is also difficult to separate them from the benefits of having a loyal work force (Japanese factories have little unexcused absenteeism). Taken together, these aspects of work force management clearly account for much of the Japanese advantage in production.

It is sometimes argued, by the way, that the union-management relationship in the United States helps explain the superior Japanese performance in productivity and product quality. There is no doubt that the industrial relations system in the U.S. auto industry is a critical element in its performance. Nor is there any doubt that many aspects of that system do not square with the new facts of competitive life. Yet to lay these problems at the door of the union–and only there–is misleading.

Employment contracts and collective bargaining relationships do not just happen. Indeed, a contract provision that a company today finds dysfunctional often was initiated by management some time in the past. Moreover, the production

Exhibit III

Ratings of body and mechanical repair frequency
average = 10; maximum = 20; minimum = 0

Make all models	Body 1980	Mechanical 1980
Domestic		
Buick	9.3	9.4
Chevrolet	8.4	8.9
Dodge	10.0	10.0
Ford	7.2	9.2
Lincoln	8.1	8.4
Oldsmobile	8.4	9.3
Volkswagen	11.3	8.6
Imports		
Datsun	15.3	10.8
Honda	16.0	11.1
Mazda	17.5	12.7
Toyota	16.9	12.4
Volkswagen	11.3	10.0
Volvo	11.9	10.5

Source:
Consumer Reports annual auto issue, April 1981.

Note:
The data cover repair frequency of mechanical systems, components, and body (structure and finish). Ratings are given in five categories: average, below average, far below average, above average, and far above average. Beginning with a score of zero for far below average, we have assigned values of 5, 10, 15, and 20 to the other categories. The sum of the scores on body and mechanical systems gives the total score.

Exhibit IV

Customer loyalty
percent who would buy same make/model again

	Domestic	Imports	Total
Subcompact	77.2	91.6	81.2
Compact	74.2	91.4	72.4
Midsize	75.3	94.5	76.9
Standard	81.8	–	–
Luxury	86.6	94.6	87.2
Weighted average	78.7	91.8	–

Source:
Rogers National Research, *Buyer Profiles*, 1979.

2. See Robert H. Hayes, "Why Japanese Factories Work," HBR July-August 1981, p. 56.

Exhibit V **Seven factors affecting productivity: comparison of technology, management, and organization**

Factor, with ranking and relative weights	Definition	Comparative practice, Japan relative to United States
Process systems		
Process yield 1 (40%)	Output rate variations in conventional manufacturing lines; good parts per hour from a line, press, work group, or process line. Key determinants are machine cycle times, system uptime and reliability, affected by materials control methods, maintenance practices, and operating patterns.	Production-materials control minimizes inventory, reduces scrap, exposes problems. Line stops highlight problems and help eliminate defects. Operators perform routine maintenance; scheduling of two shifts instead of three leaves time for better maintenance.
Quality systems 5 (9%)	Series of controls and inspection plans to ensure that products are built to specifications.	Japanese use fewer inspectors. Some authority and responsibility are vested in production worker and supervisor; good relationship with supplier and very high standards lead to less incoming inspection.
Technology		
Process automation 4 (10%)	Introduction and adaptation of advanced, state-of-the-art manufacturing equipment.	Overall, state of technology is comparable. Japanese use more robots; their stamping facilities appear somewhat more automated than average U.S. facilities.
Product design 6 (7%)	Differences in the way the car is designed for a given market segment; aspects affecting productivity: tolerances, number of parts, fastening methods, etc.	Japanese have more experience in small car production and have emphasized design for manufacturability (i.e., productivity and quality). Newer U.S. models (Escort, GM J-car) are first models with design/manufacturing specifications comparable to Japanese.
Work force management		
Absenteeism 3 (12%)	All employee time away from the workplace, including excused, unexcused, medical, personal, contractual, and other reasons.	Levels of contractual time off are comparable; unexcused absences are much higher in United States.
Job structure 2 (18%)	Tasks and responsibilities included in job definitions.	Japanese practice is to create jobs with more breadth (more tasks or skill per job) and depth (more involvement in planning and control of operations); labor classifications are broader; regular production workers perform more skilled tasks; management layers are fewer.
Work pace 7 (4%)	Speed at which operators perform tasks.	Evidence is inconclusive; some lines run faster, some appear to run more slowly.

philosophy embodied in a contract may have had its origins in the very early days of the industry, long before unionization. Finally, many of the systems and practices that inhibit performance have little to do with a collective bargaining agreement.

Superior manufacturing performance, the key to the Japanese producers' competitive success, is therefore not the fruit of government policy, technical hardware, or national culture (Quadrants 1, 2, and 3). Instead it derives simply from the way people and operations are organized and managed (Quadrant 4).

Technological renewal

Having looked at causes, we now turn our attention to cures. In a time of expensive energy, by their success in the marketplace Japanese producers have rekindled interest in the automobile—especially the small, fuel-efficient automobile—as a product and thus have opened the way for technology to become the relevant basis of competition in the American market. As one General Motors executive remarked, "We took a look at the Honda Accord and we knew that the game had changed."

But does the American auto industry—or, for that matter, do government bureaucrats, lenders, and suppliers—really understand that the game has changed? Our investigation indicates that it has not—yet. We often hear two interpretations of the current crisis, both of them deeply flawed. By extension, both of these interpretations can apply to other sectors of the U.S. industrial economy.

Misperceptions of causes

The first of these interpretations, which we call "the natural consequences of maturity," holds that what has happened is the natural consequence of life cycle processes operating internationally on mature industrial sectors. Once an industry reaches the point where its production process has been embodied in equipment available for purchase—that is, once its mode of production is stable and well known—the location of factories

3. Edward M. Graham, "Technological Innovation and the Dynamics of the U.S. Competitive Advantage in International Trade," in *Technological Innovation for a Dynamic Economy*, edited by Christopher T. Hill and James M. Utterback (Elmsford, N.Y.: Pergamon Press, 1979), p. 152.

becomes a simple matter of exploiting geographic advantages in the relative costs of production. In this view, it makes perfect sense to move these facilities out of the United States as lower cost opportunities become available elsewhere.

Many economists argue that rather than coming to the aid of threatened industries, government and management should follow the path of least resistance, so to speak, and let the life cycle work its will. They recommend a policy not of intervention but, in the phrase of Edward M. Graham, of "positive adjustment." "Government should not," he writes, "protect or subsidize industries that are threatened by imports or [are otherwise] noncompetitive internationally, but should take concrete steps to encourage the transfer of resources from less into more competitive industries." [3]

The question of who is sufficiently infallible to be entrusted with the nasty job of picking winners and losers is, of course, conveniently left unanswered. The evidence to date suggests that no one is.

The second line of interpretation, which we call "transient economic misfortune," is a considerably more optimistic point of view. It holds that the present difficulties with automobiles are temporary, the result of rapid changes in oil prices and consumer preferences. Cost or quality is not the problem, but inappropriate capacity: too many facilities for building big cars.

The forces needed to right the competitive balance are even now locked into place, their happy result merely a matter of time and of bringing the needed capacity on line. Understandably, this view of things appealed strongly to many in the Carter administration, who could use it to rationalize a firm policy of doing nothing.

Both of these interpretive schemes are inadequate—not only because they ignore differences in Quadrant 4 management but also because they count on future stability in technology. Adherents of the maturity thesis assume an irreversible tendency of products to become standardized—that is, technologically stable over time. Adherents of the misfortune thesis, assuming that all outstanding technological problems have been solved, see the industry as needing only to bring the requisite capacity on line to recapture its competitive standing.

Both groups of adherents argue from a set of familiar but outdated assumptions about the relation of technology to industrial development. Looking back on the years since World War II as a period of competition in autos based mainly on economies of scale, styling, and service networks, they persist in viewing the car manufacturers as constituting a typical mature industry, in which any innovation is incremental, never radical, and is thus—in marketing terms—virtually invisible.

Exhibit VI **Determinants of process yield**

Rated machine speed total parts per hour	x	**Uptime** hours per year	x	**1-defect rate** good parts/ total parts	=	**Annual output of good parts**

Fluidity versus stability

Times have changed. Environmental concerns and the escalating price of oil have combined since the oil shock of 1979 to change the structure of market demand fundamentally. Technological innovation—in its radical as well as its incremental forms—again has vital competitive significance.

Changes in product technology have become at once more rapid and more extreme. Unlike most of the postwar period, recent technical advances have spawned a marked diversity in available systems and components. In engines alone, the once dominant V-8 has been joined by engines with four, five, and six cylinders, diesel engines, rotary engines, and engines with turbocharging and computer feedback control.

Moreover, these kinds of product innovation are increasingly radical in their effects on production processes. We have moved from a period in which product innovation focused on the refinement and extension of existing concepts to a period in which completely new concepts are developed and introduced. And this transition from a time of little change in production systems to a time of great turbulence in equipment, processes, skills, and organization is only beginning.

If our assessment is right, this shift in the nature of innovation will have far-reaching implications for the structure of the industry, the strategic decisions of companies, and the character of international trade. The supposedly mature auto industry now has the opportunity to embark on a technology-based process of rejuvenation in which the industry could recover the open-ended dynamics of its youth when competitive advantage was based largely on the ability to innovate.

Research has shown that manufacturing processes, no less than the products turned out, go through a life cycle evolution. As products evolve from low-volume, unstandardized, one-of-a-kind items toward high-volume, standardized, commoditylike items, the associated processes likewise evolve from individual job-shop production toward continuous-flow production. In other words, a product-process configuration, or productive unit that is initially fluid (relatively inefficient, flexible, and open to radical change), gradually becomes stable (relatively efficient, inflexible, and open only to incremental change).

This seemingly inexorable movement toward technological stability has long been the fate of the auto industry. Economies of scale on massive production lines have for more than a generation dictated the search for ever-greater product standardization and more streamlined production. Radical change in the underlying technology of either became competitively dysfunctional; the production unit was too finely tuned to wring out the last increment of marginal cost reduction—and its management too focused on organizational coordination and control—to allow the entrepreneurially fertile disruptions caused by radically new technology.[4]

The new industrial competition, however, has dated this older logic by rewarding the ability to compete on technological grounds. It has precipitated a technological ferment, which has in turn been supported by the market's post-1979 willingness to pay a premium for vehicles boasting new technology.

Consider, for example, the rapid market adoption of General Motors' X-bodies with their transaxle and transverse mounted engines; the popularity of enhanced four-cylinder engines like Ford's compound-valve hemispherical head; or the appeal of such fuel-saving materials as graphite fibers, dual-phased steel, and advanced plastics. As a result, the industry has begun to revitalize itself in a movement back to a more fluid process-product configuration in the companies and a more lively technology-based competition among them.

Technology-driven strategies

Three factors are the prime elements in the renewal of the auto industry: (1) an increasing premium in the marketplace on innovation, (2) a growing diversity in the technology of components and production processes, and (3) an increasingly radical effect of factors 1 and 2 on long-established configurations in the productive unit as a whole. These developments, in turn, have begun to define the structure and competitive dynamics of the industry in the years ahead—and the corporate strategies best suited to both.

The conventional wisdom about industry structure and strategy accepts an implicit equation between concentration and maturity. When technology-based competition heats up, this logic runs, industry concentration loosens. In such a case, car manufacturers will know how to adjust their strategies accordingly.

To be sure, in a capital-intensive industry with great economies of scale, a period of ferment in product technology often allows manufacturers to offer an increasing variety of products at or below the cost of the old product mix. Especially when the production technology is well understood and easily procurable (in the form of equipment or human skills), companies on the fringe of the industry and fresh entrants can identify and exploit new market niches. Technological activity, market growth, and industry deconcentration usually go hand in hand.

When, however, the ferment in product technology is so extreme that it causes fundamental alterations in process technology, the same degree of activity may have very different results. In this case the immediate effect of a process-linked industry renewal may well be to *increase* the degree and the stability of concentration—that is, as many believe, to push industry structure apparently in the direction of *greater* maturity.

Where these observers go wrong is in failing to distinguish concentration from maturity or, said another way, in assuming that all evidence of frozen or rising concentration is evidence of movement toward maturity. This may, but need not, be the case.

In the auto field, for example, some corporate responses to the prospect of radical process innovation probably will take the industry farther along the road to maturity. Because truly radical product changes are still some years off and because commitments to existing process technology are large (especially in the standard model segment), it is reasonable to expect producers with experience in the older technologies to defend their positions through technical alterations that reduce costs or improve performance but do not make their processes obsolete.

Such a strategy requires the high volumes necessary for scale economies. As a result, the strategy may help concentrate production—either through greater use of joint ventures or, if the scale effects are great enough, through mergers and like forms of mature industry consolidation.

4. For a discussion of the evolution toward industrial maturity, see James M. Utterback and William J. Abernathy, "A Dynamic Model of Process and Product Innovation," *Omega*, vol. 3, 1975, p. 639.

5. Alfred P. Sloan, Jr., *My Years with General Motors* (Garden City, N.Y.: Doubleday, 1964), pp. 186-187.

Other corporate responses to process-linked renewal may have the opposite effect. Major innovations in products that are linked to innovations in process technology often permit drastic reductions in production costs or improvements in performance, thus making possible the higher volumes necessary to expand market share. These innovations, however, usually involve large capital outlays as well as development of hard-to-acquire skills on the part of workers and management. So they require large increases in volume to offset the greater investment. As a result, only the leading producers may be able to profit from the process innovations and thus, temporarily at least, enhance their market share and reinforce industry concentration.

Though this pattern of concentration may appear identical to the one we have described, nothing could be further from the truth. Here a consolidation of the market serves to throw the industry into technological ferment that stimulates further technological competition—not to lock it into older process technology.

In time, this upheaval in process technology may even provide the competitive basis for new entrants to the field. Depending on the nature of process advances in auto production, companies in related industries (electronics, for example, or engines or energy) may find invasion of the market an attractive strategic option. But even if a decade from now these new entrants have not materialized, the forces that made their participation possible will have changed the competitive structure of the industry in two fundamental ways:

Whatever its immediate tendency, industry concentration will in the long run have become far less stable than at present.

The basis of competition will have changed to reflect the now-crucial importance of technology-driven strategies.

The challenge to management

Once U.S. auto manufacturers understand that energy prices and internationalization of competition have altered the industry's old competitive dynamics, they have to decide how they want to compete under the new rules of the game. It may be best for them to avoid duplicating the Japanese pattern of competition. At any rate, after decades of the maturing process, the basis for competing is in flux for U.S. producers and radical rethinking about strategy—not blind imitation—is in order.

The industrial landscape in America is littered with the remains of once-successful companies that could not adapt their strategic vision to altered conditions of competition. If the automobile producers prove unequal to the new reality that confronts them, their massive, teeming plants will become the ghost towns of late twentieth century America. The same, of course, holds true for all companies, large and small, in those old-line manufacturing industries exposed to assault from abroad. Only those able to see the new industrial competition for what it is and to devise appropriate strategies for participating in it will survive.

Managers must recognize that they have entered a period of competition that requires of them a technology-driven strategy, a mastery of efficient production, and an unprecedented capacity for work force management. They cannot simply copy what others do but must find their own way. No solutions are certain, no strategies assured of success. But the nature of the challenge is clear.

Henry Ford, as Alfred P. Sloan recalled him, was a man who had had "... many brilliant insights in [his] earlier years, [but] seemed never to understand how completely the market had changed from the one in which he had made his name and to which he was accustomed.... The old master failed to master change." [5] That is still the crucial challenge—and opportunity.

See next page for Appendix

Appendix: The Japanese cost advantage

Table A Calculation of U.S. and Japanese labor costs for a subcompact vehicle

	1	2	3	4	5	6 [4 x 5]	7 [6 x .575]
	Share in OEM manufacturing costs	**Average OEM hours per vehicle**	**Estimated OEM employee cost per hour**	**Estimated cost per vehicle**	**Labor content**	**Labor cost per vehicle**	**U.S.-Japan difference**
OEM labor							
Hourly	.24	65	$ 18	$ 1,170	100 %	$ 1,170	$ 673
Salaried	.08	15	21	315	100	315	181
Purchased components	.39	NA	NA	1,901	66	1,255	721
Purchased materials	.14	NA	NA	683	25	171	98
Total	–	–	–	**$ 4,875**	**NA**	**$ 2,911**	**$ 1,673**

Notes:
OEM hourly labor is defined as total nonexempt and includes direct and indirect production workers. The calculations assume an exchange rate of 218 yen per dollar. The method of calculation and sources of data are as follows:

Column 1 contains estimates of the share of total manufacturing cost accounted for by direct and indirect production labor (at the OEM level), purchased components, and materials. These estimates do not reflect the experience of any one company but approximate an industry average. They are based on data prepared for the National Research Council's Committee on Motor Vehicle Emissions as well as on discussions with industry sources. The latter have also provided us with the data in columns 2, 3, and 5.

We made the calculation of U.S.-Japan cost differences in three steps. We first used the data in columns 2 and 3 to get an OEM labor cost per vehicle of $1,170, then extrapolated using the cost shares (column 1) to arrive at a total manufactured cost and the cost of purchased components and materials (column 4). We next multiplied the cost per vehicle in column 4 by an estimate of the labor content of the three categories presented in column 5. The data imply, for example, that $1,255 of the $1,901 cost of components is labor cost. Finally, we calculated the Japan-U.S. labor cost gap by multiplying the U.S. data in column 6 by 0.575, the adjustment factor derived from our estimate of the Japan-to-U.S. unit labor cost ratio.* Thus column 7 provides an estimate of the difference in the cost of producing a subcompact vehicle in the United States and Japan due to differences in unit labor costs, not only at the OEM level but also at the supplier level.

*Let C(US) and C(J) indicate unit labor costs in the United States and Japan. We estimate C(J)/C(US) = .425. We want to know C(US)−C(J). Column 6 gives us C(US). Thus, C(US)−C(J) = $\left(1 - \frac{C(J)}{C(US)}\right)$ x column 6; this result is in column 7.

Table B Ford and Toyo Kogyo's estimated per-vehicle employee costs in 1979

	Ford	Toyo Kogyo
Domestic car and truck production* in millions	3.163	0.983
Total domestic employment†		
Automotive	219,599	24,318
Nonautomotive	19,876	2,490
Total domestic employee hours‡		
Automotive in millions	355.75	46.20
Total employee cost§		
Automotive in millions	$ 7,794.50	$ 482.20
Employee hours per vehicle	112.5	47.0
Employee cost per vehicle	$ 2,464	$ 491

*Ford figure excludes 65,000 imported vehicles; Toyo Kogyo figure is adjusted for production of knock-down assembly kits.

†Data on automotive employment and costs were obtained by assuming that the ratio of automotive employment to total employment was the same as the ratio of sales. The same assumption was made to obtain Ford employment costs.

‡Ford hours were determined by assuming that each employee worked 1,620 hours per year; Toyo Kogyo hours assume 1,900 hours. These adjustments reflect vacations, holidays, leaves, and absences.

§Data include salaries, wages, and fringe benefits. Toyo Kogyo compensation data were derived by updating a 1976 figure using compensation growth rates at Toyota. An exchange rate of 218 yen/$ (1979 average) was used to convert yen.

Table C **Product mix adjustment**

	Ford	Toyo Kogyo
1. Ratio of car to total vehicle production	0.645	0.652
2. Production shares by size		
Small	0.11	0.83
Medium	0.68	0.17
Large	0.21	–
3. Relative manufacturing cost by size		
Small	1.00	NA
Medium	1.35	NA
Large	1.71	NA
4. Weighted average of relative manufacturing cost small = 1.00	1.38	1.06
5. Production of Toyo Kogyo mix at Ford level of integration		
Employee cost per vehicle	$ 1,893	$ 589
Employee hours per vehicle	87	56

Notes:
Line 2 for Ford assumes that only Pinto and Bobcat models are small; Mustang and Capri sales were placed in the medium category.

Line 5 for Ford is obtained by multiplying lines 6 and 7 in *Exhibit B* by (1.06/1.38).

Table B uses the data on manufacturing costs by vehicle size developed for the Committee on Motor Vehicle Emissions of the National Research Council in 1974. We derived estimates of the cost to Ford of producing the Toyo Kogyo mix by first computing a weighted average of the relative manufacturing cost indices with Ford's 1979 production shares by size as weights. The ratio of the comparable Toyo Kogyo weighted average (1.06) to the Ford weighted average (1.38) was used to adjust both costs and productivity as a means of estimating the effect of product mix on Ford's average cost and labor hours per vehicle. After these adjustments we estimate that Ford would require 87 employee hours to produce the average-size vehicle in the Toyo Kogyo product line, compared with 56 hours in the Japanese company. Labor cost per vehicle is just over $1,300 higher at Ford. These comparisons are based on the average-size vehicle at Toyo Kogyo. For a small vehicle (i.e., Pinto vs. Mazda GLC), the Ford estimate is 82 hours per vehicle, while the comparable Toyo Kogyo figure is 53; the corresponding costs per vehicle are $1,785 (Ford) and $566 (Toyo Kogyo). Even this adjustment may overstate costs and hours required to produce the Toyo Kogyo mix at Ford if the trucks and commercial vehicles produced by the two companies differ substantially.

4 Efficient investment capital– the hidden secret?

Can more capital buy higher productivity?

A new way to evaluate investments may help companies find the answer

Bradley T. Gale

By now, corporate managers may be tiring of the debate that has been swirling around the question of declining U.S. productivity, a debate that has generated much discussion but few practical or new suggestions for a turnaround. Often, companies have injected capital into declining industries to improve their own productivity levels without achieving any long-term, tangible objectives. According to the Strategic Planning Institute (SPI), part of the problem may be a lack of analytic tools available to top management. Instead of relegating improvement of productivity to line managers, SPI feels, top management must decide for itself where capital should be allocated. To that end, SPI is using its data base comprised of confidential information culled from more than 200 member companies to help solve the problem. In this article, the research director of SPI offers companies practical guidelines and formulas for more accurate productivity measurement and better linking of strategic planning to capital allocation.

Mr. Gale has been director of research at SPI since February 1975 and is directly in charge of overseeing the institute's Profit Impact of Market Strategy research program. He was assisted in the preparation of the article by Sidney Schoeffler, Ronald B. Boheim, Gerard Badler, Donald F. Heany, and Donald J. Swire, as well as by Ruth G. Newman on the editorial front.

Reprint number 80403

Whether you are a manager or an economist, you know about the mounting evidence of declining productivity in the United States. In fact, signs suggest that the need for productivity improvement may be our most pressing domestic economic problem—and our most difficult to solve. But before we can tackle it, we first need to find a useful way to measure operating effectiveness. If we can't accurately establish which businesses are falling behind and why, then we can't sensibly determine corrective actions.

Out of a desire to do something, business and government have promoted solutions: shop-level approaches that require cost cutting, efficiency experts, stringent controls, and behavior modification—or mechanization/automation programs aimed at increasing labor productivity, lowering costs, and boosting margins. Very frequently, not knowing the cause of the illness—in fact not even having correctly identified the patient—we prescribe medicine whose effects are at best dissipated and at worst cause havoc.

Rather than haphazardly funding individual projects, management needs to determine which businesses have the strategic characteristics that make them good candidates for mechanization. Even more important, management needs to know which businesses are poor candidates for mechanization. With appropriate measurement tools, strategic planning can be linked to the capital allocation process, and companies can avoid both unproductive investments

Editor's note: HBR readers have benefited from the SPI approach to management problems before. "Impact of Strategic Planning on Profit Performance," by Sidney Schoeffler, Robert D. Buzzell, and Donald F. Heany, was published in March-April 1974, p. 137; and "Market Share—A Key to Profitability," by Robert D. Buzzell, Bradley T. Gale, and Ralph G.M. Sultan, appeared in the January-February 1975 issue, p. 97.

and investments that gain output per employee but at excessive costs.

Many companies delegate the problem of productivity improvement to operating managers who are "close to the action." Although it is important to involve them, this focus is narrow; it misses the essential links among productivity improvement, strategic planning, and capital allocation. A broader approach involving key decision makers and long-term planning seems essential.

Rather than evaluating investment in new equipment as a simple choice between increased capital costs and reduced labor costs, management needs to consider the long-term consequences of mechanization. Increased investment always affects the competitive climate; in the short run, it almost invariably reduces ROI (return on net plant and equipment and working capital). But the long-run outcome depends on how a business is structured within its own economic environment.

The Strategic Planning Institute in Cambridge, Massachusetts has used its data base to develop guidelines for businesses contemplating new investments to increase productivity (see the accompanying ruled insert). These guidelines offer managers some practical advice for their own businesses by focusing on the following key questions:

> Which businesses should be allowed to mechanize-automate?

> Is a business's output per employee above or below par?

> How is operating effectiveness best measured?

> When do shop-level approaches to labor productivity pay off?

> How can sound portfolio management improve capital and labor productivity?

Which businesses should automate further?

The SPI data base offers empirical support for the belief that labor output can be increased by investing more capital equipment per worker. But it also tells us that labor output is influenced by other factors: a high market share or a high level of capacity utilization helps to boost labor output; unionization and new product introduction, on the other hand, tend to reduce it.

To monitor and control productivity, we must first be able to measure it. But that is not simple. Different productivity measures are needed for different purposes. They range from engineering concepts of efficiency (physical units of output per physical unit of input) to financial concepts of profitability (total revenues to total costs). And between these extremes are measures such as unit labor costs (dollars of input per unit of output) and labor output (value added per unit of input).

Most managers are familiar with Murphy's law: "If it can go wrong, it will." When it comes to measuring productivity, a less-known corollary, Howe's law, is equally compelling: "Every man has a scheme that will not work." At SPI, we prefer to use the concept of value added, which represents the amount that purchased raw materials and components increase in value when they have been converted into the products of the business or—stated another way—a firm's sales minus its purchases. Dividing value added by the number of employees gives a measure of labor output that is comparable across businesses. In addition, it reflects both the physical output of each worker and the value of that output.

The concept of value added per employee is not designed to measure every aspect of productivity. But it *is* designed to enable multibusiness general managers to compare both the level and the rate of change in output per employee across their portfolios. The value-added concept is applied in a way that takes capital (as well as labor) inputs into account and also links productivity improvement to profitability through strategic planning and sound capital allocation.

The various businesses included in the SPI data base show a wide distribution of value added per employee. Across the large sample, businesses register from less than $10,000 to more than $60,000.

Productivity & profitability

As might be expected, we have found that fixed investment increases labor output. Yet, even though investment in equipment to automate production does allow each worker to add greater amounts of value, mechanization is *not* an all-purpose panacea for problems in labor output. For most businesses, unfortunately, we have also found that increased investment intensity reduces profitability.

The explanation for this disquieting relationship is not merely arithmetic. There are several good reasons why investment intensity hurts ROI:

☐ Increasing investment can lead to aggressive competition, especially when economic conditions worsen and plant and equipment are only partially used. The resulting pressure to use capacity can explode into price and marketing wars.

The data base backup

This article is based on a study of more than 1,700 businesses included in the data base assembled by the Strategic Planning Institute (SPI), a non-profit, tax-exempt organization located in Cambridge, Massachusetts. Known as the PIMS (profit impact of market strategy) program, the data base includes the strategy experiences, both good and bad, of product and service businesses operated by the more than 200 member companies of all sizes located in North America, Europe, and Australia. Each "business" is a division, product line, or other profit center within its parent company, selling a distinct set of products or services to an identifiable group of customers, in competition with a well-defined set of companies. For each, a meaningful separation can be made of revenues, operating costs, investments, and strategic plans.

SPI disguises and summarizes the information in the data base before making it available to member companies. It documents the actions taken by each business, the market it serves, its competitive environment, and the financial results achieved. Included in the data are over 200 separate characteristics of each business experience, not only traditional balance sheet and income statement data but also information about market share, investment intensity, productivity, product quality, and unionization.

□ Heavy fixed investment acts as a barrier to *exit*. When the business cycle turns down or when the real growth rate of an industry declines, investment-intensive businesses are hurt the most. (Heavy investment intensity does not represent a barrier to *entry*, because investment is measured as a ratio to employees, not as an absolute amount of investment required.)

□ Managers sometimes focus on a normal return on sales, forgetting the heavier than normal investment per dollar of sales required for some projects. A normal return on sales combined with a greater than normal amount of investment per dollar of sales yields a lower return on investment.

There are many examples of investment-intensive, low-profit businesses—commodity paper, chemical and steel products, to name a few. For the average business (neither a good nor a bad mechanization candidate), ROI will fall with increased investment in mechanization.

Even with this likelihood, such an investment may still be desirable. Those projects that indicate a negative net prospect for percentage ROI often promise a favorable one for dollar results because the lower percentage is applied to a larger investment base. In such cases, it seems that management faces a difficult decision: it must choose between increased sales and dollar profits on the one hand and a decreased rate of profitability on the other.

But our findings also show that certain conditions —a large market share, low rate of new product introduction, and good capacity utilization (see *Exhibit I*)—enhance the benefits of investment intensity and alleviate the threats to profitability and thus help ease management's task.

Relative market share

Relative market share has a positive effect on value added per employee. A large share relative to competitors usually allows greater labor specialization and economies of scale within the business, resulting in increased efficiency. Large-share businesses also enjoy economies of cumulative volume, which reduce unit costs by the experience-curve effect and by spreading set-up costs over a longer production run.

At first glance, it seems that higher investment greatly helps value added per employee, regardless of whether market share is large or small (see *Exhibit II*). For large-share businesses, the difference in value added between high-investment and low-investment businesses ($51,000 minus $20,000) is $31,000. For small-share businesses the comparable difference is $25,000. However, closer inspection shows that the positive effect of investment on value added is greater when the market share is large. Moreover, this greater increment of value added allows large-share businesses to sustain their very high rates of return on investment even though they have much more investment per employee at stake.

In contrast, small-share businesses do not have a big enough value-added increment to prevent their already low rate of profit from being lowered further by investment intensity. The average ROI of small-share businesses that are investment intensive is about 25% lower than those that are not investment intensive—13% versus 17% (see *Exhibit II*).

Rate of new product introduction

New product introduction is usually associated with a reduction in labor output and profits (*Exhibit III*). Manufacturing a new product often requires reorganizing the production process. New methods of production must be perfected and learned by workers, so downtime and waste tend to be greater during the early life of a product.

For businesses with a low rate of new product introduction, the value-added differential between high-investment and low-investment businesses is $32,000, or $49,000 minus $17,000 (see *Exhibit III*). For businesses with a high rate of new product introduction, the corresponding differential is only

$21,000, probably because the effectiveness of a mechanized production system is disrupted by the continuous appearance of new products.

Even though they have more investment at stake, businesses with a low rate of new product introduction get a large enough boost from value added to allow them to sustain their ROI. In contrast, businesses with a high rate of new product introduction do not. In fact, the average ROI of businesses with a high rate of new product introduction and high investment per employee is about 30% lower than that of low-investment businesses—17% versus 24% (see *Exhibit III*).

Other influences

While the preceding variables may carry the greatest weight in determining a particular business's relative capacity to improve its productivity, other—perhaps less tangible—factors can affect its chance of success as well, including the degree of unionization, capacity utilization, real market growth, and the extent to which its product lines are standardized or made to order.

Heavy unionization: This often leads to low profitability and labor output, perhaps by work rules that inhibit production and by impediments to the rate of technological change. Frequently, unions bargain for work rules that result in slower production or lower production quotas. Unions also resist any reduction in the work force implied by an employer's move toward additional automation. Sometimes, unions bargain for a larger portion of value added as wages, thus leaving a smaller one for profits.

Even more significant, unions may actually reduce the amount of value added per employee available to be split between wages and profits (see *Exhibit IV*). Alternatively, perhaps businesses with a low level of labor output are more likely to become unionized, while those where morale is good and productivity high may be less susceptible to unionization.

Capacity utilization: At high operating levels, fixed costs are spread over a large volume of output and usually reduce unit costs. High capacity utilization also tends to elevate selling prices and profit margins, considerably boosting ROI.

Surprisingly enough, however, capacity utilization has only a weak, though positive, impact on value added per employee, because marginal, inexperienced employees are hired during peak operating times, while more experienced employees are re-

Exhibit I

Some businesses are good candidates for mechanization; others are not

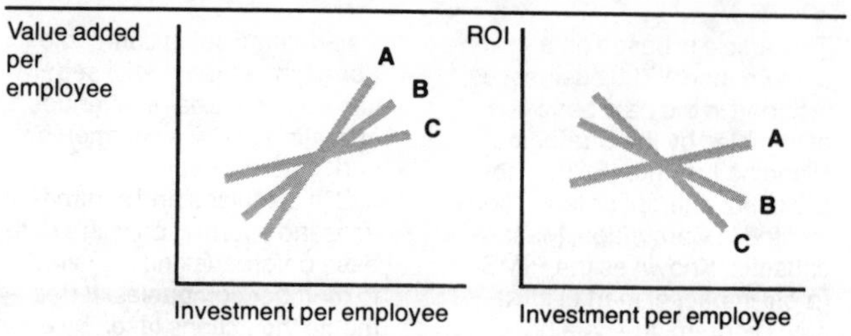

A: Good candidate for mechanization (high share, low rate of new product introduction, good capacity utilization, rapid real market growth, etc.)

B: Average business

C: Poor candidate (low share, high rate of new product introduction, low capacity utilization, negative real market growth, etc.)

Exhibit II

High-share businesses get a bigger output boost from heavy investment

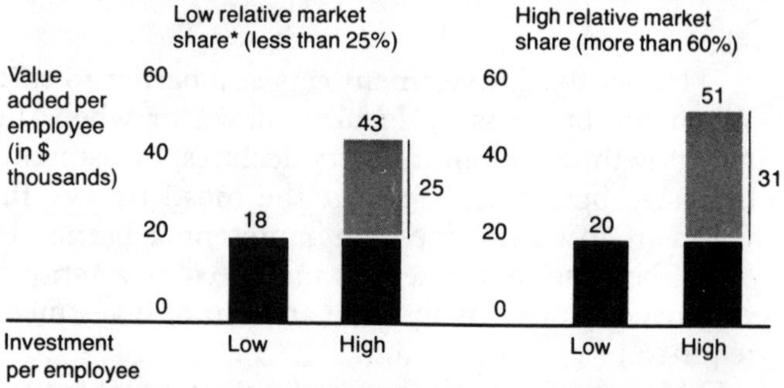

***Note:** Relative market share is defined as a business's share of its served market divided by the combined shares of its three largest competitors.

High-share businesses are better able to maintain ROI, no matter how investment intensive

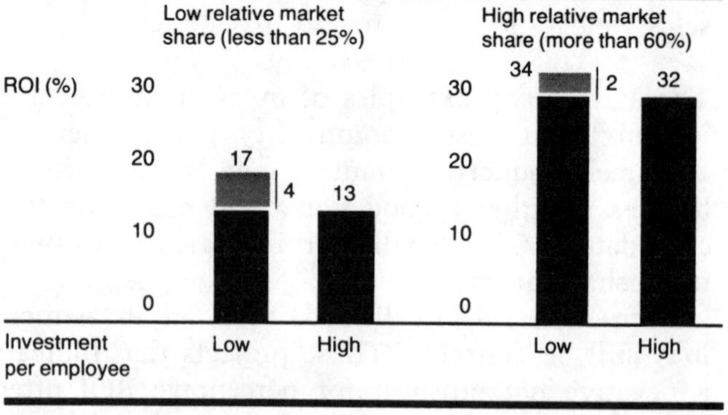

Exhibit III

Businesses with a low rate of new product introduction get a bigger output boost from heavy investment

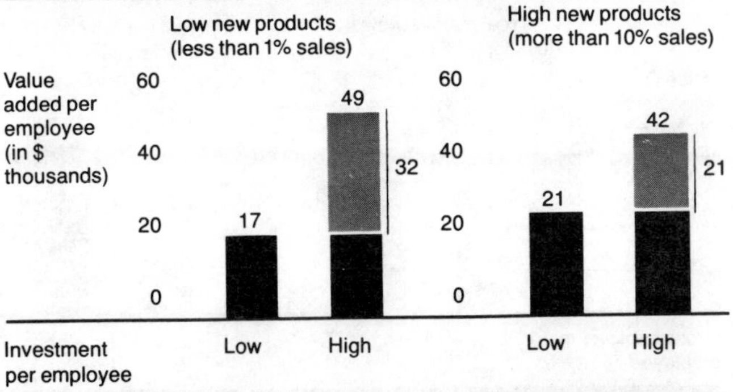

Among investment-intensive businesses, those with a low rate of new product introduction are better able to maintain ROI

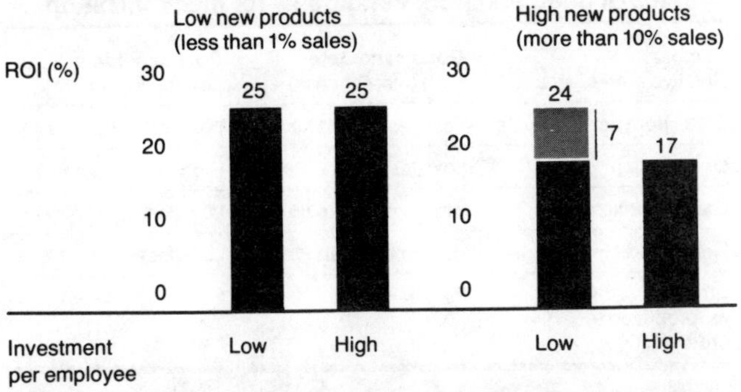

Exhibit IV

Businesses with a low degree of unionization* get a bigger output boost from heavy investment

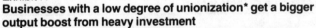

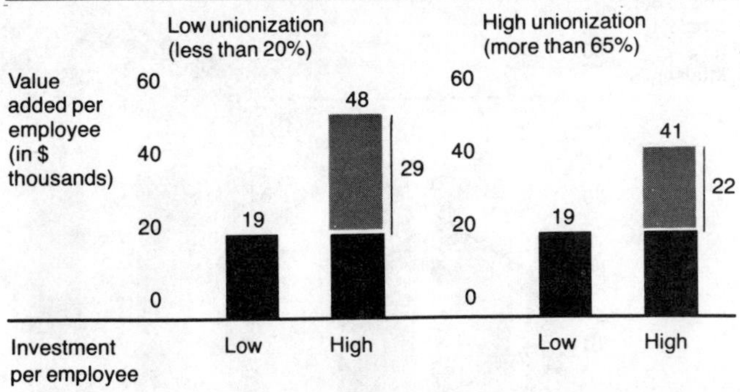

***Note:** Unionization is measured as the percentage of unionized employees in a business (managerial and nonmanagerial, salaried and hourly).

tained at low ones. (For businesses with high fixed capital intensity, the positive effect is somewhat stronger.)

Real market growth: Real market growth helps value added per employee, especially when fixed capital intensity is high (see *Exhibit V*). Slow growth rates may depress margins, particularly when growth is negative and plant and equipment cannot be liquidated easily. Rapid growth will tend to increase sales margins when the increase in demand is not fully anticipated and supply is short. Rapid growth does not increase ROI very much, because new plant and equipment are required, frequently at an inflated cost that has only partially been depreciated.

Standardized vs. made to order: Product differentiation tends to be more prevalent among businesses producing made-to-order goods. When a business carries a high level of investment per employee, product differentiation provides some insurance against price or marketing wars. By contrast, businesses that make nondifferentiated products are subject to severe price competition, especially when demand is slack and a lot of investment is at stake.

Scoring your mechanization payoff

From our findings, profiles can be constructed that indicate the strength of a particular business as a candidate for increased mechanization (see *Exhibit VI*). Generally speaking, good candidates can be identified by high market share, low rate of new product introduction, nonunionization, high capacity utilization, rapid real market growth, and differentiated products.

If one of your businesses closely matches the profile of a good candidate, then mechanization could result in dramatic increases in its labor output with almost no injury to profitability. On the other hand, if a business looks like a poor candidate, automation is likely to seriously injure profits while only slightly increasing labor output.

You can score your own businesses on their potential mechanization payoffs by referring to the percentage ranking for good and poor candidates in *Exhibit VI*. Give a business 3 points for any attribute that puts it on the good-candidate list, 2 points for a percentage rank that puts it midway, and 1 point for an attribute that categorizes it as a poor candidate. Using this tabulation, you will see that the average business will receive 12 points; the range will be from 6 points for a particularly doubtful candidate to 18 points for an excellent candidate.

Some companies allocate resources by funding individual projects that are designed to carry them over a particular hurdle; more suitably, they should set business strategies and provide the required investment funds for the entire program. A narrow focus is frequently accompanied by optimistic financial projections that are not borne out by the realities of the business's strategic position. Companies that fund projects rather than business strategies should reconsider any mechanization projects approved for businesses with scores of 10 points or less.

Is your value added per employee above or below par?

Can you judge whether your business is appropriately productive, given your amount of fixed investment? You can–if you use your fixed investment per employee as a measure. Suppose, for example, your business averages $35,000 of output per employee. If you compare this figure with the average for a business with your amount of investment per employee, you can judge how you are doing (see *Exhibit VII*).

Let's say your investment is between $7,000 and $12,000. Your business is doing very well indeed, because the average output for a business with this investment intensity is only $25,000. If your fixed investment is between $30,000 and $40,000, however, your value added level of $35,000 is well below the norm ($55,000) for businesses with this high a level of investment intensity. But if your fixed investment is between $17,000 and $27,000, you are right on target–you might reasonably expect a value added of about $35,000.

The basic tool we use is shown in *Exhibit VII*, which provides a benchmark for comparing productivity levels (value added) of businesses with different amounts of fixed investment. Here's how it works: (1) calculate the dollar amount of plant and equipment per employee for your business, (2) position your business along the horizontal axis of *Exhibit VII*, and (3) use the trend line to find the level of value added per employee normally achieved by businesses with your amount of fixed investment. A business with $36,000 of fixed investment would have a value added norm of about $44,000. Check to see where your business falls in relation to the trend line.

Exhibit V

Businesses in growing markets get a bigger output boost from heavy fixed investment

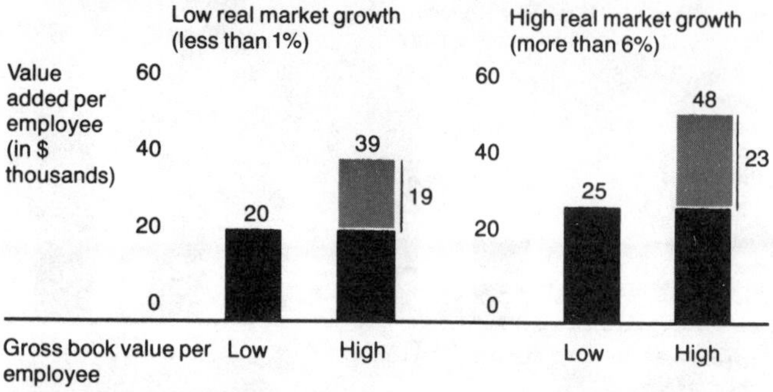

Exhibit VI

Profiles of good and poor candidates for mechanization

Factor	Good candidate	Poor candidate
Relative market share	High (more than 60%)	Low (less than 25%)
Sales from new products	Low (less than 1%)	High (more than 10%)
Unionization	Low (less than 20%)	High (more than 65%)
Capacity utilization	High (more than 85%)	Low (less than 70%)
Real market growth	High (more than 6%)	Low (less than −1%)
Standardized (S) vs. produced to order (PTO)	PTO	S

Exhibit VII

Setting benchmarks for value added per employee (based on a single factor)

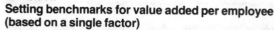

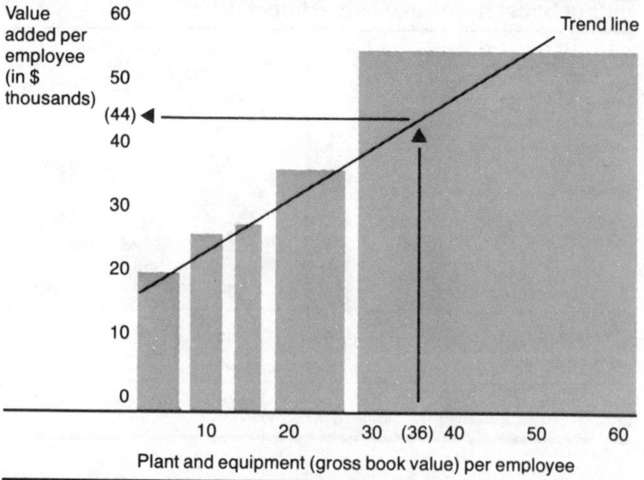

Exhibit VIII
Business profiles and corresponding par levels of value added per employee

Businesses	A	B	C
Relative market share (%)	15%	130%	130%
Sales from new products	30	2	2
Unionization	85	0	0
Capacity utilization	60	90	90
Real market growth rate	1	8	8
Standardized (S) vs. produced to order (PTO)	S	PTO	PTO
Fixed investment per employee	$30,000	$30,000	$15,000
Par value added per employee	$24,000	$41,000	$30,000

Exhibit IX
Operating effectiveness has a dramatic positive effect on profitability

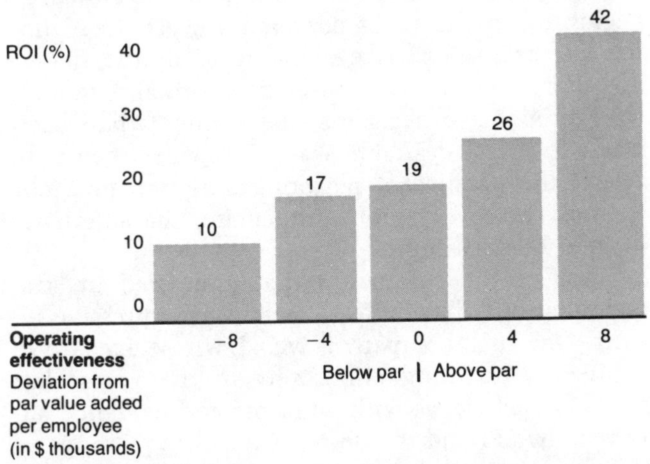

So far, we have used fixed investment alone to establish a benchmark. However, suppose two businesses each have $36,000 of fixed investment per employee, but one is serving a rapid-growth market and the other, a declining market. If we look back at the findings about real market growth (*Exhibit V*), we find that investment-intensive businesses in rapid-growth markets average $48,000 value added, while those in declining markets average $39,000. The norm of $44,000, based solely on fixed investment, can be refined, therefore, by incorporating information on the real market growth rate.

Since several other factors besides fixed investment influence value added per employee, it is possible to establish a more realistic benchmark or par by adjusting the norms from the trend line in *Exhibit VII* up or down depending on a business's capacity utilization, market share, market growth rate, degree of unionization, and rate of new product introduction. The SPI data base has been used to develop a model that, when applied to data from different time periods, automatically makes adjustments for the effects of inflation. Factors included in the model are: (1) consistent with economic theory, (2) reasonable to knowledgeable businessmen, (3) statistically significant, and (4) controllable by management. Once par has been established for each business, a manager can assess the actual value added of each business in the portfolio against par.

To illustrate this par concept, *Exhibit VIII* shows profiles of three businesses and indicates the par level of value added per employee for each. Business A (par $24,000) and Business B (par $41,000) have the same fixed investment per employee. However, in contrast to Business B, Business A has a weak relative market share, is highly unionized, offers standardized products, and serves a slow-growth market. One might say A has a weaker strategic position and therefore a lower par.

By comparing Businesses B and C (par $30,000), you'll see they differ only in fixed investment per employee. Since Business B has a stronger strategic position than A and more investment than C, Business B has the highest par. Given the productivity-influencing characteristics of your business, you can estimate the level of value added per employee that is your par.

How can you measure operating effectiveness?

Differences between actual and par arise from factors not included in the model used to establish par, such as employee motivation and morale or management's organizational ability.

How should you interpret the difference from par? After taking into account the effects of key structural influences (e.g., fixed investment per employee), the deviation from par can be considered as a measure of *operating effectiveness* relative to other businesses. Its impact is positive and dramatic (as shown in *Exhibit IX*); moving a business from well below par to near par roughly doubles its ROI.

Separating actual value added into its par and deviation from par components helps to indicate the kind of action management should take to improve labor productivity. As we discuss in the following section, the appropriate action depends on whether the par for the business is low or the business itself is below par.

When does tradition pay off?

Managers responsible for a portfolio of businesses can rank those businesses according to their differences from par. Businesses that are below par need more traditional, shop-level productivity programs, such as those to improve either managerial effectiveness or worker motivation.

By contrast, consider one of your businesses that should have a very low par but is performing somewhat above par. Because it is already above par, its operating effectiveness has probably received management attention and is under control, so a shop-level program is less likely to succeed. The par/deviation from par framework indicates instead that the low level of output per employee is due to the production structure, market environment, and competitive position of the business (the low par).

Whether such a business is a good candidate for mechanization to increase value added per employee (without reducing ROI) can be analyzed by scoring the business's mechanization payoff potential. If the business has several structural characteristics that place it in the poor-candidate category, these weaknesses should be addressed before attempting a mechanization strategy.

Exhibit X
Improvements in Mead asset mix and return on net assets

	Asset mix		Return on net assets	
	1972	1976	1972	1976
Inappropriate businesses for Mead	13.2%	2.1%	2.4%	4.2%
Businesses with good strategies in place	38.5	53.4	8.8	9.6
Businesses undergoing strategic changes	48.3	44.5	2.8	11.8
Total corporate return on net assets			4.7%	10.4%

How to manage a portfolio to improve productivity

In the past, most efforts to improve productivity were tactical actions at the shop level. However, beginning in the 1950s companies began to realize the importance of strategic planning. By the 1960s—and more prevalently in the 1970s—formal structures were brought to decisions that formerly had been made in a less desirable way. Companies began to accept the practice of performing a strategic audit to analyze the key profit-influencing characteristics of their business units.

Some of the companies that pioneered in strategic planning have already achieved impressive results. One such company is Mead, whose executives evolved a planning philosophy in the 1970s that blended their ideas with concepts and evidence advanced by SPI and the Boston Consulting Group.[1]

In 1972, Mead conducted an extensive review of its market segments and product lines. The major objective was to focus incremental capital on businesses where cost-effective leadership was possible. To implement this strategy, Mead concentrated on three factors: capital allocation, people management, and asset management. Specifically, Mead executives decided to:

> Eliminate low-growth businesses with low market share.

> Move emphasis from lower-priced, commodity-type businesses to higher-priced, value-added lines.

> Obtain market leadership if possible (e.g., in paperboard, focus on market share and specialty products; in paper, focus on product lines where technical capability exists).

> Monitor significant drifts toward investment intensity by individual businesses.

> Discourage investment-intensive solutions to business problems and encourage, through business

1. This section draws on two 1977 Mead Corporation booklets, "Why Strategic Planning?" and "Mead Executive Management Presentation to Paper and Forest Products Analysts." (Available from Mead World Headquarters, Courthouse Plaza Northeast, Dayton, Ohio 45463.)

planning and capital-project review, creative solutions that are not investment intensive.

Major divestitures made by Mead during the past few years include a pig iron business, two soil pipe plants, two container plants, a lime business, a cement business, an upholstery operation, a school and commercial supply business, a company making paper plates, a partnership in a Belgian paper mill, a ferroalloy business, a distribution chain for educational products, and a 50% interest in an asbestos and plastic pipe business. For the most part, these divested businesses produced commodity-type undifferentiated products, had small market shares, and their percentage in Mead's asset mix declined from 13% in 1972 to only 2% in 1976 (see *Exhibit X*).

By contrast, the percentage of Mead's asset mix in businesses that had good strategies increased from 39% to 53%. In addition, about half of Mead's assets were tied up in businesses undergoing strategic changes in 1972. These businesses increased their return on net assets from 2.8% in 1972 to 11.8% in 1976. Thus, by shifting its asset mix toward more profitable businesses and improving the profit rate of businesses undergoing strategic change, Mead was able to achieve a dramatic increase in corporate profitability.

Mead also devoted a great deal of attention to people management in these five years. The company held a seminar for some 300 of its managers to familiarize them with the new approach to financial and strategic planning. In addition, Mead reorganized several businesses, made changes in management, and improved productivity by monitoring and reducing the number of employees per dollar of sales.

Mead's concentration on people and asset management achieved substantial results. Investment per employee between 1972 and 1976 measured in current dollars increased about 40%, or 7% at an annual rate, a slight decline in real terms. By contrast, value added per employee measured in current dollars increased by 80%, or about 12.5% per year. By improving its strategic position, Mead was thus able to increase its value added per employee without a corresponding increase in investment per employee. In addition, Mead's asset-management program resulted in an 18% reduction in investment per dollar of sales.

Taken together, the capital-allocation, people-management, and asset-management programs allowed Mead to more than double its return on total capital, from 4% in 1972 to 11.2% in 1976. In addition, Mead's standing in terms of return on total capital improved among the 16 largest forest products companies, from 12th in 1972 to 4th in 1976.

How these comparisons can help

Investment in new plant and equipment is often evaluated in terms of increased capital and reduced labor costs. This conventional perspective is incomplete because it ignores key factors that affect capital and labor productivity. It is also misleading because no consideration is given to the way increased investment affects the competitive climate and, inevitably, selling-price levels in the industry.

Executives need an objective benchmark to help them evaluate actual versus potential levels of output per employee. The methods of comparison presented here allow them to pinpoint which businesses need which kinds of productivity-improvement programs. Those businesses that are below par for value added per employee probably need more traditional, shop-level productivity programs.

To balance capital and labor productivity, a business's production structure as well as its competitive position and market environment must be considered. The score for mechanization-payoff potential can help decision makers determine which businesses contemplating mechanization are likely to achieve anticipated cost reductions and avoid unanticipated price declines and, perhaps more important, which will be ineffective users of investment funds.

Let's stop eating our seed corn

Tax laws and regulations must preserve capital to ensure future industrial productive capacity

Lawrence Revsine

In a world of economic uncertainty, there is a demand for bold solutions to complex problems. Once these solutions are put forth and endorsed by experts, the public tends simply to sit back and watch what happens. Little time is spent analyzing possible consequences.

One such solution is the FASB's approach to inflation accounting. While the author believes that the FASB's approach is a step in the right direction, he also argues that the latitude permitted by the FASB in defining and presenting inflation-adjusted income may have dangerous long-term consequences. He feels the FASB's approach does not necessarily stress maintenance of physical capacity. Because of this, even adjusted profits may appear "obscene" to the public. This perception may well influence legislation and regulation—with the result that corporations will not be able to husband enough resources for future development. The author believes his alternative could generate much better results in the long term.

Mr. Revsine is the Eric L. Kohler Professor of Accounting and Information Systems at Northwestern University. His book *Replacement Cost Accounting* (Prentice-Hall, 1973) presented one of the earliest analyses of distributable income and physical capital maintenance. The author of numerous books and articles on a range of accounting topics, Revsine has served as a consultant to various policy groups—such as the SEC and the FASB—as well as to many corporations.

Reprint number 81108

Because of the prevailing gloom in current economic headlines, it is easy to forget that these same headlines portrayed 1979 as a year of record corporate profitability. And once a recovery gets under way, it should not be long before we are deluged by another flood of optimism.

But the optimism will be misplaced. Inflation renders much of the so-called profit heralded by the headlines nonexistent. Because past costs are much lower than current costs, the traditional historical cost assumption used by accountants creates the illusion of prosperity—particularly for capital-intensive companies with older assets.

For example, the Commerce Department estimates that profits reported in 1979 were overstated by approximately 50% due to inflation. In individual cases distortions can be even more extreme; after eliminating the effects of price increases, Southern New England Telephone's 1979 income from continuing operations was a full 92.4% less than the traditional profit number.

But it is the illusory profits that seem to have the greatest impact on the general public, legislators, and policymakers. In the words of SEC Chairman Harold Williams, this situation "leads . . . to [misguided] demands . . . to moderate these profits." Most important, since taxes are also based on the illusory figures, retained profits are already inadequate to maintain existing productive capability in certain industries.

As the 1979 annual report of the Dillingham Corporation points out: "Under present laws the effective tax rate has risen to confiscatory levels, resulting in after-tax earnings that are insufficient to replace assets, provide a positive return to shareowners and generate the cash required for growth. As the new methods of inflation accounting indicate

. . . our 1979 effective tax rate rises from 46% in the conventional statement to . . . 89% using the current cost method." And the imposition of new taxes (like that on windfall oil profits) worsens the capital formation crisis and could threaten the very survival of essential business sectors.

Financial decision makers are trying to help alter this trend by providing Congress, policymakers, and the general public with more relevant accounting data; some even view the FASB's recent inflation accounting statement as a solution in itself.[1] But that oversimplifies matters. The many forms of inflation accounting do not necessarily highlight the real inflation-induced threat to productive capacity. Some systems even ignore the issue—and if used may make things worse by stimulating restrictive taxes and regulations.

This article evaluates the threat to business's survival when inappropriate inflation-adjusted income numbers are used as a basis for national policy decisions. It counters the mistaken impression that a simple move to inflation accounting protects business capacity. It also outlines features of a system designed both to forestall potentially dangerous legislative and regulatory actions and to provide a more realistic picture to policymakers.

Where to begin?

Accounting statements are used as a basis for regulation and help shape the public's opinion about business. A good financial reporting system should give accurate data about the economic performance of individual companies, thus promoting economic strength. It should neither report illusory profits nor hide excessive returns.

To develop this type of system, the focus must shift from income to capital. This is not especially difficult, since any framework for accounting income is linked conceptually to maintenance of capital. For example, income is usually defined as the maximum amount of inflow during a period that can be consumed without dipping into the start-of-period capital. More succinctly, income is what remains after the company has set aside enough resources to preserve its starting capital position.

This immediately raises the question of how the starting capital position ought to be defined. In other words, what capital should we, as an economy, attempt to maintain? There are essentially two options: (1) maintenance of *physical* capital and (2) maintenance of *dollar* capital.

The choice between these two options is an important one since the alternatives lead back to profoundly different views of income—views that affect public policy in very different ways. Ideally, what we are looking for is a system that can adjust income for inflation at the same time that it stimulates the most desirable economic and social policy actions.

Physical capital maintenance

To understand the basic characteristics of the physical capital-maintenance approach, consider the following situation:

On January 1, 1980, a company owned two units of inventory with a total historical cost (and current value) of $40. It also had two fixed assets with a total historical cost book value (and current value) of $150. One fixed asset was new; the other, one year old. Each cost $100, had a two-year life, and experienced a straight-line decline in service potential. The company's balance sheet on that date was:

Assets			Equities	
Inventory		$ 40		
Fixed assets	$200			
Less: accumulated depreciation	(50)			
		150	Owners' equity	$190
		$190		$190

On January 2, 1980, the replacement cost of the fixed assets increased by 10%; the new asset then cost $110 and the one-year-old asset, $55. These new fixed asset prices remained in effect during 1980.

On December 31, 1980, the replacement cost of the inventory was $24 per unit. The company sold one unit of inventory on December 31, 1980 for $150—which was received in cash on that date.

We also assume that the company wished to distribute a cash dividend equal to 100% of its "income" (however defined).

Given these data, current cost financial statements that are prepared using the *physical* capital-maintenance assumption look like the statements in *Exhibit I*.

Under the physical capital-maintenance approach to inflation accounting, income equals $16. This

1. Financial Accounting Standards Board, "Statement of Financial Accounting Standards No. 33: Financial Reporting and Changing Prices" (Stamford, Conn.: September 1979).

Exhibit I
Current cost financial statements
physical capital maintenance

Statement of income and retained earnings
year ended December 31, 1980

Sales revenues		$150
Current cost of goods sold	24	
Current cost depreciation expense [($110 ÷ 2) + 55]	110	134
Current cost income from continuing operations		16
"Holding gain" (a direct credit to retained earnings – *not* income); inventory, $8 + fixed assets, $15		23
Dividend paid (100% of income from continuing operations)		(16)
Net addition to owners' equity		**$ 23**

Statement of financial position
December 31, 1980

Assets			**Equities**	
Cash		$134		
Inventory		24	**Owners' equity:**	
Fixed asset	$110		January 1, 1980 balance	$190
Less: accumulated depreciation	(55)	55	Addition during 1980	23
		$213		**$213**

number, called "current cost income from continuing operations" is one of the disclosures now required by the FASB.[2]

To understand the physical capital-maintenance view, it is important to understand precisely why income is considered to be $16:

□ The company started 1980 with two units of inventory and two fixed assets (one that is new and one that is one year old). Thus the starting capital position is defined in physical terms.

□ Units of inventory cost $24 each on December 31, 1980; and, when new, fixed assets cost $110 each (they cost $55 after one year).

□ If "income" of $16 is "consumed" (paid as a dividend), there is $134 left of the original inflow from sales revenues ($150 cash inflow minus the $16 dividend).

□ The $134 retained is precisely equal to the amount needed to purchase another unit of inventory and another fixed asset (to replace the one asset that wore out during 1980): 24 + 110 = 134.

□ If this is done, the company will once again have two units of inventory and two fixed assets (one that is new and one that is one year old). Notice that this is precisely equal to its start-of-period capital position expressed in physical terms.

□ Thus a dividend of $16 (equal to 100% of current cost income from continuing operations) allows the company to begin its next year of operations at the same physical capital level as it did the year before.

Notice that here income exists only after a company generates sufficient resources to maintain the level of physical capacity at which it started.

Dollar capital maintenance

If we look at the previous example from the dollar capital-maintenance approach, current cost financial statements look like *Exhibit II*.

In order to understand what capital is being preserved in the dollar capital-maintenance approach, it is necessary to explain why income is considered to be $39. The analysis proceeds as follows:

□ The company started 1980 with assets that had an aggregate market value of $190. Thus, the starting capital position is defined in dollar (rather than physical) terms.

□ If "income" of $39 is "consumed," this will retain $111 of the original inflow from sales revenues ($150 cash inflow minus the $39 dividend).

□ The $111 holdback can then be used to purchase an additional $111 of assets (for example, one new fixed asset for $110 and 1/24th of a unit of inventory for $1). Asset purchases totaling $111 (in any configuration) would again leave the company with assets having an aggregate market value of $190 ($111 + 55 [fixed asset] + 24 [inventory]), which is precisely equal to its start-of-period market value of assets.

□ Thus, a dividend of $39 (equal to 100% of total current cost income) allows the company to reestablish its start-of-period capital position, defined in dollar terms—that is, nominal dollar market value.

Consequences of the alternatives

The choice of physical or dollar capital maintenance, as the example illustrates, determines what number one gets for current cost income ($16 or $39). In Statement No. 33, the FASB explicitly chose not to express a preference for either concept. Instead, companies are simply required to disclose holding gains on assets next to the figure for income from continuing operations. Whether these gains are to be included in total income (the dollar capital-maintenance approach) or excluded (the physical capital-maintenance approach) is left to the discretion of the reporting companies and the readers of their financial statements. This latitude may prove disastrous in the long term since the messages conveyed by each approach differ radically and could thus elicit divergent policy responses. To illustrate, consider what happens if the company in the example decides to distribute a $39 dividend—the amount of income shown in *Exhibit II* for the dollar capital-maintenance approach. After paying a $39 dividend:

> The amount of cash left over ($111) is only sufficient to buy, say, one new fixed asset and 1/24th of a unit of inventory at year-end prices.

> While the company has indeed maintained the market value of its assets at $190, in physical terms its assets have been reduced.

> This means that the remaining productive capacity is insufficient to maintain the previous level of physical operations.

Current cost income based on the dollar capital-maintenance concept could thus result in a level of consumption (not just dividends but also taxes and adverse regulatory decisions) that decreases the company's future capacity to produce real goods and services. This result arises because holding gains (increases in beginning-of-the-period market values) are treated as income in a dollar capital approach. But, as *Exhibit I* shows, holding gains cannot be consumed or taxed away without diminishing future productive capacity.

If the public believes that these holding gains constitute real income, legislative and regulatory pressures may be exerted to eliminate them; but confiscating these holding gains reduces the productive capacity of business. From a social standpoint, any payout of holding gains—as dividends, taxes, or whatever—is tantamount to eating our seed corn.

In contrast, current cost income based on a physical capital-maintenance concept considers income to exist only insofar as inflows exceed the amount needed to maintain physical productive capacity. This figure for current cost income is the more relevant yardstick for national policy decisions because only by maintaining existing production potential do we provide an undiminished opportunity for future inflows and future prosperity.

Windfall profits tax

Many recent taxation and regulatory debates reveal a widespread misunderstanding about the nature of holding gains. Consider the controversy about the windfall profits tax on oil. Part of the reason that the oil companies' profits appeared excessive to the public is because these profits were measured on a historical cost basis and are distorted by inflation.

Using our previous example, notice that historical cost profit would be $30 (revenues of $150 minus original costs of $20 for inventory and $100 for fixed assets) which is $14 greater than current cost income computed on a physical capital-maintenance basis. This $14 difference consists of realized holding gains. That is, the historical cost profit number includes $4 of realized holding gain on the unit of inventory actually sold during the period (the cost increased from $20 on January 1, 1980 to $24 on December 31, 1980) and $10 of realized holding gain on the two fixed assets. (The cost increase for fixed assets was $10 on the new asset and $5 on the old asset. Since the new asset was depleted by 50% and the old one totally "consumed," $10 of fixed asset holding gains are implicitly "realized" under traditional historical cost accounting.)

2. Financial Accounting Standards Board Statement No. 33, 1979, p. 11; the physical capital-maintenance concept was also explored in a slightly different context by Richard F. Vancil, "Inflation Accounting—The Great Controversy," HBR March-April 1976, p. 58; and in my book, *Replacement Cost Accounting* (Englewood Cliffs, N.J.: Prentice-Hall, 1973).

Exhibit II
Current cost financial statements
dollar capital maintenance

Statement of income and retained earnings
year ended December 31, 1980

Sales revenues		$150
Current cost of goods sold	24	
Current cost depreciation expense [($110 ÷ 2) + 55]	110	134
Current cost income from continuing operations		16
"Holding gain" (an income component in this concept); inventory, $8 + fixed assets, $15		23
Total current cost income		39
Dividend paid (100% of total current cost income)		(39)
Net addition to owners' equity		**$ 0**

Statement of financial position
December 31, 1980

Assets			**Equities**	
Cash		$111		
Inventory		24	**Owners' equity:**	
Fixed asset	$110		January 1, 1980 balance	$190
Less: accumulated depreciation	(55)	55	Addition during 1980	0
		$190		**$190**

Note: FASB Statement No. 33 computes the "holding gain" (which the FASB calls "increases or decreases in current cost amounts") net of overall inflation. For expository ease, I ignore this complication since it does not affect my analysis or conclusions. In Statement No. 33, this holding gain number is not directly added to current cost income from continuing operations, but the FASB does indicate that such cost changes are an element of income in a dollar capital-maintenance approach.

The historical cost method automatically includes realized holding gains on assets sold or used in the bottom-line number and does not differentiate between these "holding gains" and income from continuing operations.

The effect is anything but trivial. Here's an illustration: Mobil Corporation reported that in 1979 39% of its third quarter historical-cost earnings increase from foreign sources was attributable to holding gains on inventory. But that's not all. The cost of replacing fixed productive capacity also keeps increasing; and the impact is cumulative since fixed assets have long lives. Accurate adjustments for the additional overstatement due to fixed asset holding gains are harder to come by, but undoubtedly the distortion is considerable. For example, Shell Oil Company's 1979 ratio of income from continuing operations to shareholders' equity declines from 18.4% on a historical cost basis to 5.1% on a physical capital-maintenance basis (after eliminating illusory holding gains on both inventory and fixed assets).

As *Exhibit I* shows, holding gains must be retained within the company to maintain physical capital. If these "gains" are taxed away, Congress essentially confiscates a portion of productive capacity. Since remaining resources are insufficient to start the cycle again, a tax on holding gains—which is essentially what the windfall profits tax is—really represents a tax on capital. (The fact that the tax, as finally enacted, is an excise rather than an income tax makes this a little harder to see but does not change the ultimate economic effect.)

Is this tax consistent with the expressed policy of encouraging greater domestic energy investment? Clearly not. After paying the tax, companies that want to reestablish their previous level of operating capacity would require an infusion of new outside capital just to put themselves back where they started from. But new capital will be more expensive since the windfall profits tax reduces real profitability.[3]

Such legislation could easily worsen an already difficult energy situation. Furthermore, even a move to inflation accounting won't automatically solve the problem of oil companies' illusory profits. Only if inflation-adjusted income is based on a physical capital-maintenance concept will holding gains be excluded from income. Only then can legislators, regulators, and the general public get financial data that are relevant for evaluating social policy issues.

Far-reaching impact

The side effects of dollar capital maintenance afflict all U.S. enterprises, not just oil companies. Evidence raises the disturbing possibility that many capital-intensive companies may be dissipating productive capacity. For example, approximately one-third of the 30 Dow-Jones industrials are estimated to have paid dividends in excess of their current cost income from continuing operations in each of the years 1976, 1977, and 1978.[4]

The problem is reduced only slightly for less capital-intensive companies. For example, American Hospital Supply Corporation made the following disclosure in its 1979 annual report: "Cash dividends paid in 1979 were 26% of reported net earnings. The payout was . . . 81% of net earnings adjusted for changes in specific prices [that is, current cost income from continuing operations]." Thus, after adjustment for inflation, income holdbacks are far lower than the reassuringly comfortable percentages often cited.

Additional erosion of productive capacity occurs because of regular corporate income taxes as well. As Koppers noted in its 1979 annual report: "[Inflation accounting] does suggest the significant hidden impacts of income taxes in periods of high inflation and the adverse effects on a company's ability to retain earnings to meet the escalating cost of replacing and expanding its productive capacity. It therefore emphasizes the need to reconsider national tax policies in order to give recognition to the reality of inflation."

These adverse tax effects arise because the existing tax laws are based on historical cost income and thus automatically include realized holding gains in taxable income. Since "holding gains" must be retained within the company to maintain physical productive capacity, taxing any portion of these so-called gains runs the risk of reducing future productive capabilities. Furthermore, these effects do not fall equally on all. The real tax burden tends to be higher for capital-intensive companies with relatively older assets, raising the potential for subtle but significant redistributions in favor of service-oriented industries.

Physical capital maintenance is also an especially important concept in regulated industries where rates must be high enough to ensure continuation of the regulated service. But if regulators treat holding gains as income, then rate relief is less likely and long-term physical capital maintenance is endangered.

The role of debt

One frequently advanced argument is that companies benefit from having outstanding debt during inflation; thus some contend that a gain on debt must be included in the determination of inflation-adjusted income. Doing so offsets, to a degree, the adverse effects on profitability; when these gains on debt are added in, inflation appears much less damaging.

Because of this factor, some people have resisted accounting and tax reforms since "things aren't as bad as inflation accounting makes them appear to be." Nor has the FASB settled the issue. According to Statement No. 33, the gains on debt must be disclosed but do not have to be included in the determination of total income.

Our previous discussion helps to resolve the controversy over debt. The key question becomes: Is a business in a better physical capital position because it issued debt in a period of inflation? Clearly not. To see why, return to the example for which I drew up the statements in the exhibits.

Assume that all facts are the same but one. Assume that the company was financed with $100 of debt and $90 of equity on January 1, 1980. Further assume that overall inflation was 10% during 1980. Following FASB 33, we report a gain on debt of $10 ($100 of book value times 10% inflation) to reflect the fact that the debt will be paid back with "cheaper" dollars. What's important to understand, however, is that the so-called gain on debt simply doesn't exist under a physical capital-maintenance concept. That is, the $10 "gain" is not income in a physical capital view and cannot legitimately be added to the $16 of current cost income from continuing operations, as some would have us do.

The proof is straightforward. If we treated the so-called gain on debt as income, the new income fig-

3. On this point also see Paul Craig Roberts, "The Windfall Illusion," *Wall Street Journal*, November 28, 1979.

4. These estimates are from Sidney Davidson and Roman L. Weil, "Excerpts from Estimated Financial Statements Complying with FASB Statement No. 33 for the Dow-Jones Industrials" (unpublished manuscript, University of Chicago, 1980).

ure would be $26—that is, $16 from *Exhibit I* plus $10 of "gain on debt." (For simplicity, interest on the debt is ignored. This simplification does not affect the conclusion.) Given our assumption of a 100% dividend payout, the ending cash balance would be $124. But since it now takes a total of $134 to replace the unit of inventory ($24) and one fixed asset ($110), a payout of $26 does not allow the firm to maintain its original physical capital.

The "shortage" is $10, precisely equal to the "gain on debt." In other words, this $10 cannot be income in a physical capital-maintenance sense. If we treat this item as income to the entity, we would face the risk of taxing away resources that are needed internally to maintain physical productive capacity.

(Some people might argue that this $10 of "extra" payout may be recouped by issuing additional debt. Unfortunately, this misses the entire point of physical capital maintenance. That is, amounts that are needed within the corporation in order to maintain productive potential shouldn't be taxed away in the first place! What is the rationale for instituting an income measure that could force companies to reshuffle their financing in order to stay even?)

To summarize, if the policy objective is to maintain physical capital, then there is no such thing as an inflation gain on debt. Those who argue otherwise are implicitly adopting a dollar capital-maintenance view of income, a view that could easily lead to decreases in productive capability.

The downward spiral

Given the enormous social impact of accounting numbers, there is some truth to the old adage that "accounting is far too important to be left solely in the hands of accountants." I feel we urgently need a reporting system that will provide accurate information about real underlying performance. Whether industry is maintaining its existing production capacity is crucially important to America's future.

Inflation accounting provides useful data for social policy decisions only if physical capital maintenance governs the preparation of reports. While the two options—"physical" and "dollar"—use the same measurement techniques, they classify certain items differently and result in different final income figures. Do not underestimate the importance of this difference. At stake is the entire question of how corporate performance is communicated to legisla-

tors, regulators, and to the public. How these groups see corporations' profit situations in turn influences whether they try to dampen or brighten the business climate.

If holding gains on assets or gains on debt are treated by accountants as an element of income, it is difficult for most people to see just how severely businesses are suffering from inflation. Under the dollar capital approach, we run the risk of taxing and otherwise distributing resources that must be retained within the business in order to maintain productive capacity.

The physical capital view considers maintenance of productive capacity to be of utmost importance. In this view, income exists only after continuation of physical capital is ensured; thus, neither asset-holding gains nor gains on debt are counted as income.

An economy's performance can be monitored intelligently only if policymakers and the public have a clear idea of what is happening to its long-term productive capability. When financial reports convey the message more accurately, a climate will be created in which the problem can be resolved. Then policymakers will be encouraged to formulate laws that allow the nation's economy to build for the future rather than to inadvertently consume existing capital.▽

Printed in U.S.A. by
Harvard University Printing Office,
Boston, Massachusetts 02134.

[redacted]